THE ICONOGRAPHY OF HELL

THE ICONOGRAPHY OF HELL

edited by

Clifford Davidson and Thomas H. Seiler

Early Drama, Art, and Music
Monograph Series, 17

Medieval Institute Publications

WESTERN MICHIGAN UNIVERSITY

Kalamazoo, Michigan
1992

Cover design by Linda K. Judy

ISBN 1-879288-01-X (casebound)
ISBN 1-879288-02-8 (paperback)

Contents

Illustrations   vii

Preface   ix

Pamela Sheingorn
"Who can open the doors of his face?
The Iconography of Hell Mouth   1

Barbara D. Palmer
The Inhabitants of Hell: Devils   20

Clifford Davidson
The Fate of the Damned in English Art
and Drama   41

Philip Butterworth
Hellfire: Flame as Special Effect   67

Richard Rastall
The Sounds of Hell   102

Thomas H. Seiler
Filth and Stench as Aspects
of the Iconography of Hell   132

Ann Faulkner
The Harrowing of Hell at Barking Abbey
and in Modern Production   141

Peter Meredith
    The Iconography of Hell in the English
    Cycles: A Practical Perspective   158

Cecile Williamson Cary
    "It circumscribes us here":
    Hell on the Renaissance Stage   187

Index   209

Illustrations

Plates

1. Detail of Last Judgment. Wall painting (restored), Church of St. Thomas of Canterbury, Salisbury.

2. Damned being tormented by Devils and Snakes. West Front, Lincoln Cathedral.

3. The Damned assailed by dragons. West Front, Lincoln Cathedral.

4. The Devil tortures two of the Damned. West Front, Lincoln Cathedral.

5. Fall of Rebel Angels, Creation, Fall of Man. Icelandic Old Testament (Stjórn's translation)

6. Doomsday from N-town Pageants. Staged by the Graduate Centre for the Study of Drama, University of Toronto.

7. Detail from Doom. Wall painting, Guild Chapel, Stratford-upon-Avon.

8. Salvation and Damnation. *Carthusian Miscellany*.

9. *Revelations* 6.7-8. Opening of the Fourth Seal: Pale Horse. Cloisters Apocalypse.

10. Opening of the Fourth Seal: Pale Horse. Harley Apocalypse.

11. Opening of the Fourth Seal: Pale Horse. Alexander Minorita Apocalypse.

12a-12b. Hieronymus Bosch, Monsters. Bister and pen drawings.

13. Mace, from London.

14. Flesh-hooks, from London.

15. Detail of Doom. Painted Glass, Church of St. Mary, Fairford.

16. Devil with Flesh-hook. Misericord, Sprotbrough, West Yorkshire.

17. Hell Mouth, swallowing human figure. Bronze Closing Ring. Adel, West Yorkshire.

18. Harrowing of Hell. *Holkham Bible Picture Book.*

19. The Last Judgment. *Holkham Bible Picture Book.*

20. The Weighing of Souls (above), the Ladder of Salvation, and Hell. Wall painting (restored), Church of SS. Peter and Paul, Chaldon, Surrey.

21. Punishment of the Wrathful. *The Kalender of Sheephardes* (c.1570).

22. The Barking Harrowing Play, produced by the Chicago Medieval Players, 1989.

23. The Dead Rising. York Doomsday Play. York Festival, 1988.

Preface

Hell, a constant topic of popular interest over the past millenium, has to some extent receded from the public consciousness in spite of the popular resurgence of Fundamentalism in the United States. Fewer people than a generation ago fear the fires of hell, or they fear them for different reasons than in the past. Hell and its denizens are now less likely to be blamed for the immoral acts of individuals, and the initial effort of Satan to subvert the race in the Garden of Eden is usually regarded as a deeply perceptive story rather than a fact of history. Yet evil persists, and in our view of it we continue to be influenced by the past understanding of its source in the fallen angels, who are resident in the deep pit of hell.

The present volume cannot claim to provide a history of hell, but rather concentrates on some questions concerning belief in its reality and on some ways in which hell was understood in the late Middle Ages and Renaissance. The focus is on England, especially on the art and drama and music of that country, although we know that belief in hell extended throughout the entire region influenced by Christianity in the Middle Ages and thereafter. In her paper in the present volume, Pamela Sheingorn examines the opening to hell in popular iconography—the hell mouth, which appears in the visual arts and also in drama. The opening to hell according to the traditional view appeared to us to provide a useful opening point for this book.

Those who have lost all hope, the fallen angels—metamorphosed into hairy and dirty devils from their original heavenly brightness—and the souls of the damned, are the unhappy inhabitants of this anti-bliss so devoutly to be avoided by men and women who considered themselves sensible and responsible. In painted glass by John Thornton of Coventry in the Great East Window of York Minster the prelude to history is represented by a panel that depicts the disobedient and proud angels falling across the cosmos, to which God will now give shape and life. The fallen angels provide a paradigm for the future, for as they themselves fell, so also one of their number, Lucifer, will successfully tempt Eve—who, in turn, will successfully tempt Adam—to fall by disobeying the divine command. Thus death came into the world, and the two paths, represented by Cain and Abel, the sons of Adam and Eve, became available to all those who came after. The one path would lead upward to the reward of heavenly bliss, the other would lead down to deserved punishment in the place of darkness. The myth was not only one that exercised very great fascination for the West, but also penetrated the deepest recesses of the Western mind.

Devils and the damned are the topics of papers by Barbara D. Palmer and Clifford Davidson, while another dimension of the popular understanding of hell is treated by Philip Butterworth, who writes about hellfire as represented in the drama and theater of the late Middle Ages. The development of the technology of explosives and flame had a use that was quite practical for the theater person, and hence effects dependent on this technology made a significant contribution to plays. Yet another dimension, and one not normally considered, involved the sense of smell, which was an important aspect of the conception of hell. Hell was, as Thomas Seiler reminds us, odoriferous as well as dirty, and it was this hell that was represented in the medieval religious drama. Hell was, in short, hardly a nice place to meet one's friends in the hereafter.

In contrast to the perfect harmony of the music of heaven, hell was most often associated with cacophony and unpleasant sound, as Richard Rastall reminds us. In iconography, devils may blow horns, but can we assume therefore that these creatures of darkness are particularly musical? The horns blown by devils in such examples of medieval art as the wall paintings at Stratford-upon-Avon in England and Fjälkinge in the province of Skåne in southern Sweden could never take their place in a well-tuned medieval orchestra such as the choir of angels in painted glass at the Beauchamp Chapel in Warwick. Nevertheless, music of a more pleasant sort may also have a demonic function as an agent of temptation used by evil characters.

Practical aspects of staging hell are treated in the present book by Ann Faulkner and Peter Meredith. Faulkner reports on a production of the Barking Abbey Harrowing, which is particularly noteworthy because of the role of an abbess of Barking in bringing the Latin text into being and functioning as its producer (in the American sense of the word)—a role that she undertook for the sake of the spiritual welfare of the abbey. Meredith, on the other hand, surveys the theatrical presentation of hell in vernacular drama with the eye of a performer and director, and he also brings a certain healthy skepticism to his topic. Modern production, of course, does not demand that the original conditions under which a play was performed be replicated (nor could such an effort succeed for any number of reasons), but we do need to keep in mind two points concerning early performances that lie in part outside his argument: (1) local actors and directors would have tended to visualize hell in ways familiar to them, and thus would have been influenced not only by texts but also by those local examples familiar to them; and (2) the preparation of such stage properties as hell mouth would have required the assistance of carpenters and painters, the latter likely to rely on pattern books in their possession for the design of the property.

Hell was also, as Cecile Cary reminds us, a presence on the English Renaissance stage, where it could appear as an actual prop (as in Marlowe's *Doctor Faustus*) but more often found its way into the imagery expressed by the text (as in the case of the character who imagines himself porter of the gate of hell in *Macbeth*). Renaissance dramatists, prevented by legal restrictions from dealing with purely religious topics on the English stage, nevertheless used the awareness of hell to deepen the aesthetic structure of tragedy and to elicit a stronger emotional response to drama than otherwise would have been the case.

All except three of the contributions in this book began as conference papers read at the International Congress on Medieval Studies in 1990. The conference papers were thoroughly revised and expanded, and the papers by Butterworth, Rastall, and Meredith were added. The editors appreciate the effort which the authors have made in preparing their work for publication, and also acknowledge the assistance of Juleen Eichinger, Linda Judy, and Earl Hawley toward preparing the book for the printer.

"Who can open the doors of his face?"
The Iconography of Hell Mouth

Pamela Sheingorn

The metaphorical language of *Job* ("Who can open the doors of his face?" [41.5]), suggesting that Leviathan's mouth functioned as a portal to a prison for humankind, assimilates an inorganic structure (it is buildings that have doors) with an organic being (it is creatures that have faces).[1] But as long as the metaphor remained in the realm of the verbal there was no need to work out the details of this horrific mechanism. Concretizing the image was the task of the pictorial arts, including drama, and the results of that concretization are the subject of this paper.

Throughout Northern Europe in the late Middle Ages, people were familiar with the image of the gaping jaws of a bestial monster that served to indicate the entrance to hell. In England this hell mouth loomed before them perhaps most memorably in the Doom paintings found so frequently over chancel arches, as at the Church of St. Thomas of Canterbury in Salisbury (fig. 1).[2] Doomsday, combined with the Rood, was painted even in relatively small churches where it was frighteningly close to the congregation, as at Dauntsey in Wiltshire.[3] On the Continent the large tympana carved in relief over entrance doors, and frequently painted in bright colors, often represented the Last Judgment, complete with hell mouth, as at the Church of St. Foy in Conques. But hell mouth was also to be seen on a smaller scale on church façades, as in the narrative reliefs on the west front of Lincoln Cathedral (figs. 2–4), and on capitals such as one from Ripoll in Catalonia.[4] It could be found woven into tapestries such as the well-known set at

Angers illustrating the Apocalypse,[5] and carved on liturgical objects—e.g., a crozier head, now in the Staatliche Museum in Berlin, with hell mouth forming its base. Hell mouth appeared in altarpieces—especially in the alabaster Passion altarpieces made in England and exported to the Continent and to Iceland.[6] And, of course, hell mouth made its most frequent appearances in manuscript illustration. The accessibility of this image and, therefore, the immediate understanding of its symbolic meaning, were crucial to its use on the stage and need to be established from the outset. Although the widespread deterioration, if not destruction, of wall painting forces some reliance on manuscript evidence in this paper, most people in the Middle Ages knew this symbol from public art.[7]

The omnipresence of the image of hell mouth only confirmed what people knew in the Middle Ages—that there was another world in addition to the earthly world and, as Gurevich puts it, that the other world "was perceived as part of the same universe as the earth, and presented no riddle to medieval people."[8] This perception was confirmed by the popular genre of literature recording visionary visits to the other world. In the widest-known example of this genre, *The Visions of Tondal*, written about 1149, the soul of an Irish knight is given an escorted tour of hell, purgatory, and heaven by his guardian angel, and he returns to his body to tell his tale.[9]

There was no doubt about the existence of hell, but there was concern regarding its precise location. Gregory I assumed that hell lay under the earth.[10] In Northern Europe there was a belief that hell was located on a distant island, while Gurevich explains that in Italy "'Sailing to Sicily' was a synonym for departing to the Other World, since the craters of Sicilian volcanoes led directly to hell, according to contemporary beliefs (inherited from Antiquity)."[11] In Caesarius of Heisterbach's *Dialogue on Miracles* the novice asks, "What must we think of these mountains Stromboli, Etna and Gyber? As souls are sent into them, is purgatory there, or hell?" The narrator-monk replies, "They are said to be the jaws of hell, because none of the elect, but the wicked only are sent into them. . . . Hell is supposed to be in the heart of the earth, so that the wicked may not see the light of heaven."[12] Those who constructed complete cosmologies situated hell mouth in various places. In her *Liber divinorum operum*, Hildegard of Bingen describes a vision of the cosmos in which "darknesses appear towards the west outside the curve of the earth" and "between the west and north corners the darknesses split like a terrible mouth that was flung open for the purpose of engulfing."[13] The miniature illustrating this vision in the early thirteenth-century manuscript of the *Liber divinorum operum*, now in Lucca, shows what Rita Otto describes as a dragon-like head with glowing eyes and sharp teeth, jaws spread wide against the circle that, according to Otto, represents the cosmos.[14] On the other hand, the Sphere of John Peckham, a diagram of concentric circles representing "the spheres of the universe from Hell to the Empyrean," places a burning hell mouth inside the innermost circle and thus at the center of the cosmos.[15]

The point is that the mental image of the world included heaven and hell somewhere, and therefore it should not surprise us to find a representation of hell, or at least of its entrance, on the stage of the world as well. As A. C. Cawley observes, "The medieval theatre readily invites the imagination to see it as a symbol of the universe in miniature. It embraces Heaven, Hell and Middle Earth, and the dramatic action moves freely between them."[16] Thus there was a fixed location called hell in circular playing areas, in place-and-scaffold productions of the English cycle plays, and in Continental plays like those at Lucerne and Valenciennes, and the entrance to that hell was most frequently represented as the gaping jaws of a beast. In both art and drama, hell is present not just in sacred narratives where it is specifically mentioned, such as the Harrowing of Hell and the Last Judgment, but also in subjects treating the history of the Church on earth—that is, in the lives of the saints—and in subjects treating the life of the individual Christian, such as those dramatized in morality plays. To make a quick survey, hell occurs in these narrative subjects from the Hebrew Bible: it is most frequent in the fall of the rebel angels, illustrated, for example, in miniatures for Chapter I in manuscripts of the *Speculum humanae salvationis*,[17] and plays of that subject seem to require at least an entrance to hell. In the twelfth-century Anglo-Norman *Jeu d'Adam* devils appear at the death of Adam and Eve to take them to hell, from which smoke arises and the banging of pots and cauldrons may be heard.[18] Though the story of Cain and Abel does not often include a representation of hell mouth in the pictorial arts, the smoke from Cain's burning sacrifice turns downward into hell mouth on fol. 5 of the *Holkham Bible Picture Book*,[19] and in the Towneley cycle Cain admits, "In hell, I wote, mon be my stall" (l. 375).[20]

In illustrations of New Testament narrative, hell mouth appears, though quite rarely, in the Temptation of Christ, and is a standard if not indispensable feature in the apocryphal Harrowing of Hell as well as in the Last Judgment. In a stationary staging, it is quite plausible that the devil should enter and exit via hell mouth in the Temptation play, and an entrance to hell is certainly required in dramatizations of the Harrowing and the Judgment. In addition, illustration of the parable of the Wise and Foolish Virgins includes hell mouth—for example, on the lintel of the fourteenth-century chapel portal at Marienburg (Malbork) Castle, the stronghold of the Teutonic Knights. The dramatization of the parable in the eleventh-century *Sponsus* play from St. Martial of Limoges and in the Künzelsauer Fronleichnamspiel requires an exit identified as hell.[21] Pictorial treatments of the parable of Lazarus and the rich man also include hell mouth, and there is a record from Sterzing in 1541 indicating that a hell was constructed out of cloth for use in a play of the rich man and poor Lazarus.[22] And, of course, hell mouth appears almost obsessively in illustrations to that great eschatological vision, the Apocalypse.

In the lives of the saints hell mouth concretizes the punishment of those who persecute the saints, as in the representation of the death of Nero in a fourteenth-century manuscript life of St. Denis. Contrast heightens Nero's fate, since this scene shares the page with the martyrdoms of SS. Peter and Paul. Their souls receive angelic escort to heaven while demons snatch Nero's soul and take it to hell, inscribed INFERNUS.[23] The famous miniature of St. Apollonia from the Hours of Étienne Chevalier tells us that hell mouth occurred in saints' plays as well,[24] and in the Digby *Mary Magdalene* we find the stage direction: *"Here xal entyr the prynse of dyllys in a stage, and hell ondyrneth that stage"* (l. 357*sd*).[25] An Anglo-Norman tract on the Mass advised its readers to form a mental picture of hell mouth when they meditated upon holy subjects during the Mass. The tract counsels readers that during the Introit they should "think on the desire that the holy patriarchs and prophets had, that our Savior come to rescue them," an instruction illustrated by a miniature showing, at the left, the hand of God extended towards the patriarchs and prophets held captive in hell mouth, while at the right two worshippers stand behind a priest in a chasuble praying before an altar with an open book on it.[26] In the pictorial arts the Tree of Vices often grows out of hell mouth, teaching the lesson that all sin originates in hell and reminding us that Pride, Wrath, and Envy dwell with Belial on the scaffold of the devil in *The Castle of Perseverance*. And souls suffering in purgatory are shown confined in hell mouth—a reflection of the same concern with the eternal fate of the soul so apparent in morality plays.

We can certainly conclude from this rapid survey that hell mouth appeared with great regularity in both pictorial and dramatic arts. Next we turn to a consideration of the placement of hell mouth within a larger pictorial composition[27] and then to an examination of the specific forms it might take. Some subjects virtually require a vertical composition with heaven at the top, earth (or middle earth) in the center, and hell at the bottom. In a fourteenth-century Icelandic miniature, based on English (especially East Anglian) models, showing the fall of the rebel angels, the villains plummet the whole length of the page (fig. 5),[28] and a thirteenth-century psalter illustration seems especially close to stage composition with the fall of the angels indicated by their disappearing feet, their heads and shoulders emerging into hell mouth at the bottom, and the creation of Adam and Eve taking place in between, on middle earth.[29] Play texts of this subject put so much emphasis on the physical action of falling that the stage composition *must* be vertical, and in modern productions of the English cycle plays, acrobatic actors have shown us that vertical motion is dramatically quite effective. The iron swing used by God "when he sall sty vppe to heuen" in the Last Judgment play of the York Cycle, a property listed in the Mercers' indenture of 1433,[30] may also have been used by Lucifer in the Fall, according to Peter Holding.[31] If so, the swing's motion would have contributed to the verticality of the stage composition.

The Harrowing of Hell, on the other hand, is usually composed horizontally in the pictorial arts, partly because the entire scene is set in hell. A horizontal motion communicates Christ's act of freeing those in Limbo.

In the pictorial arts the Last Judgment combines horizontal orientation (hell is at Christ's left hand) and vertical motion (sinners plunge downward into hell).[32] But a vertical composition was more likely to have been used in pageant wagon staging and in a single stationary staging, as was the case in the very successful production of the N-town cycle at the University of Toronto in May of 1988 (fig. 6). Alexandra Johnston and Margaret Dorrell (now Rogerson) suggest that since the Mercers' indenture from York lists hell mouth separately it must have been an individual prop, placed on the ground below the pageant wagon itself,[33] an arrangement that would create a vertical composition. Bakhtin argues in favor of vertical composition when he says, "In the medieval picture of the world, the top and bottom, the higher and the lower, have an absolute meaning both in the sense of space and of values. . . . Every important movement was seen and interpreted only as upward and downward, along a vertical line. All metaphors of movement in medieval thought and art have this sharply defined, surprisingly consistent vertical character."[34]

Now that we have a picture of the possibilities for the placement of the entrance to hell in pictorial and stage composition, we need to investigate next its specific form. How did the pictorial arts come to prefer the image of hell as a bestial mouth? The imagery of the Hebrew Bible, and especially the Psalms, inspired the earliest representations of hell. In the Utrecht Psalter, a ninth-century manuscript with illustrations providing a literal interpretation of the language of the Psalms, we find several different ways of imaging hell. In the lower right corner of the illustration to Psalm 1 an immense figure personifying Hades embraces the souls of the damned.[35] Another favorite image was the pit, often filled with snakes and other chthonic creatures, as in the illustration to Psalm 6 of the Utrecht Psalter (fol. 3ᵛ).[36] Envisioning the entrance to hell as a pit remained a viable choice and was especially popular in the pictorial arts at the end of the Middle Ages. In the York play of the Harrowing of Hell,[37] Satan cries as he falls: "Allas for dole and care,/ I synke into helle pitte" (ll. 347–48). In the Renaissance theater the entrance to hell could be a trap door creating the effect of hell pit. Glynne Wickham reminds us that in *Gorboduc* "Act IV is introduced by a spectacular dumb-show presenting the furies rising through a stage-trap out of hell. . . ."[38]

It was in Anglo-Saxon England that hell mouth took shape as the jaws of a devouring beast. Gregory the Great had already gathered all the relevant biblical quotations in his *Moralia,* and had used the image of a monstrous beast to convey Satan's evil nature. In Gregory this monster is initially identified as "a Behemoth, or huge land beast, and [then as] the Leviathan or sea monster, his shape shift[ing] from lion to dragon to whale to bird."[39] Joyce Galpern explores the reasons that this imagery took concrete form as open jaws to represent the entrance to hell in her dissertation, "The Shape of Hell in Anglo-Saxon England." She argues that the "conjuncture of the late tenth-century monastic reform and the Danish invasions in England" led to a "search for an iconography of hell that could be understood by pagan and Christian alike."[40] Although some early images show a dragon or snake-like body attached to the head with its gaping jaws, the pictorial arts soon came to prefer the disembodied head, as if to figure the unidirectionality of being swallowed by hell mouth.

Some artists multiplied the heads, creating fantastic imagery. This solution was particularly favored in Anglo-Norman Apocalypse illustration as, for example, in the Cloisters Apocalypse.[41] Some images retain the chthonic associations of the pit, as in a representation of the fall of the rebel angels in a fourteenth-century

Breviary of Love, in which hell mouth is surrounded by snakes and toads and has a snake crawling out of its ear.[42] But images like these had little possibility of realization on the stage, which preferred the stronger association of hell mouth with fire rather than with earth creatures. The Drapers' accounts from Coventry, which refer sometimes to hell head and at other times to hell mouth, have a rather consistent payment for keeping the fire there.[43] In the pictorial arts, this fiery hell mouth could create a vertical opening like a door, serving both as entrance and as cauldron of punishment. Or the jaws could function as the site of the eternally burning fire heating the cauldron as in the late fifteenth-century Playfair Hours.[44] This may have been the form of hell mouth noted by M. D. Anderson in a fifteenth-century French play of the martyrdom of SS. Peter and Paul, in which devils throw Nero into a cauldron with smoke billowing up from beneath it.[45] But stage practice is more likely to have represented jaws and cauldron separately, placing the cauldron, along with other punishments for the damned, behind the open jaws serving as the entrance to hell.

The more elaborate stationary stagings of medieval drama probably created architectural structures to represent hell, and we should not forget that another important image for the entrance to hell was hell gate, but the association of gaping jaws with the entrance to hell was so strong that the jaws were incorporated into architectural frameworks to create buildings with the quality of nightmarish reality. A particularly likely stage model is provided by a number of images that combine the jaws—providing a handy entrance and exit for devils—with the architectural structure needed for the Harrowing of Hell, which might have included a barred gate as well as parapets from which demons watched Christ's assault on hell. An illustration in an English manuscript of the mid-fourteenth century, the Fitzwarin Psalter, shows this combination quite clearly, as does an English alabaster panel of the late fourteenth or early fifteenth century in the Castle Museum at Carcassonne.[46] As Anderson observes, "This arrangement would have made it possible for the lesser demons of the *Towneley Plays* to obey Beelzebub's commands to 'go spar the gates . . . set watches on the walls' and other alabasters show these demon warders on the battlements of Hell holding horns, keys and instruments of torture." She further suggests: "It would . . . have been easier to paint the profile of a Hell-Mouth on a cutboard shape, and use this to mask a practicable doorway, than to contrive a monstrous head large enough for the actors to pass through its jaws."[47] An illustration of the Harrowing of Hell in a Dutch book of hours of about 1450–70 shows such a doorway, with its arched top forming the upper jaw of a very flattened, if not two-dimensional face.[48] We cannot deny the possibility that such profiles were used, but evidence both from pictorial arts and dramatic records suggests that, at least in some cases, the jaws of hell were three-dimensional. Along with the very important evidence of the Stratford Guild Chapel Doom painting (fig. 7), we must consider the records. The records of the Passion play performed in Metz in 1437 indicate: "The gateway and mouth of Hell in this play was very well made, for by a device (engin) it opened and closed of its own accord when the devils wanted to go in or come out of it. And this great head (hure) had two great steel eyes which glittered wonderfully."[49] This description makes one think of Cailleau's 1577 stage plan of the Valenciennes Passion of 1547.[50] The Rouen Passion Play had a hell mouth that "opened and closed when necessary."[51] One of the props for a play about Tobias put on in Lincoln in 1564 was "hell mouthe with a neithere Chap" or jaw.[52] And in a 1594 description of a fantasy theater the author gives details of a three-dimensional hell mouth: "there might you see the ground-worke at the one end of the Stage whereout the personated Divels should enter in their fiery ornaments, made like the broad wide mouth of an huge Dragon . . . the teeth of this Hels-mouth far outstretching."[53] Some representations of hell mouth in the pictorial arts suggest that it is more like a mechanism than an organism and may indicate familiarity with a hell mouth that had working jaws.

Certainly such properties were expensive and required maintenance. At Hall in the Tirol a "Lorentz maler" was paid to paint hell in 1501,[54] and at Dortmund the Antichrist play presented on 6 February 1513 included "hell with many ghastly and brightly colored devils. And it cost a great deal of money and work."[55] The records of the Lucerne Passion Play include various payments for hell mouth, including nails, while its design and location as part of the set are indicated on the stage plan of 1583.[56]

Payments without such a drawing as the Lucerne plan, although they indicate that there was a property called hell mouth, do not, however, tell us much about its form. Like the Lucerne plan, the Stratford painting and the Valenciennes drawing corroborate the view that complex, multi-level architectural structures may have been built for the most elaborate stagings. A simpler solution would have been a scaffold of the type seen in the martyrdom of St. Apollonia in Jean Fouquet's Hours of Étienne Chevalier[57] and possibly represented in the graffito at Stetchworth, according to John Marshall.[58] In a scaffold staging, hell mouth could have been painted on canvas with a flap serving as entrance and exit, while the activities in hell took place on the more visible platform above. Another possibility, in combination with place-and-scaffold staging, is suggested by an extremely crowded opening in a fifteenth-century English manuscript, the Carthusian Miscellany (fig. 8). The general theme of the contrasting paths to salvation and damnation is illustrated through a combination of biblical stories (the Expulsion in the upper right), parables (the foolish virgins entering hell in the center right), and lessons about good behavior (the sacraments pictured at the top). As Francis Wormald has observed, stage practice is indicated by the separate pavilions for each sacrament and the architectural structures for Paradise. Wormald, comparing these illustrations to the Fouquet miniature of the Martyrdom of St. Apollonia, concludes, "It is of course impossible to be certain that we have here a reflection of a mise-en-scène of a medieval play, but it does not seem an impossibility to suggest it."[59] Wormald's suggestion is reinforced by the unusual form of hell mouth. With its long, worm-like scalloped body, it resembles nothing so much as cloth stretched over a series of rings like those purchased for a Passion play in Montferrand in 1477: "Item: the

said Percheron [*one of the town consuls*] has given to the said
Colas 15d for a bundle of rings (*faysse de cercles*) to make the
Hell's mouth."[60] Such a hell mouth could easily have been as-
sembled for each year's performances. Of course if there were no
scenes set *in* hell, hell mouth might simply serve as a stage door,
either in two- or three-dimensional form.

Another way of presenting hell mouth in the pictorial arts
appears at first to be merely a visual oddity but cannot be disre-
garded as a stage possibility. It occurs in Apocalypse illustrations,
specifically in miniatures accompanying the text describing the
opening of the fourth seal, *Revelations* 6.7–8: "And when he had
opened the fourth seal, I heard the voice of the fourth living creature saying: Come, and see. And behold a pale horse, and he that
sat upon him, his name was Death, and hell followed him." Frequently and most familiarly the illustration for this text shows the
horse and rider exiting from hell mouth. However, some artists
who paid closer attention to the text noted that the subject, hell,
was accompanied by a verb of motion—"et infernus sequebatur
eum"— and hell was following him. How, exactly, might hell follow? There is a certain ambiguity in the representation of this
scene in the Cloisters Apocalypse (fig. 9)—is hell mouth stationary
or, as the modern commentary to the manuscript suggests, does it
follow "closely like a float in a parade"?[61] And there may even
be ambiguity in a fourteenth-century German version in which hell
mouth, containing a personification of hunger, is attached to the
tail of the lion on which Death is seated.[62] But there is no doubt
that hell is in motion in some other examples. In a French prose
version of the Apocalypse illustrated in a fourteenth-century manuscript (fig. 10) hell mouth is tied by a rope, apparently to the hal-
ter of the striding horse,[63] and in an Apocalypse manuscript
made in England in the late fourteenth century, a similar rope is
tied to the horse's tail. A different interpretation is even more
startling. In these renditions, the gaping mouth of hell has grown
functional, if slightly disproportional legs, enabling this truly sur-
real monster to follow death by walking along behind (fig. 11).
This walking hell mouth occurs in illustrations of the Opening of

the Fourth Seal in Apocalypse manuscripts, and may have its roots in the twelfth century.[64] It is especially associated with illustrations to the commentary on the Apocalypse by Alexander Minorita.[65] Another especially suggestive context is the Harrowing of Hell, as in a thirteenth-century German Psalter from Blankenburg.[66] And if this monster could migrate out of Apocalypse illustration into New Testament narrative, it is certainly possible that it found a way into dramatic productions as well, for it is hard to imagine that an audience would not be impressed by such an apparition. Evidence from the pictorial arts suggests that the jaws could be oriented either horizontally or vertically, but would be most impressive if they were belching smoke and fire.

It may seem that this paper has slipped into the world of pure fantasy by proposing that evidence from the hallucinatory world of Apocalypse illustration has anything to do with the concrete reality of stage properties, but there is some supporting evidence for the suggestion. Although it is late in date (1606), it cannot be ignored. In an engraving representing the entry of a group of players at a Rhetoricians' festival in Haarlem, the Devil and Death march together. Between them, clearly labelled "Hel," comes a figure wearing a black sack that emits smoke.[67]

NOTES

1. Much of the research for this paper was conducted at the Index of Christian Art, Princeton University. I wish to acknowledge here not only the research capabilities that the Index offers but also the unparalleled resource of its superb staff, to all of whom I am grateful both for their wide knowledge of medieval iconography and for their friendship.

2. For a photograph showing the entire wall painting, see David Bevington et al., *Homo, Memento Finis: The Iconography of Just Judgment in Medieval Art and Drama*, Early Drama, Art, and Music, Monograph Ser., 6 (Kalamazoo: Medieval Institute Publications, 1985), fig. 14. This wall painting was restored with oils in the nineteenth century, however.

3. See Aymer Vallance, *English Church Screens* (New York: Charles Scribner's Sons, 1936), p. 20.

4. This cloister capital, according to François Bucher, "has an unhinged, abstract quality" (*The Pamplona Bibles* [New Haven: Yale Univ. Press, 1970], I, 51; for an illustration of the capital, see fig. 60).

5. For illustrations of these tapesteries, made in the late fourteenth century and preserved in the Tapestry Museum, Château d'Angers, see Geneviève Souchal, *Les tapisseries de l'Apocalypse d'Angers*, introd. René Planchenault (Milan: Hachette-Fabbri-Skira, 1969).

6. See Francis Cheetham, *English Medieval Alabasters* (Oxford: Phaidon Press, 1984), pp. 223–70.

7. For a survey of hell mouth in the pictorial arts, see Ernst Guldan, "Das Monster-Portal am Palazzo Zuccari in Rom: Wandlungen eines Motivs vom Mittelalter zum Manierismus," *Zeitschrift für Kunstgeschichte*, 32 (1969), 229–61. I am grateful to Gary D. Schmidt for supplying me with this reference.

8. Aron Gurevich, *Medieval Popular Culture: Problems of Belief and Perception*, trans. Janos M. Bak and Paul A. Hollingsworth (Cambridge: Cambridge Univ. Press, 1988), p. 183.

9. See Thomas Kren and Roger S. Wieck, *The Visions of Tondal from the Library of Margaret of York* (Malibu: J. Paul Getty Museum, 1990), who reproduce all the illustrations from Getty MS. 30, the only illustrated text among the 243 manuscripts that survive. See also Eileen Gardiner, *Visions of Heaven and Hell before Dante* (New York: Italica, 1989), pp. 149–95.

10. As Gurevich notes, "Gregory I found it difficult to respond to a question on this point: some assume that hell is somewhere within the earth's limits, while others incline to the opinion that it is under the earth. Proceeding from the etymology of the word *infernum* ('quia inferius jacet'), Gregory himself thought that hell was located just under the earth" (*Medieval Popular Culture*, p. 130, citing Gregory, *Dialogues* IV.xliv.1).

11. Gurevich, *Medieval Popular Culture*, p. 130.

14   Pamela Sheingorn

12. Caesarius of Heisterbach, *The Dialogue on Miracles*, trans. H. von E. Scott and C. C. Swinton Bland (New York: Harcourt, Brace, 1929), II, 302.

13. Hildegard von Bingen, *Welt und Mensch: Das Buch "De Operatione Dei" aus dem Genter Kodex*, ed. Heinrich Schipperges (Salzburg: Otto Müller, 1965), p. 188, as cited by Rita Otto, "Zu den gotischen Miniaturen einer Hildegardhandschrift in Lucca," *Mainzer Zeitschrift*, 71–72 (1976–77), 117 (translation mine).

14. Lucca, Biblioteca Statale, MS. 1942, fol. 88^v; illustrated in Otto, "Zu den gotischen Miniaturen," fig. 36b. Though it is dated after Hildegard's death, the manuscript was probably produced in the Rupertsberg scriptorium and copied from an exemplar made under Hildegard's supervision.

15. This sphere is illustrated in the fourteenth-century Psalter of Robert de Lisle (British Library MS. Arundel 83, fol. 123^v). The miniatures in this manuscript are reproduced by Lucy Freeman Sandler, *The Psalter of Robert de Lisle in the British Library* (London: Harvey Miller, 1983); see also Lucy Freeman Sandler, *Gothic Manuscripts, 1285–1385*, Survey of Manuscripts Illuminated in the British Isles, 5 (London: Harvey Miller, 1986), No. 38.

16. A. C. Cawley, "The Staging of Medieval Drama," in *Medieval Drama*, ed. Lois Potter, Revels History of Drama in English, 1 (London: Methuen, 1983), p. 6.

17. See Adrian Wilson and Joyce Lancaster Wilson, *A Medieval Mirror: Speculum humanae salvationis 1324–1500* (Berkeley and Los Angeles: Univ. of California Press, 1984), p. 142.

18. *Le Jeu d'Adam* [*Ordo Representationis Adae*], ed. Willem Noomen (Paris: Champion, 1971), pp. 53–54.

19. W. O. Hassell, *The Holkham Bible Picture Book* (London: Dropmore Press, 1954).

20. *The Wakefield Pageants in the Towneley Cycle*, ed. A. C. Cawley (Manchester: Manchester Univ. Press, 1958).

Hell mouth can also appear in pictorial representations of an incident in the life of Moses, the destruction of Korah, as in the opening page to *Genesis* in the Schocken Pentateuch made in southwestern Germany about 1300: Jerusalem, Schocken Collection, MS. 14840, fol. 1^v; see Joseph Gutmann, *Hebrew Manuscript Painting* (New York: George Braziller, 1978), p. 74, Pl. 18. I know of no example of the dramatization of this episode.

21. For *Sponsus*, which includes the stage direction "Modo accipiant eas Demones, et precipitentur in infernum," see Karl Young, *The Drama of the Medieval Church* (Oxford: Clarendon Press, 1933), II, 364, and for a discussion of this play in the context of Last Judgment iconography, see Pamela Sheingorn, "'For God is Such a Doomsman': Origins and Development of the Theme of Last Judgment," in *Homo, Memento Finis*, pp. 15–58. See also the edition of Raffaello Monterosso and D'Arco Silvio Avalle, *Sponsus: Dramma delle Vergine Prudenti e delle Vergine Stolte* (Milan and Naples: Riccardo Ricciardi, 1965), and the commentary by Clifford Davidson, "On the Uses of Iconographic Study: The Example of the *Sponsus* from St. Martial of Limoges," *Comparative Drama*, 13 (1979–80), 300–19. For the Künzelsauer play, which specifies, "Und so führen die Teufel sie zur Hölle," see *Das Künzelsauer Fronleichnamspiel vom Jahr 1479*, ed. Albert Schumann (Öhringen: F. Rau, n.d.), p. 182.

22. Bernd Neumann, *Geistliches Schauspiel im Zeugnis der Zeit: Zur Aufführung mittelalterlicher religiöser Dramen im deutschen Sprachgebiet* (Munich: Artemis Verlag, 1987), Nos. 2567–72, 2574, 2583–86.

23. Bibliothèque Nationale, MS. fr. 2091, fol. 64^v; this illumination is reproduced by Charlotte Lacaze, *The "Vie de St. Denis" Manuscript (Bibliothèque Nationale, MS. fr. 2090–92)* (New York: Garland, 1979). On this manuscript see also Ingeborg Bähr, *Saint Denis und seine Vita im Spiegel der Bildüberlieferung der französischen Kunst des Mittelalters* (Worms: Wernersche Verlagsgesellschaft, 1984).

24. Jean Fouquet, *The Hours of Étienne Chevalier*, introd. Claude Schafer (New York: George Braziller, 1971), Pl. 45.

25. *The Late Medieval Religious Plays of Bodleian MSS Digby 133 and E Museo 160*, ed. Donald C. Baker, John L. Murphy, and Louis B. Hall, Jr., EETS, 283 (London, 1982). The editors comment: "The stage of Hell is specifically called a stage . . . and has a top area and a Hell-mouth beneath."

The saints are also subject to visions of hell and its torments, as in the case of St. Colette of Corbie, who was protected by an iron cage attached to her cell during her vision; for an illustration of this scene, described in Pierre de Vaux's life of St. Colette and represented in a miniature in the late fifteenth-century manuscript of that life given to the Poor Clares of Ghent by Charles the Bold and Margaret of York and still in their possession (Ghent, Monasterium Bethlehem, MS. 8, fol. 19^r), see Charles van Corstanje *et al.*, *Vita Sancta Coletae (1381–1447)* (Leiden: Brill, 1982), Pl. 6.

26. For this tract on the Mass in Anglo-Norman French, see Paris, Bibliothèque Nationale MS. fonds français 13342, fols. 45^r–48^v; I cite Francis Wormald, "Some Pictures of the Mass in an English XIVth Century Manuscript," *Walpole Society*, 41 (1966–68), 40, Pl. 37.

27. For a general and theoretical discussion of the application to drama of the principles of composition found in the pictorial arts, see Pamela Sheingorn, "The Visual Language of Drama: Principles of Composition," in *Contexts for Early English Drama*, ed. Marianne G. Briscoe and John C. Coldewey (Bloomington: Indiana Univ. Press, 1989), pp. 173–91.

28. For a discussion of the manuscript, see Selma Jónsdóttir, *An Eleventh Century Byzantine Last Judgment in Iceland* (Reykjavik: Almenna, 1959).

29. Paris, Bibliothèque Nationale, MS. lat. 10434, fol. 9^v.

30. *York*, ed. Alexandra F. Johnston and Margaret Rogerson, Records of Early English Drama (Toronto: Univ. of Toronto Press, 1979), I, 55.

31. Peter Holding, "Stagecraft in the York Cycle," *Theatre Notebook*, 34 (1980), 51–52.

32. For extensive analyses of stage picture in Last Judgment plays in relation to composition in the pictorial arts, see the essays in *Homo, Memento Finis, passim*.

33. Alexandra F. Johnston and Margaret Dorrell, "The Doomsday Pageant of the York Mercers, 1433," *Leeds Studies in English*, 5 (1971), 31.

34. Mikhail Bakhtin, *Rabelais and His World*, trans. Hélène Iswolsky (Bloomington: Indiana Univ. Press, 1984), p. 401; see also the discussion in Clifford Davidson, "Space and Time in Medieval Drama: Meditations on Orientation in the Early Theater," in *Word, Picture, and Spectacle*, ed. Clifford Davidson, Early Drama, Art, and Music, Monograph Ser., 5 (Kalamazoo: Medieval Institute Publications, 1984), pp. 40–46.

35. Utrecht, University Library, MS. Script. eccl. 484, fol. 1^v; for a reproduction, see E. T. DeWald, *The Illustrations of the Utrecht Psalter* (Princeton: Princeton Univ. Press, n.d.), Pl. I.

36. Ibid, Pl. V. The Utrecht Psalter also offers the Hades Head as an image of hell, as in the illustration to the verse "if I make my bed in hell, behold thou art there," where a sinner is about to be devoured by a large head (Ps. 138 [139].8, fol. 78^r; DeWald, *The Illustrations of the Utrecht Psalter*, Pl. CXXI).

37. Citations are to *The York Plays*, ed. Richard Beadle (London: Edward Arnold, 1982).

38. Glynne Wickham, *Early English Stages, 1300 to 1660*, III (London: Routledge and Kegan Paul, 1981), 245.

39. Joyce Ruth Manheimer Galpern, "The Shape of Hell in Anglo-Saxon England," unpublished Ph.D. diss. (Univ. of California, Berkeley, 1977), p. 142.

40. Ibid, p. 3.

41. See *The Cloisters Apocalypse* (New York: Metropolitan Museum of Art, 1971), II, fol. 35^r; this miniature illustrates *Revelations* 20.9–10.

42. Lyons, Bibliothèque de la Ville, MS. 1351, fol. 22^v. See also the relief at Lincoln Cathedral (figs. 2–4).

43. *Coventry*, ed. R. W. Ingram, Records of Early English Drama (Toronto: Univ. of Toronto Press, 1981), *passim* (see page references listed under *hell* in the index), but see also Philip Butterworth, "Hellfire: Flame as Special Effect," in the present volume. For a discussion of the Coventry records in relation to the hell mouth included in the Last Judgment painting in the Stratford Guild Chapel, see Clifford Davidson, "Thomas Sharp and the Stratford Hell Mouth," *The EDAM Newsletter*, 1, No. 1 (1978), 6–8, and his monograph on the Stratford Guild Chapel, *The Guild Chapel Wall Paintings at Stratford-upon-Avon* (New York: AMS Press, 1988), esp. pp. 31–32, Pl. 17.

44. Though made in Rouen, this book of hours (Victoria and Albert Museum, MS. L.475–1918) follows the Use of Sarum. Hell mouth appears in the illustration to the Office of the Dead (fol. 100^r); see Rowan Watson, *The Playfair Hours* (London: Victoria and Albert Museum, 1984), Pl. XXII.

45. *Mystères inedits du XV* *siècle*, ed. A. Jubinal (1837), I, 94–95, as cited by M. D. Anderson, *Drama and Imagery in English Medieval Churches* (Cambridge: Cambridge Univ. Press, 1963), pp. 230–31.

46. Ibid., Pl. 6c. See also W. L. Hildburgh, "English Alabaster Carvings as Records of the Medieval Religious Drama," *Archaeologia*, 93 (1949), Pl. 20c.

47. Anderson, *Drama and Imagery*, p. 127.

48. Cambridge, University Library, MS. Add. 4103, fol. 171^v; see James H. Marrow, Henri L. M. Defoer, Anne S. Korteweg, and Wilhelmina C. M. Wüstefeld, *The Golden Age of Dutch Manuscript Painting* (New York: George Braziller, 1990), p. 230, Pl. X.

49. *The Staging of Religious Drama in Europe in the Later Middle Ages: Texts and Documents in English Translation*, ed. Peter Meredith and John E. Tailby, Early Drama, Art and Music, Monograph Ser., 4 (Kalamazoo: Medieval Institute Publications, 1983), p. 90; on the technology of the eyes, see also the paper by Philip Butterworth in the present volume.

50. See Elie Konigson, *La représentation d'un mystère de la Passion à Valenciennes en 1547* (Paris: CNRS, 1969).

51. Donald Clive Stuart, "The Stage Setting of Hell and the Iconography of the Middle Ages," *Romanic Review*, 4 (1913), 339.

52. *Records of Plays and Players in Lincolnshire, 1300–1585*, ed. Stanley J. Kahrl, Malone Soc. Collections, 8 (Oxford, 1974), p. 67.

53. A. E. Richards, *Studies in English Literature*, I: *The English Wagner Book of 1594* (1907), as quoted by E. K. Chambers, *The Elizabethan Stage* (Oxford: Clarendon Press, 1923), III, 72; see also George R. Kernodle, *From Art to Theatre: Form and Convention in the Renaissance* (Chicago: Univ. of Chicago Press, 1944), p. 136.

54. Neumann, *Geistliches Schauspiel*, No. 1889.

55. "Daer waren 6 burgen to bereit. . . . Die seste was die holle mit vil gruwelichen und helschen duveln. Und koste groet gelt und arbeit" (ibid., No. 1218).

56. For records, see Neumann, *Geistliches Schauspiel*, pp. 437–574, and for its location and appearance on the Lucerne plans, see *The Staging of Religious Drama*, ed. Meredith and Tailby (inside cover).

57. Fouquet, *The Hours of Étienne Chevalier*, Pl. 45.

58. John Marshall, "The Medieval English Stage: A Graffito of a Hell-mouth Scaffold?" *Theatre Notebook*, 34 (1980), 99–103.

59. Francis Wormald, *Collected Writings*, ed. J. J. G. Alexander, T. J. Brown, and Joan Gibbs (London: Harvey Miller, 1988), II, 143.

60. *The Staging of Religious Drama*, ed. Meredith and Tailby, p. 90.

61. Jeffrey M. Hoffeld, "Commentary on the Pages of the Facsimile," in *The Cloisters Apocalypse*, II, 46.

62. Weimar, Zentralbibliothek der deutschen Klassik, MS. Fol. max 4, fol. 15^v. For description and bibliography of this and other Apocalypse manuscripts which I cite, see Richard Kenneth Emmerson and Suzanne Lewis, "Census and Bibliography of Medieval Manuscripts Containing Apocalypse Illustrations, ca. 800–1500" (Parts II and III), *Traditio*, 41 (1985), 375, 388; 42 (1986), 456–57.

63. British Library, MS. Harley 4972, fol. 11^v.

64. Guldan, "Das Monster-Portal," p. 238.

65. For a list of Alexander Minorita Apocalypses, see Emmerson and Lewis, "Census (III)," pp. 443–46.

66. Wolfenbüttel, Herzog-August-Bibliothek, Cod. Blank. 147, fol. 81^v; for an illustration of this item, see Guldan, "Das Monster-Portal," fig. 12.

67. See Stella Mary Newton, *Renaissance Theatre Costume and the Sense of the Historic Past* (London: Rapp and Whiting, 1975), fig. 1.

The Inhabitants of Hell: Devils

Barbara D. Palmer

Numerous medieval art and drama scholars have noted that while images of virtue—angels, for example—remain relatively static over time, images of evil tend to reflect their cultural environment, its values, abuses, and terrors. Throughout recorded Western art, angels normally are identified by wings and saints came to be identified by halos, whereas devils have assumed a baffling variety of shifting shapes. Such an observation may help to trace, if not to explain, the history of diabolic iconography, which at its best is interrupted and erratic rather than continuous and linear. Modern Western conceptions of the devil have conflated its earlier representational diversity into two primary images of anthropomorphic creature with horns, tail, and cloven feet or of small, plump red demon with trident. Neither caricature does justice to the profusion of imagination which early English artists and dramatists brought to their embodiments of hell's demonic inhabitants, a subject which is the analytical focus of this paper.

A cursory historical examination of the diabolic concept sheds little light on medieval English representations. The term 'devil' itself reflects philological shape-shifting; as Rossell Hope Robbins notes, "originally distinct species of spirits were unified by interchangeable translations of devil, demon, fiend,"[1] an observation buttressed by the textual designations of "serpente," "dyvell," and "Demon" within the same sentence in the Chester Cycle Fall of Adam and Eve.[2] Although theologians went to some lengths to distinguish individual types of diabolicalness, their designations never seem to have attached themselves to unique artistic forms.

One thus is free to hypothesize that both the concept and also the forms of a devil derive from the animistic world of pernicious wildlife and physical environment, acquire additional attributes from social ills and dangers, and further embody man's psychological, spiritual, and moral terrors. First as reality and then as

> imagination bodies forth
> The forms of things unknown, the poet's [or illustrator's] pen
> Turns them to shapes, and gives to airy nothing
> A local habitation and a name.[3]

Local diabolic habitations are consistently ubiquitous, devils showing an ongoing reluctance to stay in hell. Psellus' six eleventh-century habitats, which incorporate earlier desert visions and find later illustration in the arts, include the upper air, home of fiery devils who do not descend until Doomsday; the earthly atmosphere, home of aerial devils potentially visible to men; the earth itself, home of terrestrial tempters; the waters, home of malicious male Leviathans and female Sirens; the underworld, home of numerous old moles "work[ing] i' th' earth so fast";[4] and, finally and inclusively, all darkness, home of those "most dangerous and most unknowable" heliophobes.[5] No sphere of man's activities is safe from diabolic assault, and thus all environmental forms from every sphere are potentially appropriate for artistic representation.

Devils' numbers rather early on swell to "legion" and then, literally, to "legions." Calculating a Roman legion at 6,000 soldiers, the number of legions based on a percentage of fallen angels in turn based on a calculation of the number of original angels, Johannes Wierus, author of *De praestigiis daemonum* (1563), corrected former estimates of diabolic personnel "without any possibility of error" to "an army of 1,111 legions, each composed of 6,666 devils, which brought his total of evil spirits to 7,405,926. . . ."[6] As Tertullian characterizes the diabolic employment of these legions,

> Their business is to corrupt mankind; thus, the spirit of evil was from the very beginning bent upon man's destruction. The demons, therefore, inflict upon men's bodies diseases and other bitter misfortunes, and upon the soul sudden and extraordinary outbursts of violence. They have their own subtle, spiritual properties for assailing each part of human nature.[7]

Those "subtle, spiritual properties" require form, however, for artistic representation, and the brief discussion above of the diabolic
concept does not lead one to see easily where it acquired those
forms. Surely its multitudinous sources were far more complex
than Robbins' attribution to the Desert Fathers' "hallucinations and
recollections of replaced gods."[8] Even if such oversimplification
were helpful to iconographic analysis, one needs only to compile a
catalogue of the shapes which the Desert Fathers saw in order to
realize that the diabolic variety already has escaped orderly classi-
fication. A further source can be seen in scriptural imagery, which,
although not defining the shape of either the devil or of his demons, provided a potential iconographic vocabulary. Thus one
notes the serpent, Leviathan, dragon, sea beast, earth beast, leopard, bear, lion, locust, horse, scorpion, frog, and bird as diabolic
shapes and fire, fiery speech, smoke, chains, horns, multiple heads,
crowns, women's hair, lion's fangs, and breastplates as only a few
of their many attributes.[9]

While allowing that the vocabulary of visionary and scriptural
writings may have served later diabolic representation, a connection between early writings and early artistic representation is ten-
uous. Early Christian art represented the felicity of the faithful, not
the misery of the faithless. Sufficient torture existed in this world
without more being portrayed in the next. Unlike Roman art, early
Christian art contained no images of death, subjects which included death, or representation of life beyond death, excepting the
occasional allegorical figure of the Good Shepherd.[10] Although
diabolic iconographic forms were abundantly available with imag-
istic resources in pagan art, ordinary life, scriptures, and such visionary hermitic accounts as Athanasius' fourth-century *Life of St.
Anthony*, until, at the earliest, the seventh or eighth centuries one
finds no diabolic representations attached to the biblical scenes
that they later come to illustrate, with the very rare exception of
Adam and Eve separated by a tree with a serpent. Even early illustrated Gospels do not depict the accompanying text, their illustrations instead "signs meant to recall a certain evangelical event
rather than paintings which attempt to describe it."[11]

When, however, those biblical accounts which include or imply devils—exorcisms, the communion and death of Judas, the Harrowing of Hell, and Doomsday—do acquire diabolic imagery, no clearly causal or chronological iconographic progression emerges. Among the earliest extant New Testament scenes to find illustration are the demons from the eighteen Gospel accounts of Christ's casting them out. In an illumination in a Book of Pericopes of the first half of the eleventh century from Reichenau, St. Gall, or Einsiedeln, the offending demon takes the form of a diabolic bird with horns and sharply feathered arm-wings who emerges from the mouth of the possessed man; other demons in this illustration ride animals whose shapes eventually will become subsumed into their own.[12] The oldest extant Harrowing of Hell example is the seventh- or eighth-century fresco in the Roman Forum's S. Maria Antiqua, but iconographically this scene (like numerous others) is "a replica of allegorical representations of the victorious Roman emperor" which portray Christ as "victor over the tyrannical prince of death" rather than depictions of the struggles of hell's demons for their victims.[13] As Gertrud Schiller notes, "No Early Christian representation of the Temptation is known," with the early ninth-century *Book of Kells* (c.800) and Stuttgart Psalter (c.825) among the first.[14] The Stuttgart Psalter's two diabolic tempters are black and naked with sharply-pointed wings, distorted facial features, and elongated pointed fingers by which one holds a two-pronged poker and the other a splayed hook. Instead of being imaginative inventions, however, these demons seem rather to reflect a debased parody of angelic iconography.

Although the iconography of early Continental scenes of the communion and death of Judas is rich in a variety of diabolic forms (blackbirds; batlike, scrawny demons; dragon-fish; beastlike grotesques; even an ibex pulling the hanging rope), such scenes are very rare after the fourteenth century and even rarer at any point in England, making their influence on medieval diabolic imagery difficult to discern. A converse but equally opaque iconographic process seems to have occurred with Doomsday imagery.

Up to the twelfth century, the predominant Doomsday image was of Christ in Majesty as Judge of the World; after the thirteenth century, hell's torments dominate *dies irae* with increasingly imaginative and fanciful demons on both sides of the Channel. Instances of other iconographic dead-ends and jump-starts, including Eve's Satan-serpent, Jonah's dragon-fish, and *Revelation*'s bestiary, only serve to buttress further the generalization that diabolic imagery is as convoluted as sin itself and its forms as numerous as the demonic legions.

In the vast cauldron of diabolic imagery with either verbal or artistic authority, one can see the shape of a giant, black boy, monk, scholar, woman, wild beast, angel, adder, dragon, Leviathan, bird, smoke, fire, ibex, bee, or locust. Additional appendages are attached from ass, leopard, bear, horse, wolf, scorpion, bull, goat, and bat, with wings, horns, fangs, and body hair in varying proportions. Clad in fur, scales, cowl, hood, mitre, or horned headdress, these creatures are armed with chain, serpent-as-chain, fire-hook, flesh-hook, trident, ax, mace, club, and plate-armor forged from souls. Multi-headed or multi-faced to suggest their duplicity, some devils also are represented by further anatomic distortion as Behemoths of sexual prowess or corruption. Although usually pictured as black to signify their deprivation from light, red, blue, yellow, or green devils occur as cultural norms dictate. The devil within is a daunting *mélange* of "Jewish, Christian, heathen, elfish, gigantic and spectral stock," to quote Jakob Grimm's summary,[15] and its iconographic origins and development are no less promiscuous.

As André Grabar observes, "A new image can have as its source another image which does not resemble it formally. The link between the two is of a semantic nature. . . ."[16] One such semantic link cited above is the adaptation of Roman victor imagery to Christ's conquest of hell—incidents which are unlike in every respect except the semantic correspondence of triumph over one's enemies. Another such semantic link between the iconography of the Roman Empire and Christian diabolic representation includes the concept of persecution, torment, and torture, which Grabar mentions in passing but which warrants closer study in the elaborate imagery of circus, hippodrome, and martyrdom. Such common attributes as weapons, beasts, nets, swarming crowd, open mouths, and grotesquely bloodthirsty features would seem to bear more than passing similarity in their artistic depiction, regardless of their dissimilarity in every other context.

Yet a third possible semantic link emerges while looking for archetypes of medieval devils' weapons, which far exceed in variety the stereotypical pitchfork. The weapons of hell would seem to be not the weapons of earth, as one would expect. Instead, they are the tools of earth, transferred by the semantic links of the implements needed to do one's work and the concept of work's being literal torture. Thus one finds the appointments of ordinary domestic life perverted into instruments of torment to illustrate doing the Devil's own work. Hieronymus Bosch's fifteenth-century studies for monsters[17] (figs. 12a, 12b) as well as his application of those studies in such works as the early sixteenth-century *Temptations of St. Anthony* suggest the flexibility of domestic appointments.

Parallels to Bosch's instruments of torment are easily found in quite undiabolic sources. The ordinary medieval mace, which by the middle of the thirteenth century had developed into "a knobbed or flanged iron head set on a short wooden haft,"[18] typically appears as a demon's weapon to ward souls into hell (fig. 13). Medieval flesh-hooks, "a regular feature of any medieval kitchen[,] . . . used for examining and tasting the food while it was stewing in great cauldrons over the open fire," become demonic warders' weapons[19] (fig. 14). The trident grasped by goading devils is held by the innocent hand of a hunter spearing an otter in a fifteenth-century illumination from Bibliothèque Nationale MS. fr. 616, based on Gaston Phoebus' *The Hunting Book*.[20]

Harvest or agricultural implements serve as ready tools for diabolic illustration. Representative is the frequently reproduced illumination of the month of June from the *Très riches heures du Duc de Berry* (c.1416) by the brothers Limbourg which shows the two-pronged pitchfork, rake, and scythe in productive pastoral use.[21] Likewise, a Flemish harvest illumination from the *Livre des profits ruraux* (c.1470) by Pietro di Crescenzi depicts comely peasants wielding scythes, three-pronged pitchfork, rakes, and long-handled ax under the benignly approving eyes of priest and overlord.[22] From the *Tacuinum Sanitatis*, an eleventh-century Baghdad health manual that became popular in Europe in the late Middle Ages, a healer boils his medicine in flasks while using a fire-fork to stir the coals under his cauldron, an activity and implement frequently employed by devils in English chancel arch Doomsday paintings.[23]

The more diabolic images one analyzes, the less peculiar their individual iconographic elements become. At first glance demons appear to be horrific, nightmarish creatures escaped from another world; consequent examination reveals that the elements which compound diabolic representation are in fact simples from the world of man, of nature, and of sacred art. Bosch's startling left panel, showing St. Anthony borne aloft by demons, from the *Temptations of St. Anthony* is a case in point. The viewer immediately reacts to a world that never was and that he very much hopes will never be: suspended in a sulphurous blue sky, St. Anthony clings to a crab-like demon while assaulted on all sides by voracious flying fish, a captured sailing ship with boat in tow, and demons which range from the homicidal to the comical. Closer study, however, identifies recognizably natural details. The homicidal demon carries a leafy locust branch as his weapon, another demon a long-handled mason's mallet, and the third an ordinary hay scythe; the flying fish look like fish, the blackbirds like blackbirds, and the boats perfectly sea-worthy. Even the apparent oddity of the third demon's being propelled by a firecracker in his posterior is relatively normal in the world of medieval drama, as below.

Attributes from sacred art also are borrowed for diabolic representation. The feathered wings and tunic of a Methley Church of St. Oswald roof boss seraphim are as sharply pointed as any devil's appendages, and the Thornhill Church of St. Michael's painted glass Doom of 1492 shows a black-garbed St. Michael with unfurled black batlike wings guarding the entrance to heaven.[24] Particularly representative of the cross-fertilization between holy and hellish imagery are the numerous portrayals of John the Baptist as

wilderness preacher in his shredded skin or fur garments with un-
ruly, spiked hair and beard. The Harewood Church of All Saints
c.1480 tomb carving so cunningly tangles his bare legs with the
hooved animal legs of his garments that one finds it difficult to
determine where saint ends and beast begins.[25]

Attempting to draw rigid iconographic lines between diabolic
and non-diabolic representation is equally difficult and relatively
unproductive. The elements of diabolic representation are common,
drawn from normal activities, implements, and anatomies. Their
assembly, however, is perverse, and it is this grotesque organiza-
tional scheme that is peculiar to diabolic iconography. Hieronymus
Bosch is not the first, last, or only artist who "expresses the medieval conception of Hell as a state where the divinely ordained laws
of nature have disintegrated into chaos."[26] What distinguishes the
inhabitants of hell is the disintegration, fragmentation, incongruity,
antithesis, exaggeration, adaptation, juxtaposition, and recombina-
tion of elements into a potential "compound of all the contortions
and distortions known to exist among living things on this earth,"
as one writer puts it.[27] Karl P. Wentersdorf points to this perversion of heavenly and earthly elements, of angelic and human attributes, as a *monde renversé*, "a realm where the practices . . .
were a total reversal of everything ordained for mankind by the
Almighty."[28]

At the root of medieval English diabolic iconography would
seem to be the expression of chaos, a disorientation from that
which is recognized as divine or human order. At its root, too, is
an ironic perception of the difference between the way things
ought to be or to look and their distorted appearance in diabolic
iconography. Although far fewer examples survive than in Continental art, English devils reflect the same daunting *mélange*, the
same promiscuity of iconographic sources, and the same perverse
assembly of common elements. The creation of devils from fallen
angels is recorded whole at York's Church of St. Michael, Spurriergate, with "Lucifer yet in feathers, but other demons fully altered
with feathers replaced by hair";[29] and in the choir of York Minster Lucifer, described as "'a horrific red beast with the head of a

monkey, the breast of a serpent and the legs of a bird' falling downward across [the] water covered globe."[30] The demons' feathers-to-fur transformation seems to be iconographically bifurcated, with one direction the sharply pointed batlike appendages comparable to the angularity of the Methley seraphim noted above and the other a rounded ponderousness seen in a lost Dewsbury Church of All Saints painted glass figure of a man-angel in feathered lower tunic whose face and upper body are just beginning to sink into the bestial.[31]

Satan himself, although occasionally disguised—at Dewsbury as a friar tempting a musician—or humorously depicted as at Shibden Hall, Halifax, where he carries a soul, portrayed in the painted glass quarry as a very dead sole fish, to the frying pan,[32] most frequently bears the attributes with which he is identified in the common mind: horned or pointed head sometimes with animal ears, batlike wings, hairy body, and clawed or cloven feet. Occasionally one characteristic is strikingly emphasized, as at Lincoln Cathedral where the spandrel devil high above St. Hugh's shrine bears the sinister, deceitful cross-legged posture usually given to Herod, which may here be conflated iconography appropriate to the Massacre of the Innocents, or the Fairford St. Mary's Church west window where the blaze of hellfire dominates the image itself[33] (fig. 15) or the Sprotbrough Church of St. Mary misericord (fig. 16) where Satan's priapic superiority has survived even six centuries of woodworm. Sexuality also oozes from a Leeds Church of St. John 1634 Lucifer corbel, a hermaphroditic Prince of the Underworld who balances his froglike posture atop hell mouth.[34] Other Leeds fallen angel corbels include hermaphrodites, one of which is winged, a mermaid, and a merman, the forms more suggestive of an aquatic environment than a fiery and thus oddly comparable to Bosch's environment for St. Anthony, above.

Lesser English demons most frequently are animalistic or grotesque with an assortment of pig ears, snouts, batlike wings, fanged mouths, pawlike hands, facial hair, and furry bodies. The closing ring illustrating hell mouth at Adel has such features (fig. 17).[35] When determinable, as in painted glass, their colors seem to be from the primary range as in the lost Selby Abbey Doom's shaggy yellow-furred beast with green wings and its red-furred version with blue wings or the bright blue surviving example from Fairford.[36] These lesser personnel are employed as porters, stokers and cauldron tenders, tormenters, executioners, guards, scribes and accountants, and occasionally musicians. Thus among numerous other representations, one finds demons tending souls in a cauldron and holding the chain which binds the damned at York; blowing the cauldron fire with bellows, guarding with flesh hook and club, pulling a chain around souls, carrying a soul piggy-back, flogging, and hanging a soul by a hook through his nose at Stratford; spurring on animals ridden by damned souls at Compton Wynyates; carrying off a nude alewife, reading her sins from a scroll, and playing a bagpipe at Ludlow; swallowing a man, devouring a man's leg, threatening with a mace, hanging lost souls from gibbets, and fighting with angels for souls at Rotherham; and, of course, tugging on St. Michael's balance pan at Harewood and elsewhere.

Even allowing for minimal survival of English examples, the variety of diabolic representation and occupation would seem to be high and also would seem to be quite lively, an iconography which may owe as much to medieval drama production as to more conventional art historical sources. This occasion is not the appropriate forum, if any occasion is, to argue cause-and-effect between medieval art and medieval drama. One simply can observe that both visual media within the same cultural period represented devils imaginatively and unrestrictedly. Lucifer's lines from the mid-fourteenth-century French miracle play of St. Quentin well characterize the apparent artistic license:

> Smooth Devils, Horned Devils,
> Sullen Devils, Playful Devils,
> Shorn Devils, Hairy Devils,
> Bushy Devils, Cursed Devils,
>   Foolish Devils,
> Devils, Devilesses, and Young Devils,
> All the progeny of devildom. . . .[37]

In the Continental dramatic records presented by Peter Meredith and John Tailby, indeed all the progeny of devildom seems
capable of dramatic representation. One 1536 account from the
Bourges Parade which preceded its Acts of the Apostles play notes
a float for hell which was led into the playing place by a group of
devils.

> After this infernal crew (*diablerie*) came a Hell, fourteen feet long
> and eight wide, in the form of a rock on which was constructed a
> tower, continually blazing and shooting out flames in which Lucifer
> appeared, head and body only. He wore a bear skin with a sequin
> hanging from each hair and a pelt with two [*animal*] masks (*tymbre à
> deux museaux*) adorned with various colored materials; he ceaselessly
> vomited flames, held in his hands various serpents or vipers which
> moved and spat fire. At the four corners of the rock were four small
> towers inside which could be seen souls undergoing various torments.
> And from the front of the rock there came a great serpent whistling
> and spitting fire from throat, nostrils, and eyes. And on every part of
> the rock there clambered and climbed all kinds of serpents and great
> toads. It was moved and guided by a certain number of people inside
> it, who worked the torments in the [*different*] places as they had been
> instructed.[38]

The Barcelona Corpus Christi procession property list of 1424
includes "the dragon, cross, and halo of St. Margaret, together with
the trousers of the said dragon" and "two costumes with hempen
trousers, and two masks (*testes*) for the two devils."[39] A Lucerne
Temptation of Adam and Eve costume list of 1583 has the Serpent
represented as follows:

> a venomous four-footed serpent, with female face and voice. A veil
> and a crown on its head.
> It does not join in the entry procession but hides early in the morning
> in the Mount of Olives until it is its turn to speak [*Elsewhere:* it gets
> up into the tree], and when it is cursed it crawls away on all fours
> through Hell.[40]

Intercourse with the devil, whether literal, artistic, or dramatic, is
not without its dangers, as a 1496 production account by Andrieu

de la Vigne, writer of the Mystery of St. Martin play at Seurre, tells:

> Then Lucifer began to speak, and during his speech the man who played Satan, when he prepared to enter through his trapdoor (*secret*) underground, his costume caught fire round his buttocks so that he was badly burned. But he was so swiftly succored, stripped, and reclothed that without giving any sign [*of pain*] he came and played his part, then retired to his house.[41]

The English dramatic records collected to date and the surviving play texts record nothing so elaborate nor, apparently, as dangerous but are not entirely unhelpful to diabolic iconography. Most remarked of course is the early fifteenth-century *Castle of Perseverance*'s opening stage direction, that Belial shall "haue gunnepowdyr brennynge In pypys in hys handys and in hys erys and in hys ars whanne he gothe to batayl,"[42] which obviously could be done on the stage and which Bosch illustrates in his *Temptation of St. Anthony*, above. The four surviving "cycle" texts are less descriptively forthcoming, a drama text not needing to describe what everybody can see and which repeated productions already knew how to effect. In the Chester plays, the Tanners' Creation and Fall of Lucifer has two black fiends (I.251); the Drapers' Creation and Fall of Adam and Eve's Satan disguises himself in an adder's body, adder's feet, feathered "wynges like a bryde," and "a maydens face" (II.193–96), a frequent representation in illuminated manuscripts.[43] Whether the references to hell-hounds in the Butchers' Temptation of Christ (XII.153–56) and Cooks' Harrowing of Hell (XVII.98, 151) are literal demonic representations is not clear, but whatever they are, their teeth or fangs are visible in the Harrowing. In the Websters' Judgment pageant, the second demon carries a large sack or pouch filled with the damned merchant's ill-gotten gain. The Towneley's fallen angels are black, ugly, and as tattered as fools; in the Harrowing Satan either puts on armor or at least calls for it to fight Jesus; and the second demon of the Judgment lugs a bagful of sinners' rolls.[44] York's Lucifer fades from bright to "blakkeste and blo"—i.e., "discolored"—and the Satan of the Fall is "in a worme liknes" (V.23).[45] The sole unambiguously literal diabolic description to be gleaned from the N-town text is that Lucifer wears a black costume.[46]

These are early days to generalize about diabolic iconography from the English dramatic records, but at least one observation seems not to be premature: devils' costumes were extremely expensive to construct and to maintain, they suffered regular damage and required regular repair, and one thus can deduce that they were elaborate and detailed.[47] After years of renting devil costumes, the Chester Innkeepers, for example, discovered what Philip Henslowe already knew, that owning costumes is more profitable. In 1596, they laid out 10s to Robert Lyche to make two demons' heads, 4s for eight yards of canvas for two demons' coats, 2s to make the coats, 6s 8d to paint them with oil, and 11d to transport coats and headpieces, an amount which suggests either the costumes' unwieldiness, their fragility, or their distance from the Midsummer Show's route.[48]

If one borrows the Ludlow misericord representation of similar subject, the false-measuring alewife seized by devils and thrust into hell mouth, to illuminate the Chester Innkeepers' pageant, one can hypothesize that these devils' oversize heads had horns, rounded animal ears, animal-grotesque faces, and pleated attached tippets which served to balance the head on the shoulders. The Ludlow devils' coats, which essentially are short tunics, have feathers, flames, and faces.[49] The additional Ludlow details of paw-hands, cloven feet, and batwings could be constructed amply from the four-yard canvas piece specified above for each Chester coat. In an entry less open to speculation, the Chester Butchers' Temptation of Christ devil had feathers, which in performance got "all Rugged and rente."[50]

The York Mercers' three Judgment devils apparently were Janus-faced; the Devon records yield one Ashburton payment for devils' heads;[51] and Cambridge's astonishingly sparse diabolic materials of record note "ij blak develles cootes with hornes" in a St. John's College 1548 inventory and a devil's coat and face in the 1546 Queen's College inventory.[52] Wymondham, Norfolk, paid out 4d in 1538 "for a payer of devyls shoes"[53] but failed to specify whether they bought claws, hooves, paws, or talons. Whatever the shape, they seem to have gotten good value, as the Coventry Drapers' paid 11d in 1568 "for cambes [?claws] for one of the devells hose."[54]

The Coventry records for 1544 supply the Cappers' 8d payment "for a yard of canvas for ye devyll*es* mall & for makyng" in their Harrowing of Hell segment, and it was repainted in 1571. 'Mall' linguistically would seem to be mallet, but here it seems to have been "the devells clvbbe" which was again repainted in 1576 and could well have resembled the mace described earlier.[55] The Drapers' Doomsday pageant accounts record two demons' masks, coats, the clawed hose noted above, and two "farryshe hatt" which required "ij pound of heare for ye Same."[56] Although the accounts do not specifically describe the Coventry devils' appearance, their costumes seemed to disintegrate regularly into chaos: the records note frequent expenses for "points" and "newe ledder to the same Garment."[57]

The Norwich Grocers' inventory of 1564 records the famous "Cote with hosen & tayle for ye cerpente stayned w*ith* a w*hitte* heare" and a 1534 entry the "new Heer w*ith* a crown for ye Serpent 6d."[58] A much more remarkable set of Norwich entries, however, provides a diabolic iconography which conflates Satan, demons, serpent, and St. George's dragon into a beast of distinguished but not unique anatomy. Similar anatomical conflation occurs in the twelfth-century Volterra stone relief where Judas is pursued under the communion table by a winged, fish-bellied serpent dragon with Satanic head or in the fifteenth-century painted glass from the Convent of St. Lambrecht, Austria, where Jonah has encountered a dragon-fish with immense fangs.[59] The Pickering Church of SS. Peter and Paul wall painting of c.1450, though restored in the nineteenth century, probably provides the closest English visualization of what the Norwich records seem to describe. In the wall painting, a mounted St. George confronts a puff-bellied red and yellow dragon whose prone length far exceeds the charging horse's; scaled in plate-armor with a fish's lower torso, the dragon also has batlike wings and a dog-devil's face and snout. Like the modern popular concept of the Loch Ness monster, the medieval dragon seems to have appropriated natural parts and juxtaposed the recognizable into the fantastical.

The Norwich dragon was constructed from hoops of iron and, apparently, of wood which were nailed together: the 1583 St. George's Guild accounts yield payments of 8d "to Henry Radoe for A hoope of yron for the dragon and for naylles for ye same"; 6s "to A Coup*er* for putting in hoopes to sett it owt in the bellye"; 3s 6d "to A Carpenter for amending the Dragon and for the stuff [w*hich*] wherwith it was doone"; and 6s 8d "for payntyng of ytt."[60] Covered with canvas to which cloth wings were attached,[61] this wonder was repainted and equipped with "ffur & tayles" in 1622,[62] and one discovers from the 4s 6d spent in 1626 "for the Dragon paynting & mending the Broken plotes"[63] that it also boasted accessory scales. If the snap dragons currently in Norwich Castle indeed resemble earlier versions, St. George's adversary was some twenty feet long and painted green with yellow trim. Other English dragons seem to have been somewhat smaller and more portable, although size alone of course does not warrant effect. Newcastle's 1510 version required twelve yards of canvas in the construction, only three times more than one Chester devil's coat.[64] Ripon's dragon, which annually processed during the three-day celebration of Rogation and Feast of the Ascension, was carried by one man.[65]

The common thread through all of these diabolic images, however diverse and whatever their context, is that they represent man's attempt to portray disorder, the disorder which threatens his physical, psychological, social, or spiritual stability. The inhabitants of hell as depicted in medieval art and drama figure an assault on the ordinary, the regular, the anticipated. Man calculates that if he follows the rules which he either has been taught or has learned empirically the affairs of his life are likely to go in a certain more or less predictable way. If alewives pour to set measure, if clerks keep honest account books, if dragons do not transgress Rogation bounds, tomorrow is likely to run a recognizable course. If, however, man does not follow the rules, he allows a chaotic latitude that seems to find artistic expression in the iconographic diversity of medieval devils. Open to boundless images from the natural and man-made world, whirled in the maelstrom of the artist's imagination, and only slightly steadied by his realities of stone, wood, canvas, glass, or dramatic impersonation, devils present an extraordinary opportunity for innovation, individuality, and artistic evolution. By definition of the invasive, perverted, and damnable nature of the evils which it represents, diabolic iconography survives all forms of censorship—Church, state, social, and personal—to remain the means by which is expressed that which all men in all ages have most feared: chaos.

NOTES

1. Rossell Hope Robbins, *The Encyclopedia of Witchcraft and Demonology* (London: Peter Nevill, 1959), p. 131.

2. Play II.160*sd*; citations to the Chester plays are to *The Chester Mystery Cycle*, ed. R. M. Lumiansky and David Mills, EETS, s.s. 3 (London, 1974), Vol. I.

3. *A Midsummer Night's Dream*, V.i.14–17; quotations from Shakespeare in my text are from *The Complete Works of Shakespeare*, ed. David Bevington, 3rd ed. (Glenview, Ill.: Scott, Foresman, 1980).

4. *Hamlet* I.v.163.

5. Guazzo, *Compendium Maleficarum* (1608), as quoted in Robbins, *Encyclopedia*, p. 133.

6. Maximilian Rudwin, *The Devil in Legend and Literature* (LaSalle, Ill.: Open Court, 1931), p. 25.

7. Tertullian, *Apology* XXII.4–5, in *Apologetical Works*, trans. Rudolph Arbesmann and Sister Emily Joseph Daly, Fathers of the Church (Washington, D.C.: Catholic Univ. of America Press, 1950), p. 69.

36   Barbara D. Palmer

8. Robbins, *Encyclopedia*, p. 132.

9. See *Revelation* 9, 12–13, 16–17, and 20 for diabolic attributes; accounts of the Tempter in *Genesis, Matthew*, and *Luke* give no specific description that would assist artistic representation.

10. André Grabar, *Christian Iconography: A Study of Its Origins*, Bollingen Series, 35, Pt. 10 (Princeton: Princeton Univ. Press, 1968), pp. 11, 14–15.

11. Ibid., p. 92.

12. Gertrud Schiller, *Iconography of Christian Art*, trans. Janet Seligman (Greenwich, Conn.: New York Graphic Society, 1971), I, fig. 528.

13. Grabar, *Christian Iconography*, p. 126.

14. See Schiller, *Iconography*, I, 143–44, fig. 389.

15. Jakob Grimm, *Deutsche Mythologie*, as quoted in Rudwin, *The Devil*, p. 3n.

16. Grabar, *Christian Iconography*, p. xlviii.

17. Bosch is used as an example here not because of a dearth of English representation but because his sketches and paintings abundantly and concisely illustrate the use of domestic implements to diabolic purpose.

18. London Museum, *The Medieval Catalogue* (London: HMSO, 1954), pp. 74–75. The mace illustrated in my fig. 13 is from the fourteenth or fifteenth century and was found near the Bank of England.

19. The examples illustrated in my fig. 14 are from the London Wall and the Thames at London, while other examples appear in the Bayeux tapestry and the Lutrell Psalter; see ibid., p. 127.

20. Gabriel Bise, *Medieval Hunting Scenes*, trans. J. Peter Tallon (Fribourg: Productions Liber SA, 1978), p. 83.

21. *The Très Riches Heures of Jean, Duke of Berry* (New York: George Braziller, 1969), Pl. 8.

22. Pierpont Morgan Library MS. M.232, now in the Metropolitan Museum of Art; illustrated on the front cover of *The Secular Spirit: Life and Art at the End of the Middle Ages* (New York: E. P. Dutton, 1975).

23. Ibid., p. 50, Color Pl. 2. See also the Stratford-upon-Avon Guild Chapel wall painting over the chancel arch, c.1531–45, for demons and their implements: for the drawing from Thomas Sharp, *A Dissertation on the Pageants or Dramatic Mysteries* (Coventry, 1825), see fig. 7.

24. See Barbara D. Palmer, *The Early Art of the West Riding of Yorkshire*, Early Drama, Art, and Music, Reference Ser., 6 (Kalamazoo: Medieval Institute Publications, 1990), pp. 33, 158.

25. Ibid., p. 95.

26. Walter S. Gibson, *Hieronymus Bosch* (New York: Praeger, 1973), p. 60.

27. Rudwin, *The Devil*, p. 36.

28. Karl P. Wentersdorf, "The Symbolic Significance of *Figurae Scatologicae* in Gothic Manuscripts," in *Word, Picture, and Spectacle*, ed. Clifford Davidson, Early Drama, Art, and Music, Monograph Ser., 5 (Kalamazoo, Medieval Institute Publications, 1984), p. 4.

29. Clifford Davidson and David E. O'Connor, *York Art*, Early Drama, Art, and Music, Reference Ser., 1 (Kalamazoo: Medieval Institute Publications, 1978), p. 19.

30. Ibid., p. 19, quoting *Friends of York Minster: Annual Report*, 19 (1947), 26.

31. Palmer, *The Early Art of the West Riding*, pp. 30–31.

32. Ibid., pp. 39, 254–55.

33. See also June Osborne, *Stained Glass in England* (London: Frederick Muller, 1981), p. 57, Pl. XXI; Hilary Wayment, *The Stained Glass of the Church of St. Mary, Fairford, Gloucester* (London: Society of Antiquaries, 1984), Pl. XXII, Colour Pl. VId. This late fifteenth-century Last Judgment devil also has yellow eyes, scales, and a double head to receive souls.

34. Palmer, *The Early Art of the West Riding*, pp. 40, 42–43.

35. See ibid., p. 39.

36. Illustrated in John Baker, *English Stained Glass of the Medieval Period* (London: Thames and Hudson, 1978), Pl. 57; see also my fig. 16 and Wayment, *The Stained Glass of the Church of St. Mary, Fairford*, Pl. XXII.

37. J. Charles Wall, *Devils* (1904; rpt. Totowa, N.J.: Rowman and Littlefield, 1974), p. 2; trans. from the French text in Adolphe Napoleon Didron, *Christian Iconography*, trans. E. J. Millington (1886; rpt. New York: Frederick Unger, 1965), II, 146.

38. *The Staging of Religious Drama in Europe in the Later Middle Ages: Texts and Documents in English Translation*, ed. Peter Meredith and John E. Tailby, Early Drama, Art, and Music, Monograph Ser., 4 (Kalamazoo: Medieval Institute Publications, 1982), p. 91.

39. Ibid., pp. 127–28.

40. Ibid., p. 130.

41. Ibid., p. 261.

42. *The Macro Plays*, ed. Mark Eccles, EETS, 262 (London, 1969), p. 1; on the use of gunpowder effects, see also the paper by Philip Butterworth in the present volume.

43. See Clifford Davidson, *From Creation to Doom: The York Cycle of Mystery Plays* (New York: AMS Press, 1984), pp. 15–16, and J. K. Bonnell, "The Serpent with a Human Head in Art and in Mystery Play," *American Journal of Archaeology*, 2nd ser., 21 (1917), 255–91.

44. *The Towneley Plays*, ed. George England and Alfred W. Pollard, EETS, e.s. 71 (London, 1897); see Plays I, XXV, XXX.

45. Citations are to *The York Plays*, ed. Richard Beadle (London: Edward Arnold, 1982).

46. Proclamation; Fall of Lucifer, ll. 81–82; and The Temptation, l. 198; for the N-town plays, see *Ludus Coventriae*, ed. K. S. Block, EETS, e.s. 120 (London, 1922).

47. See Meg Twycross and Sarah Carpenter, "Masks in Medieval English Theatre: The Mystery Plays, 2," *Medieval English Theatre*, 3, No. 2 (1981), 69–89, for a compilation of production evidence on devils in medieval drama.

48. *Chester*, ed. Lawrence M. Clopper, Records of Early English Drama (Toronto: Univ. of Toronto Press, 1979), p. 183.

49. Francis Bond, *Wood Carvings in English Churches*, I: *Misericords* (London: Oxford Univ. Press, 1910), p. 148.

50. *Chester*, ed. Clopper, p. 244.

51. *York*, ed. Alexandra F. Johnston and Margaret Rogerson, Records of Early English Drama (Toronto: Univ. of Toronto Press, 1979), I, 55; note that Roger Burton's 1415 pageant list includes six devils for the Mercers (I, 24), and see also Davidson, *From Creation to Doom*, pp. 32–33; and *Devon*, ed. John M. Wasson, Records of Early English Drama (Toronto: Univ. of Toronto Press, 1986), p. 25.

52. *Cambridge*, ed. Alan Nelson, Records of Early English Drama (Toronto: Univ. of Toronto Press, 1988), I, 146–47, 161.

53. *Records of Plays and Players in Norfolk and Suffolk, 1330–1642*, ed. David Galloway and John Wasson, Malone Soc. Collections, 11 (Oxford, 1980–81), p. 129.

54. *Coventry*, ed. R. W. Ingram, Records of Early English Drama (Toronto: Univ. of Toronto Press, 1981), p. 246.

55. Ibid., pp. 167, 255–56, 278.

56. Ibid., pp. 246–47, 259.

57. Ibid., p. 60 and *passim*.

58. *Norwich, 1540–1642*, ed. David Galloway, Records of Early English Drama (Toronto: Univ. of Toronto Press, 1984), pp. 53, 340.

59. For an illustration of Judas' Last Supper, see Schiller, *Iconography*, II, fig. 93; for Jonah, see Lawrence Lee, George Seddon, and Francis Stephens, *Stained Glass* (New York: Crown, n.d.), p. 25. Davidson, *From Creation to Doom*, pp. 140–41,

notes this interesting conflation of images with Christ as "a kind of divine angler" and the devil as "a ravenous fish."

60. *Norwich, 1540–1642*, ed. Galloway, pp. 69–70.

61. Ibid., p. 78.

62. Ibid., p. 169.

63. Ibid., p. 195.

64. John Anderson, "The Newcastle Dragon," *Medieval English Theatre* 3, No. 2 (1981), 67–68.

65. University of Leeds, Brotherton Library, Ripon MS. 183, Chamberlains' Rolls 2 and 3 (1439–40, 1447–48).

The Fate of the Damned in English Art and Drama

Clifford Davidson

Émile Mâle, insisting on the influence of the mystery plays on the visual arts, believed that depictions of the punishments of the damned inside of hell in representations of the Last Judgment in the visual arts were the result of the influence of the drama of the later Middle Ages.[1] Mâle's theory of influence has been much criticized, and few today would be so bold as to claim the theater as the driving force behind the iconographic and stylistic changes occurring in the fourteenth, fifteenth, and early sixteenth centuries. Yet he quite correctly notes an increased interest among artists in depicting the tortures of hell—an increased interest that will be obvious also in the writings of theologians and religious writers, among whom such depictions were particularly emphasized in the Reformation and Counter-Reformation alike. Under the influence of Calvinism's rigid theology, the morality drama would also be converted from a genre that allegorically described God's mercy to a type of play that emphasized the tragic downfall of sinful man. The difference is easily charted between two plays, *The Castle of Perseverance* (c.1425) and W. Wager's *Enough is as Good as a Feast* (c.1570). The first dramatizes the story of God's merciful acts that will aid even the selfish Humanum Genus to escape from a quasi-purgatory of punishment in the hands of devils—he is saved ultimately by his deathbed repentance—while the second shows Worldly Man, having provoked God's vengeance, going to the fate he deserves, which is eternal damnation within the confines of hell where he will be "rewarded . . ./ In everlasting fire that burneth forever" (ll. 1470–71).[2]

41

If the fear of hell and depiction of its punishments are not at the center of medieval theology, they nevertheless serve as a point of focus for believers, who saw life as pilgrimage directed toward the other world with two paths, the broad one that leads to the everlasting bonfire as well as the narrow one that leads to bliss at the end of the earthly journey. The wall paintings of the Last Judgment placed over the chancel arch in English churches were a sign of warning and hope to parishioners;[3] at the left of Christ the Judge, the mouth of hell would be gaping and open to receive those whose lives merited pain rather than joy. In the restored wall painting above the chancel arch at St. Thomas of Canterbury, Salisbury, those being rounded up by devils include a high ecclesiastic (a bishop, identified by his mitre) as well as lay persons (two figures have crowns, and the dishonest alewife is prominently present[4]), all of them nude[5] (fig. 1). The largest group is encircled by a great chain, a conventional piece of equipment for this scene in the visual arts; as early as the twelfth century, the chain had been described in *Sawles Warde* as red hot: "an unrude raketehe gledread of fure."[6] The chain, ubiquitous in the visual arts—there is a fine example in the Munich Psalter (Bayerische Staatsbibliothek Clm. 835, fol. 30), illustrated at Oxford in the early thirteenth century[7]—was also probably present in the Chester play, since one of the devils explains that he has the wicked all "tyed upon a rowe" (XXIV.547). In the Towneley *Judicium* or Doomsday play, they are treated like animals as they are herded by the devils into the mouth of hell; the terms chosen to encourage them on their way are derived from words and phrases used to herd animals: "hyte hyder warde, ho. . . . War oute!"[8]

Technically, the wicked in Last Judgment scenes should not be identified simply as "souls," since they are in fact the resurrected bodies once again animated by the souls of the unredeemed. In the Towneley *Judicium*, the devils know that the Last Judgment has arrived because hell has been emptied of the souls of the wicked who have been gathered there since the time of Cain, the first murderer: "all oure saules ar wente / and none ar in hell" (XXX.116).[9] The souls were consigned to hell at death at the Particular Judgment when each was found wanting; now at the General Judgment (Doomsday) they will come before the great high Judge reunited with their bodies, and once again they will be confirmed in their eternal destiny. In the Chester Judgment play, for example, the emperor whose soul has spent a thousand years in the "woe and teene" of purgatory has at last experienced the reuniting of his body and soul; he gives praise to God who has "made [me] in flesh to ryse" (XXIV.90, 102) in eternal health. In the York Doomsday play, an angel (St. Michael) orders:

> Goode and ill, euery-ilke a gaste,
> > Rise and fecche youre flessh þat was youre feere,
> For all þis worlde is broght to waste.
> > Drawes to youre dome, it neghes nere.[10]

The Second Angel echoes:

> Body and sawle with you ye bring,
> > And comes before þe high justise.
> For I am sente fro heuene kyng
> > To calle you to þis grette assise,
> Þerfore rise vppe and geue rekenyng. . . .
> > (XLVII.91–94)

Three types of persons will thus come before the Last Judgment: those who have been admitted into heaven for the goodness of their lives, those who have had their sins purged away in purgatory, and those who have lived unrepentant lives of wickedness.

The particular Judgment that has previously given reckoning to souls is, however, rarely seen in representations in the visual arts, though a useful example is present in an illumination in an English Book of Hours (Bodleian Library, MS. Gough Liturg. 3, fol. 95ᵛ) from c.1470–80.[11] The soul, a small nude figure with hands joined in prayer, kneels on the ground between a standing angel in an alb at his right and a devil with batlike wings and a tail at his left. Above, God, in a cloud with an angel flying in the air on each side, lifts his right hand in blessing. The angel at the soul's right is gesturing by counting his good deeds on his fingers, while the devil grasps in vain toward the soul. The scene is designed to be seen as following hard upon another tableau, that of the end of earthly life, depicted normally as a dying man with his doll-like soul issuing from his mouth with his last breath and being a point of conflict between the person's guardian angel and an attendant demon. The guardian angel and attendant demon at the deathbed of good and bad persons represented, of course, a long tradition, dating from at least the *Visio Pauli* or *Apocalypse of St. Paul*, which described first how the evil angels would come for the soul of the good individual and would gnash their teeth in frustration when it was denied to them. On the other hand, the soul of the sinner will be abandoned by his guardian angel because he has not repented and hence has "lost the time of repentance."[12] Thus, according to this account, the damned soul will be presented to God so that it might know what has been lost, whereupon it will be judged accordingly, surrendered to the devil, and cast into the "outer darkness" of hell to await "the great day of judgement."[13]

In a twelfth-century manuscript of St. Augustine's *City of God* (Bodleian Library MS. Laud. Misc. 469, fol. 7ʳ), Christ sits as Judge above, and in a compartment below the soul of a dead man (in appearance like a baby) is rescued from the claws of the devil through a collaboration between the Blessed Virgin Mary and his guardian angel.[14] In the illustrated poem *Of the Seuen Ages*, dated in the fifteenth century and contained in British Library MS. Add. 37049, the entire life of man is depicted as acted out between the bad angel on one's left and the good angel on one's right; in the end, the soul (white, and like a doll with hands joined in prayer) of the man lying on his deathbed is rescued and carried upward while the bad angel, departing in anger, complains:

> Here the saule is gone fro me, allas!
> Al my labour is turned in vayne
> That I purposed in many a place,
> And supposed hafe getyn him to payne.
> Bot mercy has taken hym to grace,

For that he has lyfed in this warld here;
And els in helle he hade had a place,
Emange fyre and fendes of vgly chere.[15]

In contrast, therefore, if the soul is a wicked one, as in the case of representations of Dives on a tympanum in the Yorkshire Museum or on sculpture on the west front of Lincoln Cathedral, it would presumably have been colored black and indeed would be captivated successfully by the devil.[16] The soul of Herod in the N-town plays is received thus by a devil, who claims the bad king's soul as his property[17] and consigns him to the pit of hell where he will be treated worse than swine (XX.237, 252–53). The punishment that he describes is exactly the inverse of heavenly bliss: "ffor in oure logge is so gret peyn/ þat non erthely tonge can telle" (ll. 239–40). Citing a Continental play, Lynette Muir has noted the unambiguous stage business involved in the portrayal of the death of Judas in the French Passion by Michel:

> devils stand round the hanging corpse clamouring, but no soul appears because it normally comes out of the mouth (with the breath) and this black soul cannot pass the lips that have kissed Christ. Then the devils rip open the body which has a bag of pig entrails hanging under its robe and seize the soul . . . [which] in this play . . . speaks as it is dragged off, so the scene must have been played over a trap-door through which it could emerge.[18]

A much more ambiguous death will be dramatized in *The Castle of Perseverance*, where the devil takes away the soul, which later is rescued following the reconciliation of the Four Daughters of God.

That death could often be thus ambiguous is most clearly shown by the Chester Judgment play which, as indicated above, stresses the punishments of purgatory for imperfect souls. As the most recent editors of the Chester cycle indicate, purgatory, designed for those who have committed venial rather than mortal sins, or for those who have failed to complete penance in this life for sins committed prior to death, is the fate for a longer or shorter time of the majority of Christians.[19] The punishments of purgatory are severe, but they are limited temporally, in contrast to the punishments of hell meted out to the wicked, who are assigned *eternal* residence in hell at the time of the Particular Judgment and again at the General or Last Judgment.

The resurrection of the bodies of both good and wicked persons and the union of their bodies with their souls was apparently vividly portrayed in the staging of the great medieval English cycle drama. While physically awakening and arising from their tombs in the N-town cycle, all would loudly and incoherently cry: "ha aa · ha aa · ha aa" (XLII.26*sd*). At Chester, those granted salvation arose from their tombs[20] and spoke first, followed by a pope, an emperor, a king, a queen, a judge, and a merchant who are among the damned. The first of these laments:

> Alas, alas, alas, alas!
> Nowe am I worse then ever I was.
> My bodye agayne the soule hasse
> that longe hase benne in hell.
> Together the bee—nowe ys noe grace—
> fyled to bee before thy face,
> and after my death here in this place
> in payne ever to dwell. (XXIV.173–80)

At York where, as at Chester, the plays were produced on pageant wagons, the Mercers responsible for the Doomsday play had obtained, perhaps in 1463, a separate pageant "for ye sallys to ryse owtof," for in this year a payment was made for five yards of new canvas to this pageant, which is described as new.[21] From this pageant arose both the good and the bad, those disposed to pray and those whose response to the allegedly "hydous horne" of the Last Trumpet would be fear of the devils that stand by and of their hellish fate. In this play, St. Michael, presumably using a sword to divide them,[22] will separate the good from those fated to enter the hell mouth—a stage property listed in the 1433 inventory of the York Mercers' pageant[23]—located at the left hand of the Judge (XLVII.169–76). These unfortunate ones will experience "payne endles" (l. 228). In the N-town manuscript, this separation of bad from good is identified by the devil who serves as prologue to *Passion Play I* as the "dyvicion eternal" which damns the wicked: "In evyr-lastynge peyne · with me dwellyn þei xal" (XXVI.118, 120).

But, as indicated by the pope who is among the damned in the Chester Doomsday play, the judgment meted out at the General Judgment at the Last Day is only a confirmation of God's judgment at the Particular Judgment. Men and women whose souls have already been consigned to permanent residency in hell will be returned to that place of anguish and terror, while those who have suffered in purgatory will now have completed their works of expiation for their sins.

In a play such as *Everyman*, the protagonist goes forth to face his judge immediately at death; thereafter, when the time has passed that will divide the moment of death and the close of history—the day when Doomsday comes—a second Judgment scene will occur. Everyman, however, has come to a happy end, for his last lines commend his soul to the hands of the mighty God (ll. 886–87). Hence he will not experience the anguish, weeping, and howling predicted for one class of lost souls—the rich who oppress the poor—in *James* 5.1–7. His anxiety about life beyond the grave seems to have been generally shared by rich and poor alike, but at the end of his life's journey he can go forward with hope because of the promise of mercy to those who call on God's name and prepare themselves for the moment of death. It was a conclusion to life that was imitated by great numbers of people, if we are to believe the formulae with which wills begin—e.g., the will of Richard Peke of Wakefield, written on 4 June 1516 and probated on 28 October of the same year: "First, I commend my soull to God Almyghty, to our Lady Saynt Marie, and to all the Sayntes in heven, my body to be buried in the paroch churche of Allhallowes in Wakefelde, in the qwere of Saynt Nicholesse, in the myddes of the loweste goyng, even enens my stall, when God pleasse to call me to His mercy."[24] Through the invocation of the saints, especially the influential Virgin Mary, and God himself, the dying person chose a habit of mind guaranteed (with the help of the Sacraments of the Church) to achieve a "good death" that in turn would lead to bliss rather than to the fearful punishments in store for the wicked.[25] The alternative would be to fall into the hands of devils, whose grasp indeed was literally to be feared, as the revulsion on the faces of the damned in scenes in the visual arts will demonstrate. A euphemism reported for death in the late Middle Ages was "change of life";[26] for the unrepentant, the "change" was regarded as one that would come as a shock to the person involved.

Sheer terror is evidenced in the facial expressions and gestures of some of the resurrected figures in wall paintings and painted glass. In an example in painted glass originally part of a Doom in St. Michael's Church (later Cathedral), Coventry, a man is shouting as he rises from his tomb while others have their arms crossed over their breasts,[27] and in the Doom painting at Wenhaston, Suffolk, two figures at the left hand of Christ have "their hands clasped" in a traditional gesture of despair.[28] In the Chester Last Judgment, the Imperator Damnatus, utterly overcome by terror, trembles and quakes (XXIV.236), as do the wicked in the York cycle, where quaking (XLVII.137) is joined with weeping on this "day of bale and bittirnes,/ . . . Of ire, of trymbelyng, and of tene" (ll. 239, 242). The damned grimace and cry out, "reemynge and grennynge verey fervent" (*Chester* XXIV.578)—cries that reflect the biblical text predicting the wailing and gnashing of teeth of the wicked at the Last Day: "So it shall be at the end of the world. The angels shall go out, and shall separate the wicked from among the just. And shall cast them into the furnace of fire [in caminum ignis]: there shall be weeping and gnashing of teeth" (*Matthew* 13.49–50; Douay-Rheims).[29] In N-town, the damned "rubbe," "rave," and beg for mercy (XLII.68–69).

In the dramatic literature, the despairing persons facing Judgment are sometimes presented also as having corrupted and rotten bodies; as the Mercator Damnatus in the Chester play complains, his body is the opposite of the incorruptible state promised to those who are to receive salvation:

> My fowle body, that rotten hath be,

and soule together nowe I see.
All stynketh, full of synne.

(XXIV.326–28)

The motif is one that had been exploited in sculpture at Bourges
Cathedral, where the corrupt bodies of the damned are literally
eaten by toads and snakes.[30] Not surprisingly, damned souls upon
confrontation with their fate may scratch or otherwise inflict injury
on themselves (e.g., when they "rubbe," as in N-town [XLII.68]).
And in color their normal hue is black, contrasting with the white
of those who have merited salvation.[31] At Coventry, the Drapers'
accounts for their Doomsday play in 1561 list payment to three
"whyte Sowles" and three "blank [i.e., black] Sowles"[32]—souls
which are in 1565 noted as being "Savyd" and "dampnyd."[33] The
damned are color-coded by having them share the dark and dirty
hues of hell, in the suburbs of which Adam, Eve, David, and the
other patriarchs had waited until their release by Christ at the
Harrowing of Hell. The Harrowing is the bringing of light into the
darkness of limbo, of wisdom entering into a "speciall space"
(York XLVII.110) associated with folly, of divine power unbinding
those who had been imprisoned as the prey of devils,[34] and it is
the rescue from darkness into light of all the patriarchs and
prophets who had lived before the Incarnation—a rescue which
brings them to salvation. The black-white symbolism of the
Coventry Doomsday play thus relies on an archetypal representation of evil and good which also appears in dramatic records
in the case of the Majorca Last Judgment play where the following
costume is specified for them: "black cassocks (sotanes), and on
their heads white, black, or reddish wigs," garments which contrast
with those of the saved, who wore albs covered by an overgar-
ment, "a light colored cape," and black wigs with "bands on their
foreheads."[35] The possibilities for vivid representation of corrupt
souls were even greater in the Last Judgment play at Rouerge,
since dummies were used, and the torments were clearly of a surprisingly harsh nature: the devils used wheels, pitchforks, and
flesh-hooks to torment the damned who had been consigned to the

pit of hell.[36]

The test of a person's worth before the divine Judge is the weighing of the soul by St. Michael, often, as in painted glass of c.1330 at the Church of St. Michael-le-Belfrey in York, shown in terms of a contest between good and evil, the latter depicted by a devil attempting to weigh down the scale pan associated with evil deeds.[37] In the Doom at Wenhaston, a small figure presumably representing the soul is weighed in one scale pan against a demonic figure representing his or her evil deeds in the other.[38] In iconography, it is conventional for the weighing of souls to depict those whose good deeds outweigh the bad,[39] sometimes through the intervention of the Blessed Virgin Mary who may throw a rosary onto the side of good to weigh in on the side of salvation.[40] But, reassuring as depictions of this kind might have been, individuals looking on such a scene as illustrated in the visual arts would know that a good ending was not inevitable and that for those who failed there was a place prepared of the greatest unpleasantness. In this house of pain they were "In dole to dwelle for euermare" (*York* XLVII.320).

The earliest depictions of the Last Judgment do not seem to focus on the fate of the damned. Pamela Sheingorn calls attention to an early Christian sarcophagus lid which shows the separation of the sheep and the goats—i.e., the saved from the damned.[41] Early illustrations showing Christ as the Judge only depict him like an emperor presiding over a temporal judgment scene.[42] In the earliest Last Judgment in the West, an eighth- or ninth-century Anglo-Saxon ivory in the Victoria and Albert Museum,[43] the unpleasantness to be experienced by the damned tends to be implied rather than depicted graphically, for the damned are merely herded to the hell mouth which swallows them and are not thereafter shown being punished in hell itself—a pattern that endured in large numbers of examples to the time of the Reformation.[44] A more vivid depiction seems to have been initiated, however, in the Winchester Psalter and the famous twelfth-century tympanum at Conques; in the latter, the separation of the wicked from the saved also includes specific representation of the damned, who are literally crammed into the compartments below and at the left of the Judge. Here their physical discomfort is extreme.[45] Some attempt is also made to make the punishment fit the crime, as in the instance of the poacher who is trussed up and placed over fire like an animal being prepared for the table.[46] The Winchester Psalter (c.1140) contains two illuminations showing (1) hell mouth, filled with tortured figures of the damned and St. Michael turning the key to lock them in forever, and (2) two scenes of torture in which the wicked are punished in various ways. In the lower compartment, one is having his arms cut off, another is being gnawed upon, a third is pushed downward by a devil with a flesh hook, while a group of the damned is being thrust down into a cauldron by a devil with a two-pronged pitchfork.[47]

In England, the so-called Doomstone at York Minster, sculpture believed to have been part of the twelfth-century façade of the Norman nave of the cathedral before the structure was rebuilt in the thirteenth century, provides an English example of the punishments that will be awaiting the damned in the interior of hell presumably from a series of carvings showing the Last Judgment.[48] The iconography utilized in this stone carving joins the design of the hell mouth with the cauldron, which is otherwise extremely widespread and appears in sculpture not only at Conques but in such well-known stone carving as a tympanum at the Cathedral at Reims, where the damned are being led by means of a chain directly to the cauldron.[49] In the York Doomstone, the cauldron-hell mouth is filled with the figures of the damned who are being tortured by demons and snakes; it is being heated on a fire which devils are attending and using to punish one of the wicked whom they have pinned down with pitchforks. Such treatment of the wicked involves iconography that after the twelfth century is quite conventional, though it is less frequently utilized than the depiction of the fate of the damned culminating at the Last Judgment merely in their entrance into hell mouth in the company of devils.[50] Unlike the York Doomstone, the mid-thirteenth-century frieze on the west front of Lincoln Cathedral remains in situ, though it is quite worn and hence has lost the sharpness of detail that originally would have given very specific representation to the fate of the damned, who were not only tormented by devils but also assailed by serpents or worms and dragons (figs. 2–4). Here, however, the hell mouth, located to the right of the depiction of hell, is shown in a Harrowing of Hell scene and not in a Last Judgment context.[51] The Lincoln frieze, to be sure, is based on Italian models, and hence may be less useful for the study of English iconography than the York Doomstone.

Nevertheless, the appearance of reptiles, snakes, and worms at Lincoln and elsewhere, including the Winchester Psalter, is significant since it represents a tradition shared with Continental art. As Martha Himmelfarb has noted, this tradition is grounded in biblical sources.[52] In *Mark* 9.42–48, worms as well as fire are identified as characteristic of hell, a place "Where their worm dieth not, and the fire is not extinguished." The reference in this passage is to a verse in *Isaiah*: "And they shall go out, and see the carcasses of the men that have transgressed against me: their worm shall not die, and their fire shall not be quenched: and they shall be a loathsome sight to all flesh" (66.24). There are also two further important references to worms and fire that connect them with hell: the Greek text of *Sirach* 7.17 ("the punishment of the ungodly is fire and worms") and *Judith* 16.17 ("fire and worms he will give to their flesh").[53] Himmelfarb notes that worms were appropriate to the Hebrew Sheol, which was a dark and damp location—a pit— while fire was associated with the valley of Gehenna, a place of punishment initially invoked by Jeremiah.[54] The medieval hell thus drew upon the Hebrew conceptions of both Sheol and Gehenna, and added specific details such as the use of a cauldron to be placed over the fire in this place of horrors.

Once introduced, the cauldron as a punishment for the damned continued to appear in England until the Reformation.[55] An anonymous and undated broadside ballad entitled *The Dead Mans Song* specifies that the cauldron contains "poyson'd filth." In the wall painting of c.1521–45 discovered in the early nineteenth century over the chancel arch of the Guild Chapel at Stratford-upon-Avon,[56] the cauldron, in keeping with the specification which requires a "furnace" in *Matthew* 13.50, was of a technologically improved type and was fanned by devils operating bellows (fig. 7). At the left of the cauldron, devils with two-pronged pitchforks were harrassing a group of persons, whose bare feet stand in fire—obviously painful, since they are attempting out of pain to raise their feet from the ground. M. D. Anderson has called attention to a vision that was described in a Middle English translation of the *Gesta Romanorum*: "sone aftyr come ij. deuyls yellyng, and broughtyn a Cawderon full of hote wellyng brasse, and sette it downe . . . and after hem came othere ij. deuyls, Cryinge, and broughtyn a man; and after hem Came othere ij. deuyls, with grete noyse, and broughtyn a woman. than the ij. deuyls tokyn bothe the man ande the woman that they brought, and Caste hem into a Cawderon and helde hem there, till the fleshe was sothyn from the bone."[57] At Stratford, one has crossed his arms in a gesture that is indicative of very great discomfort. A man on his knees at the right of the cauldron was attempting to pray though such an act would not be effective in relieving his discomfort, since, as Jesus explains in the Chester Doomsday play, the "tyme of grace" is past (XXIV.609): "Noe grace may growe through theire prayere" (l. 617). A similar warning comes from Lazarus in the Towneley plays: "To shrife no man thaym may/ After youre endyng day" (XXXI.169–70). Over the cauldron itself a devil held a scourge of some kind designed to prevent the figures in the cauldron from escaping from whatever molten liquid it contains. Unfortunately, this portion of the wall painting is too eroded at the present time to study except from drawings made in the early nineteenth century.

The intensity of the pain inflicted on the damned in the cauldron in hell is emphasized interestingly in the fourteenth-century *Holkham Bible Picture Book*; in this illuminated manuscript, as part of the depiction of the Harrowing a great iron kettle holding seven men (and women?) is placed above a fire issuing from hell mouth (fig. 18). A devil seems to be forcing them down into the heated vessel with a ladle. Above the cauldron is a metal hood of a type introduced not long prior to the illumination of the manuscript.[58] The fourteenth century had seen the invention of the blast furnace and the discovery of techniques to make cast iron;[59] almost immediately, therefore, the technology of the blast furnace was adapted to the iconography of hell and to the punishment of the wicked and damned. In another illumination in the *Holkham Bible Picture Book*, showing the final stage of the Last Judgment (fol. 42ᵛ), two cauldrons are shown, one of which is attached by chains under a chimney (fig. 19). Below the lower cauldron is the mouth of hell out of which flames again issue. A devil is force-feeding one of the damned in this cauldron with a ladle. In contrast to the noise and boistrous action at the bottom of the illumination and at the left side of the Judge which contains the scene from hell, the righteous are being welcomed into heaven on the right with music played by angels on a trumpet and portative organ. In the York Doomsday play, God speaks with a certain irony of the damned: "Of sorowes sere now schall thei syng" (XLVII.378). In contrast to the unmelodious sounds from hell, however, the play ends with heavenly music as the angels cross the pageant stage back and forth. The Towneley manuscript specifies that the music which concludes the pageant should be the *Te Deum* (XXX.620). The final impression is one of harmony and joy rather than of the chaos and disharmony of the wicked, and yet the text of the *Te Deum* also concludes with a supplication to Christ to preserve Christians from hell and to bring them "with your saints to glory everlasting."

Technology is again drawn upon for the depiction of hell in the design for the painted glass (c.1500) in the Great West Window in Fairford Church in Gloucestershire (fig. 16). In this Last Judgment window, the tortures are very severe—the damned are carried to hell by frightening devils, and are placed by them on sharpened spikes in addition to the expected roasting in the furnace. They are ground by a machine into a vat, and thereafter they descend into a cauldron, while others (their faces are distorted with terror) are swallowed like fish by a great hell mouth—an allusion to the great leviathan Satan who lures souls into this unfortunate fate.[60] The portion of the window described here is in very good condition and has not suffered from restoration as has been the case in the upper half of the window.

Another important example of the tortures of hell in the visual arts in England that requires mention is the wall painting of c.1200 at Chaldon, Surrey[61] (fig. 20). In this restored wall painting, the cauldron is present and is set on a tripod over a fire on the left, below a scene showing St. Michael weighing souls. A small figure is being hurled into the cauldron (he seems suspended above it), and two devils are pushing down on those already in the cauldron with two-pronged pitchforks. Behind one of the devils one of the damned is reclining on spikes, and another devil seems to take joy in impaling others on his pitchfork as they fall from the ladder of salvation (which in this case, following early Byzantine models, is also paradoxically the ladder of damnation, since some are falling from it while others climb successfully) in the center of the wall painting.[62] On the bottom right of the wall painting, below a representation of the Harrowing of Hell, is an equally interesting scene, for here a usurer or miser is made to eat coins as he sits over a pile of money heated to redness by fire—punishment that would recur in Dunbar's followers of Covetousness, who, however, first vomit up hot molten gold, which then is reinserted into their throats by devils:

Out of thair thottis thay schot on udder
Hett moltin gold, me thocht a fudder,
As fyreflawcht maist fervent;
Ay as thay tomit thame of schot,
Feyndis fild thame new up to the thrott
With gold of alkin prent.[63]

Above the miser in the Chaldon wall painting, two devils hold a spiked board upon which several more damned, all of them apparently small tradesmen, are painfully attempting to cross.[64]

More tortures for the damned were devised by the artists of the fifteenth and early sixteenth century in depictions of hell. A woodcut by Lucas Cranach, for example, shows a scene in the flames of hell in which an ugly devil is fondling a woman's breasts and raping her.[65] It should be noted that there was often a relationship between such punishments and the visualizing of the Seven Deadly Sins. For example, at Stratford, Gluttony and Envy appear immediately behind the mouth of hell where the latter is suspended by the waist and beaten by the devil with a flabby bag attached to a stick—an instrument reminiscent of a fool stick. The former is hung by the nose, and a third figure between the two sins has his arms raised in terror. The presence of certain of the Deadly Sins links this example not only to the medieval Dooms-day but also to the Renaissance play of *Doctor Faustus* by Christopher Marlowe in which the Seven Deadly Sins play a definite role in bringing the protagonist to his unhappy end.[66]

Very specific punishments for sins are popularized in the late fifteenth and early sixteenth centuries by illustrations accompanying the Old French *Visio Lazari*[67] and ultimately the popular woodcuts in *Le Traité de bien vivre et de bien mourir* published by Antoine Vérard in Paris in 1492.[68] The woodcuts included with the summary of Vérard's treatise in Guyot Marchant's *Calendrier des bergers* were copies,[69] and these designs found their way to England where they were again copied in various editions of the *Shepherds' Calendar* beginning in the early sixteenth century and continuing to at least 1631.[70] These woodcuts showed some particularly brutal punishments, as in the case of the wrathful who are laid out and tied or chained to tables that in appearance are like butchers' stalls as devils thrust their spears into their flesh (fig. 21). The cauldrons, reserved for the covetous, are filled with boiling lead and oil, while the gluttons are fed fire, toads, and other indigestibles. The first of the punishments is for the most heinous of mortal sins, pride, which is punished by being placed on great wheels to which the sinful are attached by hooks and ropes. Was Shakespeare thinking of this punishment and others described in the *Shepherds' Calendar* when he gave to King Lear the lines "I am bound/ Upon a wheel of fire, that mine own tears/ Do scald like molten lead" (IV.vii.46–48)? Lear is directly contrasting his condition with that of the "soul in bliss" who in his view is Cordelia, and as audience we have a strong recognition that he has indeed been subjected to the *hell* of filial ingratitude and madness.[71]

Humanum Genus in *The Castle of Perseverance* fears that he will be hung on hooks as punishment for his sins,[72] and he is promised by the devil that he will placed "In bolnynnge bondys" where he will "brenne" and that he will be thrown "In pycke and ter to grone and grenne" (ll. 3076, 3078). Hell is a dungeon where souls are regularly beaten and otherwise mistreated. It is a house of death—"deaðes hus," inhabited by "unseligastes," according to *Sawles Warde*[73]—where terrifying sights and smells reflect a lack of light and life. The shapes of hell are deliberately distorted and painful. To those upon whom the gates of this terrible place have shut, there will be, according to a sermon by Richard Alkerton delivered in London in 1406, torture by boiling in "fyr and brymstone withouten ende. Venemous wormes and naddris shul gnawe alle here membris withouten seessyng, and the worm of conscience, that is grutching in her conscience, shal gnawe the soule." Play is converted "in to moorning" and laughter "in to sorwe" as those who do the tormenting "shul never be wery, nether dye."[74]

In the play by Christopher Marlowe, hell is described for Doctor Faustus by the Bad Angel as containing appropriate punishments, in general derived from medieval tradition or the *Shepherds' Calendar*:

> Now, Faustus, let thine eyes with horror stare
> Into that vast perpetual torture-house.
> There are the furies, tossing damned souls
> On burning forks; their bodies boil in lead:
> There are live quarters broiling on the coals,
> That ne'er can die: this ever-burning chair
> Is for o'er-tortur'd souls to rest them in:
> These that are fed with sops of flaming fire
> Were gluttons and lov'd only delicates
> And laugh'd to see the poor starve at their gates.
> But yet all these are nothing; thou shalt see
> Ten thousand tortures that more horrid be.
>   (xix.116–27)

Yet, more importantly, as Faustus' Good Angel reminds him

—"O, thou hast lost celestial happiness,/ Pleasures unspeakable, bliss without end" (xix.106–07)—hell is a place where eternal joy is missed, a place where the soul (and, later, the soul reunited with the body) will be totally alienated from God, who is the source of light and life in the universe. Such despair involves knowing that one can never achieve closeness with God again since, as the prologue Devil says (quoting a tag from the Office of the Dead) in the N-town *Passion Play I*, "Quia in inferno nulla est redempcio" ("Because in hell there is no redemption" [XXVI.48]).

NOTES

1. Émile Mâle, *Religious Art in France: The Late Middle Ages*, trans. Marthiel Mathews (Princeton: Princeton Univ. Press, 1986), pp. 417–20.

2. W. Wager, *The Longer Thou Livest and Enough Is as Good as a Feast*, ed. R. Mark Benbow (Lincoln: Univ. of Nebraska Press, 1967), p. 143.

3. See Clifford Davidson, *From Creation to Doom: The York Cycle of Mystery Plays* (New York: AMS Press, 1984), pp. 183–84.

4. For the alewife, see also *The Chester Mystery Cycle*, ed. R. M. Lumiansky and David Mills, EETS, s.s. 3, 9 (London, 1974–86), I, 337–39 (XVII.277–336). One may wonder if persons, of either high or low degree, depicted in this way were intended to be recognized as actual historical people. A case brought before the Star Chamber in the 1620's focused on a stage play involving local actors at Kendal Castle in Westmorland which had ridiculed local landowners and Puritans as well as various others by placing them in hell, represented as under the stage. A hell mouth was probably used since the play is described as "a representacion of Hell"; see *Cumberland, Westmorland, and Gloucestershire*, ed. Audrey Douglas and Peter Greenfield, Records of Early English Drama (Toronto: Univ. of Toronto Press, 1986), pp. 188–98. Subsequent references to the Chester plays in my text are to the edition of Lumiansky and Mills.

5. See especially Albert Hollaender, "The Doom-Painting of St. Thomas of Canterbury, Salisbury," *Wiltshire Archaeological and Natural History Magazine*, 50 (1942), 351–70. For a description and drawing of the wall painting prior to resto-

ration, see Robert Benson and Henry Hatcher, *Old and New Sarum*, in *The History of Wiltshire*, ed. Richard Colt Hoare (London, 1843), VI, 589 and plate following p. 588. See also Pamela Sheingorn and David Bevington, "'Alle This Was Token Domysday to Drede': Visual Signs of Last Judgment in the Corpus Christi Cycles and in Late Gothic Art," in David Bevington *et al.*, *Homo, Memento Finis: The Iconography of Just Judgment in Medieval Art and Drama*, Early Drama, Art, and Music, Monograph Ser., 6 (Kalamazoo: Medieval Institute Publications, 1985), pp. 121–45, fig. 14. Sometimes in staging the Doomsday plays in England and in certain regions on the Continent, leather body stockings were used to simulate nudity; see the stage direction in the Cornish *Creacion of the World* that indicates the costumes to be used for the nude Adam and Eve before the Fall: "Adam and Eva aparlet in whytt lether . . ." (ed. Paula Neuss [New York: Garland, 1983], p. 28). Problems involved in historical research on the appearance of the resurrected souls have been addressed by Meg Twycross, "'With what body shall they come?': Black and White Souls in the English Mystery Plays," in *Langland, the Mystics and the Medieval Religious Tradition: Essays in Honour of S. S. Hussey*, ed. Helen Philips (Cambridge: D. S. Brewer, 1990), pp. 271–86.

6. *Sawles Warde*, in *Early Middle English Verse and Prose*, 2nd ed., ed. J. A. W. Bennett and G. V. Smithers (Oxford: Clarendon Press, 1968), p. 250. The detail of the red-hot chain placed around a group of the damned is probably borrowed from one of the punishments described in the *Visio Pauli* or *Apocalypse of St. Paul*; see *The Apocryphal New Testament*, trans. M. R. James (Oxford: Clarendon Press, 1924), p. 544 (sec. 39).

7. Nigel Morgan, *Early Gothic Manuscripts, 1190–1250*, Survey of Manuscripts Illuminated in the British Isles, 4 (London: Harvey Miller, 1982), pp. 68, 70 (No. 23), fig. 87.

8. *The Towneley Plays*, ed. George England and Alfred W. Pollard, EETS, e.s. 71 (London, 1897), p. 384 (XXX.535–36).

9. The author of this play seems to have had in mind the sequence of events implied in the Fifteen Signs of Doomsday myth; see Clifford Davidson, "An Interpretation of the Wakefield *Judicium*," *Annuale Mediaevale*, 10 (1969), 113–14.

10. *The York Plays*, ed. Richard Beadle (London: Edward Arnold, 1982), p. 408 (XLVII.85–88); subsequent references to the York plays are to this edition.

11. Otto Pächt, *Illuminated Manuscripts in the Bodleian Library, Oxford*, III: *British, Irish, and Icelandic Schools* (Oxford: Clarendon Press, 1973), No. 1116. For commentary on this illumination, see Nicholas Rogers, "The Particular Judgement: Two Earlier Examples of a Motif in Jan Mostaert's Lost Self-portrait," *Oud Holland*, 97 (1983), 125–27.

12. *Apocryphal New Testament*, trans. James, pp. 529–33. The *Visio Pauli* had been an influential text in Anglo-Saxon England. Antoinette di Paolo Healey indicates that indeed it "was the chief articulator of the simple relationship between human deeds and the fate of the soul" in that period (*The Old English Vision of St. Paul* [Cambridge: Mediaeval Academy of America, 1978], p. 56).

13. *Apocryphal New Testament*, trans. James, pp. 533–35.

14. C. M. Kaufmann, *Romanesque Manuscripts, 1066–1190*, Survey of Manuscripts Illuminated in the British Isles, 3 (London: Harvey Miller, 1975), p. 87 (No. 54), fig. 147.

15. Alan H. Nelson, "'Of the seuen ages': An Unknown Analogue of *The Castle of Perseverance*," *Comparative Drama*, 8 (1974), 127–28, 130–32.

16. F. Saxl, *English Sculptures of the Twelfth Century*, ed. Hanns Swarzenski (Boston: Boston Book and Art Shop, n.d.), fig. 49, Pl. LII; cf. Meg Twycross, "With what body shall they come?" pp. 271-86.

17. *Ludus Coventriae*, ed. K. S. Block, EETS, e.s. 121 (London, 1922), p. 176 (XX.232*sd*, 233); subsequent references to the N-town plays in my text are to this edition.

18. Lynette Muir, "Aspects of Form and Meaning in the Biblical Drama," in *Littera et sensus: Essays on Form and Meaning in Medieval French Literature Presented to John Fox*, ed. D. A. Trotter (Exeter: Univ. of Exeter, 1989), p. 118. Normally a doll was used to represent the soul (ibid.).

19. *Chester Mystery Cycle*, II, 356.

20. Tombs are specified in the Chester stage directions: "et omnes mortui de sepulchris surgent" (XXIV.40*sd*).

21. *York*, ed. Alexandra F. Johnston and Margaret Rogerson, Records of Early English Drama (Toronto: Univ. of Toronto Press, 1979), I, 95.

22. Davidson, *From Creation to Doom*, p. 187.

23. *York*, ed. Johnston and Rogerson, I, 55; in the inventory of 1526, it is called a "hell dure" (I, 242).

24. *Testamenta Eboracensia*, ed. James Raine, Surtees Soc., 79 (Durham, 1884), V, 73–74.

25. See also Philippe Ariès, *The Hour of Our Death*, trans. Helen Weaver (New York: Knopf, 1981), pp. 106–98.

26. Marie Collins, "A Little Known 'Art of Dying' by a Brigittine of Syon: *A Daily Exercise and Experience of Death* by Richard Whitford," in *Dies Illa: Death in the Middle Ages*, ed. Jane Taylor (Liverpool: Francis Cairns, 1984), p. 186.

27. This glass is now in the Bishop Haigh Chapel; see Clifford Davidson and Jennifer Alexander, *The Early Art of Coventry, Stratford-upon-Avon, Warwick, and Lesser Sites in Warwickshire: A Subject List of Extant and Lost Art, Including Items Relevant to Early Drama*, Early Drama, Art, and Music, Reference Ser., 4 (Kalamazoo: Medieval Institute Publications, 1985), p. 37; see also Philip B. Chatwin, "Medieval Stained Glass from the Cathedral, Coventry," *Transactions of the Birmingham Archaeological Society*, 66 (1950), 3, Pls. VI–VII.

28. Charles E. Keyser, "On a Panel Painting of the Doom Discovered in 1892, in Wenhaston Church, Suffolk," *Archaeologia*, 54 (1894), 124; on gestures of the damned, see Clifford Davidson, "Gesture in Medieval Drama with Special Reference to the Doomsday Plays in the Middle English Cycles," *EDAM Newsletter*, 6 (1983), 13–14.

29. See also *Visio Pauli*, in *Apocryphal New Testament*, trans. James, p. 547: "And I looked from the north unto the west and saw there the worm that sleepeth not, and in that place was gnashing of teeth." This location, according to the *Visio Pauli*, is an extremely cold part of hell, which is thus not merely a place of fire only.

30. Émile Mâle, *Religious Art in France: The Thirteenth Century*, trans. Marthiel Mathews (Princeton: Princeton Univ. Press, 1984), p. 381. See also the sermon of Lazarus in *Towneley*, ll. 139–40.

31. Twycross, quoting from St. Thomas Aquinas, also notes that the damned will also "be weighed down, and heavy, and to a certain extent unresponsive to the soul" (*Contra Gentiles* 4.89, as quoted in "With what body shall they come?"). Twycross also notes that this heaviness is elsewhere related by Aquinas to the darkness of their souls, a darkness reflected in their bodies (*Compendium of Theology*, chap. 176)—an aspect foretold in *Isaiah* 13.8: "their countenances shall be as faces burnt."

32. *Coventry*, ed. R. W. Ingram, Records of Early English Drama (Toronto: Univ. of Toronto Press, 1981), p. 217.

33. Ibid., p. 230.

34. Adam and Eve had been placed in fetters by the denizens of hell as they were led off in the Anglo-Norman *Adam* (l. 590sd); see *Le Jeu d'Adam*, ed. Willem Nooman (Paris: Champion, 1971).

35. *The Staging of Religious Drama in Europe in the Later Middle Ages: Texts and Documents in English Translation*, ed. Peter Meredith and John E. Tailby, Early Drama, Art, and Music, Monograph Ser., 4 (Kalamazoo: Medieval Institute Publications, 1983), p. 89.

36. Ibid., p. 111.

37. Clifford Davidson and David E. O'Connor, *York Art: A Subject List of Extant and Lost Art Including Items Relevant to Early Drama*, Early Drama, Art, and Music, Reference Ser., 1 (Kalamazoo: Medieval Institute Publications, 1978), p. 116.

38. Sheingorn and Bevington, "Alle This Was Token Domysday to Drede," p. 123, fig. 17.

39. Mary Phillips Perry, "On the Psychostasis in Christian Art," *Burlington Magazine*, 22 (1912–13), 216.

40. Evidence from the York *Ordo paginarum* of 1415 demonstrates that the Virgin Mary was once present in the York Doomsday play; see *York*, ed. Johnston and Rogerson, I, 24. For comment which suggests the wisdom of eliminating Mary at this point in the cycle, see Rosemary Woolf, *The English Mystery Plays* (Berkeley and Los Angeles: Univ. of California Press, 1972), p. 296, who also criticizes Continental drama on aesthetic grounds for scenes in which Mary's rejected pleas "are disconcerting in their suggestion of a callous severity in Christ." But such ineffective intercessions are likely to come after the Judgment rather than before, and represent the kind of pleas by Mary to which Jesus refers in *Chester* XXIV.613–16: "And though my sweete mother deare/ and all the sayntes that ever were/ prayed for you right nowe here,/ all yt were to late."

41. Pamela Sheingorn, "'For God is Such a Doomsman': Origins and Development of the Theme of Last Judgment," in Bevington *et al.*, *Homo, Memento Finis*, pp. 21–22, fig. 1.

42. André Grabar, *Christian Iconography: A Study of its Origins*, Bollingen Series, 35, Pt. 10 (Princeton: Princeton Univ. Press, 1968), p. 44.

43. John Beckwith, *Ivory Carvings in Early Medieval England* (London: Harvey Miller, 1972), pp. 22, 24, 118–19 (No. 4), fig. 1; see also Sheingorn, "For God is Such a Doomsman," pp. 25–26, fig. 3.

44. Beckwith, *Ivory Carvings*, pp. 22, 24.

45. Émile Mâle, *Religious Art in France: The Twelfth Century*, trans. Marthiel Mathews (Princeton: Princeton Univ. Press, 1978), pp. 411-16, fig. 288.

46. Bevington *et al.*, *Homo, Memento Finis*, fig. 5; see also Mâle, *Religious Art in France: The Twelfth Century*, p. 415, for further examples: "Pride falls from his horse; Avarice, his purse tied around his neck, is hanged as Judas was hanged; a couple, chained together throughout eternity, symbolize Lust."

47. British Library, Cotton MS. Nero C.IV, fols. 38–39; reproduced in Francis Wormald, *The Winchester Psalter* (London: Harvey Miller and Medcalf, 1973), figs. 41–42 and frontispiece. For a possible connection between this manuscript and the sculpture at Conques, see Don Denny, "The Date of the Conques Last Judgment and Its Compositional Analogues," *Art Bulletin*, 66 (1984), 7–14.

48. Edward S. Prior and Arthur Gardner, *An Account of Medieval Figure-Sculpture in England* (Cambridge: Cambridge Univ. Press, 1912), pp. 212ff, fig. 192; cf. Saxl, *English Sculptures*, p. 67, Pl. XCIII.

49. Mâle, *Religious Art in France: The Thirteenth Century*, fig. 248.

50. The Provençal *Sponsus* of the eleventh century also breaks off as the Foolish Virgins are driven into the mouth of hell, and no attempt is made to follow their history further once they have entered the place of darkness; for the text of this music-drama, see Karl Young, *The Drama of the Medieval Church* (Oxford: Clarendon Press, 1933), II, 362–64.

51. The panel nearest hell mouth on the Lincoln Cathedral frieze is an early nineteenth-century replacement; this space was shown as blank in William Camden, *Britannia*, trans. and ed. Richard Gough, 2nd ed. (London, 1806), II, Pl. XI; by this date the other panels were already very weathered. See also George Zarnecki, *Romanesque Sculpture at Lincoln Cathedral* (Lincoln, n.d.), p. 10; and Saxl, *English Sculptures*, pp. 45–47, figs. 30–31, Pls. XLVI–XLIX and also LII, which shows a hell mouth receiving the soul of Dives and two others.

52. Martha Himmelfarb, *Tours of Hell: An Apocalyptic Form in Jewish and Christian Literature* (Philadelphia: Univ. of Pennsylvania Press, 1983), pp. 116–20.

53. RSV; quoted by Himmelfarb, *Tours of Hell*, p. 109.

54. Ibid., p. 108.

55. For the *Visio Pauli* as a possible source for the cauldron as a place of punishment for sinners, see the summary by D. D. R. Owen, *The Vision of Hell* (Edinburgh: Scottish Academic Press, 1970), p. 3.

56. Clifford Davidson, *The Guild Chapel Wall Paintings at Stratford-upon-Avon* (New York: AMS Press, 1988), fig. 17; Clifford Davidson and Jennifer Alexander, *The Early Art of Coventry, Stratford-upon-Avon, Warwick, and Lesser Sites in Warwickshire*, pp. 69–71, figs. 28–29.

57. *Gesta Romanorum*, ed. Sidney J. H. Herrtage, EETS, e.s. 33 (London, 1879), p. 385; cited by M. D. Anderson, *The Imagery of British Churches* (London: John Murray, 1955), p. 135.

58. W. O. Hassall, *The Holkham Bible Picture Book* (London: Dropmore Press, 1954), fol. 34, pp. 138–39.

59. Lynn White, Jr., *Medieval Religion and Technology* (Berkeley and Los Angeles: Univ. of California Press, 1978), p. 11.

60. Hilary Wayment, *The Stained Glass of the Church of St. Mary, Fairford, Gloucestershire* (London: Society of Antiquaries, 1984), p. 57, Pls. XXII, LIX, Color Pl. VIIc.

61. See F. K. N. Flynn, "The Mural Painting in the Church of Saints Peter and Paul, Chaldon, Surrey," *Surrey Archaeological Collections*, 72 (1980), 127–56; and also E. W. Tristram, *English Wall Painting: The Twelfth Century* (London: Oxford Univ. Press, 1944), pp. 36–39, 108.

62. See John Rupert Martin, *The Illustration of the Heavenly Ladder of John Climacus*, Studies in Manuscript Illumination, 5 (Princeton: Princeton Univ. Press, 1954), pp. 5–15, figs. 66–67. The Byzantine iconography is also described in *The "Painter's Manual" of Dionysius of Fourna*, ed. Paul Hetherington (London: Sagittarius Press, 1974), p. 82. For closely related iconography in a Western European example, see Herrad of Landsberg's *Hortus Deliciarum*, trans. Aristide D. Caratzas (New Rochelle, N.Y.: Caratzas Brothers, 1977), Pl. LVI.

63. William Dunbar, *The Poems*, ed. W. Mackay Mackenzie (London: Faber and Faber, 1932), p. 121.

64. Flynn, "The Mural Painting," p. 150; A. Caiger-Smith, *English Medieval Mural Paintings* (Oxford: Clarendon Press, 1963), pp. 36–37. Pl. III.

65. Warburg Institute photographic collection.

66. Christopher Marlowe, *Doctor Faustus*, ed. John D. Jump (London: Methuen, 1962), pp. 40–43 (vi.111–69).

67. See Edward J. Gallagher, "The *Visio Lazari*, the Cult, and the Old French Life of Saint Lazarus: An Overview," *Neuphilologische Mitteilungen*, 90 (1989), 331–39.

68. See Mâle, *Religious Art in France: The Late Middle Ages*, pp. 430–31, figs. 268–69.

69. Ibid., pp. 431–32.

70. *Short Title Catalogue*, Nos. 22407–23. For less slavishly copied but nevertheless rather crude woodcuts, see Wynkyn de Worde's edition of *The Kalender of shepeherdes* of 1528 (STC 22411).

71. See also Kenneth Muir's note to *King Lear* IV.vii.47 in the Arden edition of the play, 8th ed. (1952; rpt. London: Methuen, 1959).

72. *The Macro Plays*, ed. Mark Eccles, EETS, 262 (London, 1969), p. 93 (l. 3066).

73. *Sawles Warde*, p. 252.

74. British Library MS. Add. 37677, fol. 60ᵛ, as quoted by G. R. Owst, *Literature and Pulpit in Medieval England*, 2nd ed. (New York: Barnes and Noble, 1961), p. 522.

Hellfire:
Flame as Special Effect

Philip Butterworth

Representations of hell and its staging occur in all the major forms of extant English medieval theater. Even though the iconography depicting hell presents some consistent features throughout medieval Europe, its counterpart in staging terms is not always apparent. For instance, it is by no means clear that such representations *always* centered around the property or device known as hell mouth. Designation of hell in theatrical terms could also be achieved in a number of other ways, obviating in those cases the need for a physical representation of it. The naming of "infernum" in the plans contained in the Cornish *Ordinalia*, for instance, gains its symbolic and theatrical relevance by virtue of its physical position relative to other designations.[1] The same point could be made in respect to the "Northe Belyal skaffold" in *The Castle of Perseverance*.[2] Such a scaffold need not necessarily have attempted to represent hell in terms of a hell mouth device, for Belyal's occupation of the scaffold at key points may have provided sufficient symbolic identification with hell. Indeed, the mere appellation of named and nameless devils in various plays could of itself have indicated hell in some instances without there being need for a physical representation. In this respect the consistent use of "entrances," "exits," or *loci* would have been a necessary aid to communication.[3] Because the theatrical use of devils implicitly creates symbolic reference to hell, without the necessary representation of it, I intend to consider evidence concerning devils who may have operated outside the strict staging confines of hell in addition to the more traditional reference to hell mouth.

Flame and Fire at Hell Mouth. Specific references to hell mouth in the English mystery plays are to be found among the records at Coventry and York.[4] At Coventry, the Cappers and their play of the Resurrection and Descent into Hell and the Drapers and their pageant of Doomsday each possessed a hell mouth. Payments exist toward the construction, refurbishment, and maintenance of hell mouth of both guilds.[5] Yet there is one type of payment particular to the Drapers which does not exist in the accounts of the Cappers—payment referring to the keeping of fire at hell mouth. Occasionally such items refer to "kepyng of hell mowthe & the fyer."[6] One reference is made to "kepyng of the fyers."[7] Precise evidence concerning the location, duration, and number of performances given by the Drapers' guild is not extant. References to "the fyer" could be indicative of one performance or of more than one. The single reference to "fyers" indicates more than one performance and different locations. Payments for "kepyng" are the same for the singular or plural reference, namely, four pence. The Drapers' accounts seem to indicate that there were three performances—a deduction from payments, usually made to Robert Crow, for making and setting on fire "iij worldes."[8] These "worldes" seem to have been carried between performances and set on fire as part of the conflagrative climax to the play of Doomsday. If there were three performances of the Drapers' pageant, may we assume that three fires were kept? The records do not refer to the transport of fire or hell mouth between performances. Since payments in the respective accounts treat hell mouth as a separate entity, it may be supposed that hell mouth was a separate structure to the pageant and that it may or may not have been carried separately between performances.[9] It seems that some preparation of the fire at each performance would have been necessary, as at Mons,[10] if the fuel was coal or wood. Although we may be well aware of the iconographic significance of the fire at hell mouth, the theatrical purpose needs to be further considered. What was the fire required to do? Was it intended to create flame or smoke? Was it important for the audience to see the fire? Was the fire the means of creating other effects? What did the keeper of the fire do? Different theatrical statements are clearly possible, depending on the answers to the above questions.

Presumably the fire would have needed to be contained in braziers or fire-pans if the fuel was coal or wood.[11] Such provision is clearly indicated by payments for the use of "ij fyer boxes" for "a dragons head and a dragons mowthe" at Court.[12] It is, of course, possible that the fuel at Coventry was not coal or wood but spirit of some kind, in which case it would not have been necessary to prepare the fire in advance. A comparable payment to the Coventry Drapers' provision of fire is also contained in the Drapers' Repertory for June 1541 concerning the Midsummer Shows in London: "3s.8d. for a gallon of 'aqua vyte' to burn in the dragon's mouth; 16d. to him that kept fire in the dragon's mouth."[13]

Again, it is important to determine what was involved in the business of keeping the fire. Like most spirits, "aqua vyte" (brandy) burns with limited visibility and color to the flame, so it would appear that the use of burning "aqua vyte" is likely to have been similar to that of a pilot light on a modern gas appliance: it was intended to ignite other fuel. There are many references to fifteenth- and sixteenth-century dramatic or processional dragons which spouted fire.[14] No doubt the dragon to which reference is made in the London Drapers' Repertory did just that. One possible technique of spouting fire, which will be discussed below, involved blowing a mixture of powdered sulphur and "aqua ardens" over coals: this would have produced a bluish flame and might well have been accomplished by "him that kept fire."[15] The use of "aqua vyte" to ignite a sulphur/"aqua ardens" mixture would have produced the same sort of effect. Other pyrotechnic compositions might have produced flame of other colors. It must be acknowledged, however, that payments for additional pyrotechnic ingredients do not occur in the appropriate Drapers' Repertory.

The size of the Coventry Drapers' hell mouth is not recorded, but it must have been large enough to take the fire, the person who kept hell mouth, the person who kept the fire, and the two devils to which reference is made in the accounts.[16] Clearly the presence of the contained fire of itself would not have made much theatrical impact, whether it was visible to or hidden from the audience.[17] As noted in relation to the use of "aqua vyte," additions to the fire would have been necessary in order to create more spectacular light, flames, or smoke. If the fire was fueled by coal or wood, the material most likely to have been used is rosin. Payments for rosin occur in nearly all the relevant Drapers' accounts.[18] The rosin used here is probably a type known as colophone or Greek Pitch,[19] which is the residue produced when turpentine is distilled with water[20]—a residue capable of being reduced to a powder. There are, however, different kinds of rosins; while each consists of different chemical compositions and burning characteristics,[21] the principal feature common to them is that they consist of relatively high carbon content. When rosin in powder form is sprinkled onto a fire, the carbon produces a bright white flame.[22] Rosin was required "to the resurrecyon pley" at Reading, Berkshire, in 1507, and E. K. Chambers has suggested that this was "possibly for making a blaze" at the point where Pilate's soldiers "are all afraid and fall downe."[23] The "hoistmens playe" at Newcastle acquired "vj li. of rossell" (rosin) for nine pence in 1568 for what is thought to have been a Harrowing of Hell or Doomsday play. The rosin recorded here is among a list of other pyrotechnic ingredients which are clearly intended to create fire and explosion.[24] Similar payments were made for "di li of rosset iiij d" in a list of firework ingredients for use in hell at New Romney in 1560.[25]

Brief reference has been made above to the different functions of keeping the fire at hell mouth and keeping hell mouth itself. In the Coventry Drapers' accounts, payments are sometimes made to both functions, while on other occasions payments are made to each of these separate functions. Whether the single payment to both functions or separate payments to individual functions occurred, the "going rates" tended to be the same. Generally, these rates were four pence for keeping the fire and eight pence for keeping hell mouth. Occasionally when the payments were made as one, the overall payment was lower, at ten pence, to include both functions. It is not clear whether these functions were performed by one or more persons. In 1558 two payments which may serve as representative of split payments were made as follows:

payd for kepyng of hell movthe   viij d

. . .

payd for kepyng of fyer at hell mothe   iiij d[26]

Since separate payments were made in respect of these functions, what did the keeper of "hell movthe" do to warrant double the amount paid to the keeper of the "fyer"? I take the term 'kepyng' to involve more than mere minding and to indicate maintenance of some sort.[27] Whatever the tasks of the keeper of "hell movthe," they were seemingly regarded to be of greater value and/or responsibility than those involved in keeping the "fyer." Did the Drapers' "hell movthe" contain doors, gates, curtains, or a moveable mouth? If so, the keeper may well have let the devils in and out of hell. It is possible that the person who kept "hell movthe" was given iconographical significance as the door keeper or porter of hell.[28] Certainly, the opening and closing of hell mouth seem to have been a feature elsewhere. At Lincoln in 1564 when "the storye of olde thobye was playd," accounts concerning properties belonging to the play inform us of "hell mouthe w^t a neithere Chap."[29] Presumably the purpose of the moveable jaw was to enable devils to enter and exit from hell. A similar requirement is made of hell in the Cornish *Creacion of the World* by a stage direction following line 244 which instructed: "*Lett Hell gape when the Father nameth yt.*"[30] Considerable information exists in the French records concerning the opening of hell mouth. For instance, at Romans in 1508 payment is recorded to "Grégoire for two large bolts, weighing three pounds, for making Hell mouth open: in all . . . 3 sous."[31] At Mons in 1501, Master Jean du Fayt was paid "pour ii pentures à marteaux servant au pendre la gheule du Crapault d'Enffer, vi s." ("for two iron bars on which to hang the mouth of hell, 6s")[32] and "pour ii paires de pentures à marteau servant à ii huisses à l'Enfer, viii s." ("for two pairs of iron bars to be used on two doors into hell, 8s").[33] The Nativity play at Rouen in 1474 required "Hell made like a great mouth (*guelle*) opening and closing as is needful."[34] At Metz in 1437 it was reported that hell involved an "engin" operating the opening and closing of the mouth—a mouth structured as a "great head (*hure*)" with "two great steel eyes which glittered wonderfully."[35]

Although the opening and closing of hell mouth may be supported by evidence from the records, it is just as likely that this function served stage-management needs in allowing preparation time for and cueing of pyrotechnic effects such as shooting fire, creating smoke and flame.[36] However, such elaborate effects do not appear to have occurred in the Drapers' pageant at Coventry. Even though the opening and closing of hell mouth seems to have been the most likely function of the person who kept "hell movthe," absence of payments for firework ingredients other than rosin suggests only a limited use of pyrotechnics. It is possible that the two demons of the Drapers' pageant threw amounts of powdered rosin onto the fire, enabling more spectacular entrances and exits to be achieved.[37] This task could also have been the responsibility of the keeper of the fire, who seems to have maintained three separate coal fires in order to receive his four pence and to produce the required effects.[38]

Flame as Light. Reference to the use of a hell mouth device by the Cooks' Harrowing of Hell pageant at Chester (Play XVII) is not extant, presumably because the pageant vehicle itself represented hell.[39] The Norwich "Helle Carte" of 1527 appears to have been another example of the vehicle itself representing hell.[40] There are no references to the use of pyrotechnics in the Cooks' pageant, although an interesting requirement for the production of light occurs at the very beginning of the play in the following stage direction: "Et primo fiat lux in inferno materialis aliqua subtilitate machinata, et postea dicat Adam" ("And at the start let there be material light in hell created by some cunning device and afterwards Adam shall say").[41] Although the requirement made by this stage direction is imprecise to a modern reader, it does indicate that the original author recognized the need for, and the possibility of, creating such light by the use of an ingenious device. Presumably, this sort of device was capable of producing the desired effect and was a known technical possibility rather than merely a requirement as expressed in the *Gospel of Nicodemus*.[42] The Chester Cooks were not the only practitioners to make this kind of demand; the sort of requirement often found in stage directions is for "*a marvellous splendour of light*" or "a great light."[43]

How was such a light to be achieved? It might be useful at this point to consider some appropriate principles and possible techniques in an attempt to determine how the Chester Cooks' stage direction was realized. Care must be taken here in relation to the Cooks' instruction, since the terms are both ambiguous and relative. The intensity of light required by this stage direction is not likely to be that of a 2000-watt profile lantern, directed onto a round mirror, held by the angel Gabriel, as used in the National Theatre's *The Mysteries*.[44] The principal light source in this case must have been flame, whether it was provided by candle, torch, lantern, or cresset. In order to achieve the importance implied by the stage direction, the basic light source would have been required to be subjected to an arrangement involving reflectors and/or lenses. The particular characteristics of any lantern used in modern lighting depend upon the reflector-bulb-lens relationship. The ability to change this relationship determines, for example, whether soft-edged or hard-edged (profile) light is produced. Similarly, this relationship can determine whether light is focused. The principles concerning the behavior of light apply equally to the use of flame. The simplest way of increasing the intensity and illumination of a light source is to cause the source to be reflected.

Techniques of polishing metal in order to provide parabolic mirrors were known from Celtic times.[45] Lead-backed mirrors were known from the thirteenth century.[46] At Revello in 1483 the following instruction was given for the Transfiguration:

> And when Jesus is on the mountain let there be a polished bowl (*bacillo*) which makes the brightness of the sun striking the bowl reflect on Jesus and towards his disciples. Then Jesus shall let fall his crimson garment and appear in white garments. And if the sun is not shining, let there be torches and some other lights.[47]

This direction clearly demonstrates understanding of the principle of reflection to increase illumination. The reflector is not a flat mirror but a polished bowl, possibly made of copper or bronze. The value of a bowl-shaped reflector would have been to collect the available light, whether from the sun or torches, and to enable its rim to define the rough limits of direction. The depth of the bowl relative to the diameter would have affected its capacity to direct or spread light. The technique is noted by Sebastiano Serlio as follows: "if you need a great light to show more then the rest, then set a torch behind, and behind the torch a bright Bason; the brightnes whereof will shew like the beames of the Sunne."[48]

The same principle operates in modern floodlights where lenses are not incorporated and the light characteristic is determined by what is effectively a bulb in a "tin box" which contains a reflector. Light produced by this arrangement is soft-edged and relatively indiscriminate. Some direction of light clearly was possible with the Revello polished bowl. No doubt the bowl was hand-held in order to allow for the movement of Jesus in relation to the light source. It is unlikely that the "torches and some other lights" offered the same intensity of light to be reflected as would have been provided by the sun. The discrepancy may not have mattered in that the use of "torches and other lights" would have operated in a relatively darker context.

Another interesting use of the bowl-flame arrangement is contained in an account of the reception of Robert Dudley, Earl of Leicester, to the Hague and Leiden in January 1586: "against my lord's gate, a barbar had on a wall placed three score or more basons of bright copper, and in the middest of euerie one a wax candle burning was placed; in the middest of all was painted a rose and crowne: this made a faire shew, and was a pretie deuise. . . ."[49] Although this description is not conclusive in determining whether the "basons" were intended to reflect light toward the viewer, there seems little other value in designing such an arrangement. The word 'bason' indicates a relatively shallow vessel in proportion to its diameter and may therefore have reflected light fairly widely. Nevertheless, this must have been an impressive sight.

A further stage in the ability to create intensified and directed light would have required the use of a lens. The purpose of a lens is to focus or create divergence of light. Eyeglasses and the use of lenses to increase magnification were known in the thirteenth century.[50] However, the construction of a lens was not always from a solid piece of glass. Lenses could be created from round glass vessels containing liquid. Hugh Platte offered the following advice in creating a device which operated in the manner of a lens: "Cause a round & double Glasse to bee made of a large size, & in fashion like a globe, but with a great rounde hole in the toppe, and in the concaue part of the vppermost Glasse place a Candle in a loose socket, and at some hole or pipe which must bee made in the side thereof, fill the same with spirite of Wine or some other cleare distilled water that will not putrifie, and this one Candle will give a great and wonderfull light, somewhat resembling the Sun beames"[51] (see fig. A).

This double-skinned glass vessel contained "spirite of Wine" or "cleare distilled water" as a medium through which the light source —i.e., the flame—was focused by the convex outer surface of the vessel. The "Sun beames" effect referred to by Platte is likely to have consisted of slim vectors of intensified light surrounding the vessel. If placed on a flat surface, the "Sun beames" would have been seen to radiate horizontally from the

Fig. A. "How with one candle to make as great a light as otherwise with two or three of the same bignesse."

vessel. Since the description required the liquid to be poured into the vessel via "some hole or pipe," the assumption to be made is that the liquid was capable of being sealed into the vessel by removing the pipe or introducing a bung to the "hole." Platte himself indicates his surprise at the fact that "one Candle will give a great and wonderfull light. . . ."

Another example of a liquid-filled vessel acting as a lens is given by Platte: "I knewe an expert Ieweller, dwelling (whilest he liued) in the Blacke-friers, who had a Glasse with a round bellie, and a flat backe standing vpon a foote, with a Lampe placed so at the backer part thereof, as that the light thereof was iust opposite to the center of the bellie through which (the Glasse being first filled with spirite of Wine) there would so brim and glittering light appeare, as that by the helpe thereof he would graue anie curious worke in golde as well at midnight as at the noone day."[52] The principle involved here is the same as in the previous example, yet an important piece of additional information is offered in that the light source, "a Lampe," was placed "iust opposite to the center of the bellie." This exact relationship between the light source and the "bellie" of the "Glasse" would have been the means of focusing the resultant intensified light. Serlio made a similar requirement: "And behind the glasses you must set great Lampes, that the light may also be stedfast: and if the bottels or other vessels of glasse on the side where the light stands were flat, or rather hollow, it would show the clearer. . . ."[53]

The principle of focus is well illustrated with reference to a lace-maker's lamp, consisting of a globe of water suspended on a base to which is attached a moveable candle holder. According to the length of the candle, the holder is capable of being moved up or down in order that the flame might be positioned opposite the "bellie" of the globe. When the candle is in this position it produces a focused slim vector of intensified light onto the lace-maker's work[54] (fig. B).

A third method of intensifying candle light is a development of the reflector: "What light a Candle woulde shewe if it were placed in a large Cilinder like vnto a halfe Lanterne, all of Latten kept bright and glistring, the same being inwardly garnished with diuerse steele Looking-glasses, so artificially placed as that one of them might reflect vnto an other"[55] (fig. C). The arrangement of the "steele Looking-glasses" effectively enabled more lighting sources to be created which were in turn reflected and re-reflected in order to produce greater intensity and illumination.[56]

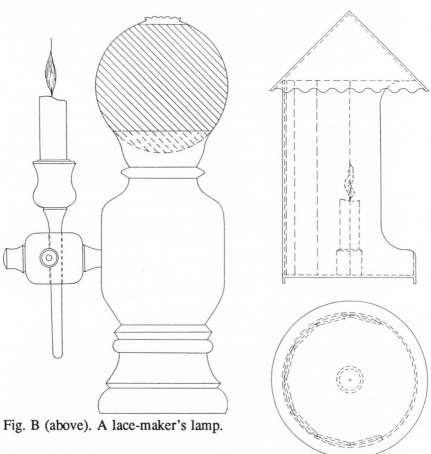

Fig. B (above). A lace-maker's lamp.

Fig. C (right). "a halfe Lanterne. . . ."

Knowledge of the principles involving reflectors and lenses was widely disseminated by the fifteenth and sixteenth centuries. The candle/globe examples given by Platte are unlikely to have produced sufficient illumination to compete with ordinary bright daylight; however, the principles to which he refers could have used stronger light sources in the form of torches, lanterns, or sunlight, as required by Serlio and the Revello stage direction.

To return to the lighting requirement made by the stage direction in the Chester Cooks' pageant, it is clear that the principles discussed above must have been employed in creating such an ingenious device. Given the relative scale of presentation—i.e., a pageant vehicle performance in the streets of Chester—I suspect that Platte's candle/globe examples would have been relatively ineffective in bright daylight and the bowl/torch method would have required some greater space in which to operate in order to be effective for an audience. This leads me to suggest that some such device as Platte's "halfe Lanterne" with "steele Looking-glasses" might have answered the intensity requirement in the relatively confined space of a pageant vehicle positioned in a Chester street. A device of this kind might also have qualified as being "cunning" or ingenious.

Flame as Heat. A recurrent image frequently found in the iconography of hell is that of the hell cauldron, many examples of which occur throughout Europe, perhaps most strikingly in the tympanum above the central doorway of Bourges Cathedral. The portrayal of this aspect, which is thought to have been based upon the apocryphal *Gospel of Nicodemus*, finds its theatrical counterpart in episodes in the drama of continental Europe, though evidence is lacking in English drama. None of the extant English medieval texts requires the use of the cauldron in representations of hell. The only specific use of a cauldron occurs in the Croxton *Play of the Sacrament*.[57] Although the cauldron in this play is not concerned with completing the imagery surrounding hell, the information offered by the stage directions may afford some insight into the theatrical requirements and possibilities of staging the hell cauldron. Such is the proliferation of hell cauldron imagery that it is quite possible that some English stage representations of hell did use the cauldron as part of the stage picture, even though the civic and guild records do not take note of its use.[58]

The cauldron in the Croxton *Play of the Sacrament* is not used to torture damned souls in boiling oil or lead.[59] In this instance it is used quite specifically to separate the severed hand of Jonathas from the host wafer. However, the basic arrangement is the same: a fire is lighted underneath the cauldron in order to boil its contents. The stage direction at line 672 indicates: "Here shall þe cawdron byle, apperyng to be as blood." This is one of the rare directions to be found among English medieval texts which explicitly refers to theatrical artifice.[60] Of importance here is the communicated appearance of boiling. References to this sort of device are found among other European texts, and evidence concerning methods of theatrical deception is sometimes explained in accompanying records.[61] The stage direction invites speculation on a number of interesting issues. First, assuming that timing was important, how did the cauldron manage to boil at the appropriate time—i.e., "on cue"? Second, what does the word 'byle' (boil) mean in this context? Did the cauldron actually boil if the contents were to appear as blood? Third, to whom was such "apperyng" apparent? Since the creation of the fire under the cauldron and the subsequent boiling happen within eight lines of the text, the requirement expressed by the stage direction occurred within shortened theatrical time and seems to have been instantaneous. Although Masphat and Malchas refer to the preparation and subsequent boiling of the cauldron, the stage direction contains information that explicitly refers to the creation of theatrical illusion. Normally the action of a boiling liquid requires that bubbles are seen as evidence of this state. Fortunately, for theatrical purposes accompanying steam, vapor, or smoke is also suggestive of this condition. Consequently, evidence of the cauldron "apperyng" to boil need not refer to the sight of boiling or bubbling liquid.[62] Of the possible vapors involved, smoke seems to have been the most likely effect. Similarly, reference to the contents of the cauldron "apperyng to be as blood" may have been to red smoke. Even if the audience were placed above the action of the play, as has been suggested, the sight of boiling liquid appearing precisely "on cue" would have proved a difficult proposition.[63] The possibility of smoke being the conductor of this effect could be more precisely identified if fireworks or firework ingredients were used. The ability to produce red smoke is likely to have been possible through the use of an ingredient such as vermillion oil mixed with other pyrotechnic ingredients. The use of "vermenioun ule" for celebratory purposes is recorded in Scotland among other firework ingredients in 1538 in the Lord High Treasurer's accounts.[64] Reference to "vermenioun ule" does not indicate certain use in the production of red smoke, for the ingredient may well have been used as a binding agent in a pyrotechnic mixture to produce, for instance, red stars for aerial use. However, vermillion has certainly been used in the production of red smoke.[65]

The use of fireworks to create the illusion of boiling is noted in a stage direction in the Majorca SS. Crispin and Crispinian play:

> The official is to go away with two or three men, and they are to bring a piece of lead and a cauldron. They are to put the two youths into a cauldron and a little fire is to be made with straw. They are to put a firework (*coet*) beneath the cauldron, and when the youths have stopped singing, they are to set fire to the firework.[66]

Although this direction does not inform us of the nature of the effect to be achieved, it seems likely that the firework was intended to supplement the "little fire" in the production of an effect. The resultant effect is more likely to have been one of flame or smoke than of noise. The production of smoke by the firework would have contributed to the illusion since fire was already in place beneath the cauldron. Additionally, smoke would produce the necessary dimension to the effect and yet remain relatively controllable.

Further support is given to this kind of boiling illusion by a stage direction from the Modane play of Antichrist in 1580: "Then they shall make water boil in the cauldron in which the seneschal is put and do it with fireworks (*fusées*) without heating the water in the best possible way."[67] The implication here is that the cauldron actually contained water which was artificially made to boil by the use of fireworks. Presumably the water was required to seethe "without heating the water." Several early pyrotechnic sources contain directions for underwater firework mixtures and devices.[68] The successful operation of these underwater devices occurred because the chemical reactions of the firework ingredients created their own oxygen supply through the inclusion of an oxidizing agent, usually saltpeter (potassium nitrate, KNO_3). Such underwater fireworks could certainly have created violent bubbles and smoke. Typically, this sort of device consisted of a canvas ball filled with a gunpowder mixture "armed" or bound with "marling" cord and coated in pitch, rosin, tallow, or other wax. Vents were left in the canvas case in order to fire the ball. The underwater balls were ballasted with stones or lead.[69] Some sleight-of-hand would have been necessary in placing this kind of firework into the cauldron, for it would have had to be fired before immersion. However, the effects of bubbling water accompanied by much smoke would have been relatively immediate and certainly capable of occurring "on cue."[70]

Flaming Devils. The relationship between the concept of hell and fire is one of ready association, for such is the biblical and traditionally historical affinity. The iconographical portrayal of this relationship is a vivid and exciting one, and the task of giving physical representation to it in theatrical form must have been difficult, dangerous, and even more exciting. The attempt to control flame for pyrotechnic purposes is indebted to military discoveries and expertise. Early writing on pyrotechnics is often unclear with regard to the distinction between military and recreational use of fireworks. Although some of the processes were identical, separation of purpose and function only becomes apparent toward the end of sixteenth century.

It is clear that different pyrotechnic processes were involved in the theatrical representations of hell. In this respect the imprecise stage directions in the Digby *Conversion of St. Paul* may serve as a useful reference point for discussion of these processes.[71] The scene between the two devils, Belyal and Mercury, thought to have been written some twenty or thirty years after the main text, contains three directions which may well exist as records of earlier staging.[72] Belyal is required to enter *"wyth thunder and fyre"*;[73] Mercury is to enter *"wyth a fyeryng"* (1. 432*sd*); and both are required to *"vanyshe away wyth a fyrye flame, and a tempest"* (1. 501*sd*). So what were these effects and how were they achieved? It is by no means certain that the effects required by these three directions were the same or produced in the same manner. After delivering his opening speech, Belyal is required *"to syt downe in a chayre."* This suggests that the *"thunder and fyre"* that accompanied him on his entrance were short lived, occupying at most the time taken to deliver three stanzas. Perhaps the simplest known technique which might have applied to these directions is that of "casting fire." This term was usually applied in England to the straightforward act of throwing fireworks, variously referred to as squibs, serpents, or fiz-gigs.[74]

In the Chamberlains Account Books at Newcastle "the chargis of the hoistmens playe" record payment of six pence to "A man that kest fyer."[75] The respective guilds which contributed to the Lord Mayor's Show in London in the second half of the sixteenth century employed wild men to "cast squybbes w[t] fyre."[76] The records of the Merchant Taylors' Company indicate the function of these figures: "And to make waye in the streetes, there are certayne men apparelled lyke devells, and wylde men, with skybbs."[77] Hughe Wattes and Chrystopher Beck were required by the Merchant Taylors to "serve for woodhousis or Ivie men" and to equip themselves with "vyssers squybbe and powdre and they to shote of Fyer wth the seid squybbes contynually."[78] This record is helpful in that it offers an explanation of the many vague and ambiguous references to shooting fire. Again in the Lord Mayor's Show, Henry Machyn recorded such an observation: "and ther was a dullvyll shuting of fyre, and won was lyke Deth with a dart in hand."[79]

The term 'squib' was often applied loosely to any firework that was thrown, but more particularly to that type of firework which issued a shower of sparks, meandered erratically, and ended with a small report.[80] The behavior of squibs was conditioned by the construction of the case or "coffin" and contained gunpowder mixtures.[81] The "coffin" was "not much thicker than a goose quill, and about foure inches long."[82] Most of the "coffin" held a basic gunpowder mixture, which would create a shower of sparks, while a small section of it was given over to a mixture of different proportions, which created the final explosion.[83]

Another method of achieving the requirements of *The Conversion of St. Paul* stage directions is that which is suggested by the well-known direction contained in the stage plan of *The Castle of Perseverance*: "and he þat schal pley belyal loke þat he haue gunnepowdyr brennynge In pypys in hys handys and in hys erys and in hys ars whanne he gothe to batayl."[84] The use of fireworks as required by this direction is immediately graphic and presumably intended to create an impact. No doubt vigorous and timed movement by Belyal would have given greater spatial and visual dimension to the overall effect. Although the "pypys" in "hys erys" and in "hys ars" appear to have been fixed, it is possible that the "pypys in hys handys" were scattered like squibs. If the hand-held "pypys" were not thrown, then their use as threatening weapons would nevertheless have completed the formidable warlike image.

The principal gunpowder mixture contained in squibs was that which was frequently used for "golden" or "silver rain."[85] The shower of sparks produced by this composition seems to be the effect sought by *The Castle of Perseverance* direction, since the requirement is for "gunnepowdyr brennynge" and not some other pyrotechnic process. The intention appears to require an incendiary effect rather than an explosive one.[86] Clearly Belyal's costume/mask contained some sort of framework, possibly of wicker or wire, built into it in order to hold the "pypys" in his "erys" and "hys ars."[87] Presumably another figure dressed Belyal with his "pypys" and ignited him.[88] The risks inherent in the creation of this effect are well illustrated by the account, already cited above by Barbara Palmer in her article in this volume, of an accident during which the actor playing Lucifer had his costume catch fire while departing into a *secret* under the set; fortunately, the actor was given quick attention and was able to go on playing his role without any indication that he was in pain.[89] Quite possibly this incident from the *Mystery of St. Martin* represents an unsuccessful version of *The Castle of Perseverance* requirement, although it could refer to the unfortunate result of another technique which required devil figures to be set on fire. A dangerous trick of this sort represents yet another possibility with regard to the respective entrances of Belyal and Mercury in *The Conversion of St. Paul* and may also have been the technique adopted by Lucifer in *The Creacion of the World* when the stage direction required him to go "*downe to Hell, apariled fowle with fyre about hem, turning to Hell . . .*" (l. 326*sd*). The clearest documentation of this method comes from *Il quaderno di segreti d'un regista provenzale del Medioevo* (*The Volume of Secrets of a Provençal Stage Director's Book*), written within a thirty-year period toward the end of the fifteenth century and in the early sixteenth century. The technique is outlined as follows:

> Finta a far
> un diable tot ple
> de fuoch: pren tre-
> mentina e bota-
> ne ab escho sus
> lo diable, e pueis [. .]
> agone de quoto
> banat an d'aigo ar-
> den e fais-lo tene
> an la trementina;
> bota-i fioch, pueis
> bota-li un quano
> de podro a quado
> pe e mai a qua-
> do mo, e un au-
> tre diable li vo[l-]
> ra bota fuoc as
> quanos e mai al qu[. . .][90]
> <. . .>

(A trick to make a devil completely full of fire: he takes turpentine and throws [?casts, ?smears] some of it with a fuel [?fuse, ?igniter] onto the devil, and then adds cotton soaked with spirit [*aqua ardens*] and makes it remain [?stick] with the turpentine; he gives it fire and then puts a reed of powder in each hand and foot, and another devil will see to setting fire to the reeds and also to . . . [?cotton].

The use of the "quano de podro" ("reed of powder") to be placed in hands and feet is essentially the same sort of requirement as that of the direction in *The Castle of Perseverance*. These are "giant" reeds and may have been larger than goose quills, almost of cane proportions. "Trementina" (turpentine) is a resin which is capable of existing as a liquid or a waxy solid. The latter form is involved here. It is smeared or pasted onto the devil's costume. The turpentine was required to produce the principal flame and smoke. The function of the cotton soaked in "d'aigo arden" (*aqua ardens*) was effectively to create a fuse.[91] Although the turpentine would burn, it would not ignite at the low temperature of the spirit; hence the impregnated cotton was fired in order to raise the temperature and to ignite the turpentine. The cotton, whether one piece or more, would have easily stuck to the waxy turpentine. Clearly, timing of ignition and suffocation of the flame was critical to the success of the effect and the well-being of the actor. We are not informed of how the actor was protected from the flame; presumably protective undergarments, possibly of thick wool, would have been used.[92] The speed with which Satan was "so swiftly succored, stripped, and reclothed" in the accident at the *Mystery of St. Martin* indicates the necessary readiness to deal with a malfunction of the effect. The need for protective undergarments is rather negatively illustrated by the well-known accident at the French court in 1393. As part of the "mummery agaynst nyght" during a wedding celebration, Hugonin de Guisay "deuysed syxe cotes made of lynen clothe, covered with pytche, and theron flaxe lyke heare. . . ." When the nobles, including the king, Charles VI, put on their costumes and were "sowed fast in them, they semed lyke wylde wodehouses, full of heare fro the toppe of the heed to the sowle of the fote." The inherent fire risk associated with the six men who were sewn into the pitch-covered garments was appreciated, and the king ordered "all the varlettes holdinge torches to stande up by the walles, and none of them to aproche nere to the wodehouses that shulde come thyder to daunce." Unfortunately, the "duke of Orlyance" and his retinue arrived after the king had given these instructions and, being intrigued by the hidden identity of the "wodehouses," took a torch "so nere, that the heate of the fyre entred into the flaxe, wherin if fyre take there is no remedy, and sodaynly was on a bright flame, and so eche of them set fyre on other; the pytche was so fastened to the lynen clothe, and their shyrtes so drye and fyne, and so joynynge to their flesshe, that they began to brenne and to cry for helpe. None durste come nere theym; they that dyd, brente their handes, by reason of the heate of the pytche."[93] Four of the men died of their burns; the king escaped, as did one who raced to the buttery and doused himself in a "vessell full of water."

While this account does not refer to an attempted trick that went wrong, it does point to the necessity of protective clothing in order to operate the trick in the *Provençal Stage Director's Book*. The "trementina" of the Provençal device could well have been the "pytche" of the French account which, ironically, was in that case merely used as an adhesive.[94]

Another technique which might have been used by Belyal and Mercury in *The Conversion of St. Paul* presumes that the figures wore masks. If this was the case, then the following instructions from the *Provençal Stage Director's Book* might be applicable:

Las caretas d[els]
diabbles qual que a[go]
una causa ala boqu[a]
coma aquesta quareta; aqu[e-]
lses que volron fa sa-
li lo fuoc per la
boqua he per las
aurelas he pel
nas.

nota

lo fuoc
salira per
aisi

il fuoco
uscirà per
qui

[E] mai hon a[ura]
pus bel deduch
a fa lor gita [lo]
fuoc per la boqu[a;]
qual que las quar[etas]
ho porto que qual [que]
entre la boqua e [la]
facha de aquel q[ue]
la portara ago u[na]
retreta de fuoc que[pu-]
esco quabe .ii. ho [.iii.]
carbos e que aquel[a]
retreta qual que s[ia]
tota bardegada d[e-]
part dedins affin [del]
fuoc que no cremes [la]
quareta.
Et qua[l . . .]
.xxx.ᵘʰo   qu[anels]
de auqua to[s]
ples de solpre
mout de dedins
an d'ayga arden,
e quant volras
fa sali lo fuoc
no qual mas que
prengos un qua-
nel de auqua
ala boqua e que
lo bufes afin que
vengo contra lo fuoc,

> e salira
> la flama tota
> blava delas lia-
> bras del fusser h[. . .]
> del diable,
> e no qual pas q[ue]
> [. . .]es affin que no
> [. . .]onbesso ala boq[ua.][95]

(The devils' masks must have something in the mouth as in the drawing, for those which want to make fire come out of the mouth, ears,
and nose.

Then it can be even more entertaining to make them blow fire out
of their mouths. These masks must include between the mouth of the
mask and the face of the person wearing it a place separated off to
hold the fire of a dimension adequate to hold two or three coals, and
this area must be all covered with mud on the inside so that the fire
does not burn the mask.

And there must be thirty or forty goose quills filled with powdered sulphur inside and *aqua ardens* and, when you want to make
the fire come out, you do no more than take a quill in the mouth and
blow so that the sulphur comes onto the fire and the flames come, all
blue, out of the lips of the devils' mask. And not so . . . in the
mouth. . . . [The text is incomplete, and probably included a warning
against breathing in sulphur.])

The purpose of the "solpre" (sulphur) and "d'ayga arden"
(*aqua ardens*) mixture was to ensure ignition. The "d'ayga arden"
would have caught fire at a lower temperature than the "solpre"
and effectively acted as a fuse.[96] The technique of blowing the
contents of the goose quills over the coals and out through the
nose and mouth seems straightforward, providing the open end of
the quill was as near to the exit hole as possible in order that the
flame did not blow back into the mask.[97] It is difficult to see how
the flame might have been projected through the ears if the coals
were placed forward of them in the snout. Although a goose quill
might have been placed so that it projected out of the side of the
actor's mouth in order to reach the ear, it is difficult to appreciate
how the "solpre" or "d'ayga arden" mixture would have come into

contact with the burning coal. Perhaps the ears were placed forward of the coal, in which case the supposed problem would not have existed. It is further possible that the technique (to which reference has been made above) of using reeds which contain a gunpowder mixture might have been adopted, and if this were so then the reeds would have been placed in the ears and presumably ignited by another devil.

The use of mud to protect the inside part of the mask which contained coals is most illuminating and similar in its purpose to the protection afforded hell mouth at Mons.[98] However, we are not informed of how the actor's face was shielded. Presumably some sort of woolen balaclava type of head covering with holes for the eyes and mouth would have been necessary.[99]

Of the pyrotechnic processes so far considered, the casting of squibs by Belyal on his entrance in *The Conversion of St. Paul* seems to have been the most likely method to have been employed, thus meeting the *"thunder and fyre"* requirements of the stage direction.[100] This approach could have been timed by the actor playing Belyal in such a way that he was also able to fulfill the rest of the stage direction which required that he *"syt downe in a chayre."*[101] The sound and light requirements contained in the stage direction concerned with the "exit" of Belyal and Mercury could also have been satisfied by the use of squibs. Mercury's "entrance" *"wyth a fyeryng"* may be only another way of expressing the same requirement as those contained in the other stage directions. However, it is just as possible that any of the foregoing techniques might have applied to the "entrance" of Mercury.

English evidence concerning the production of larger pyrotechnic effects, as frequently found in France, Spain, and Italy, does not exist in relation to the staging of hell.[102] Cannon, fire pumps, early forms of Roman candles, and air and ground rockets were used in England for ceremonial events such as royal entries, baptisms, birthdays, and weddings, but the dramatic records do not verify that they were found in the staging of hell.[103] There are many examples of fire-spouting dragons, serpents, and bulls which used the techniques previously discussed or utilized "rockets for the ground" placed appropriately in their bodies.[104] Clearly, the use of flame as a special effect in the creation of fire, light, and heat was considerably more manipulable than might be presumed. The danger associated with the foregoing effects did not stop them from being required or executed. Given the dependency upon flame to create such effects, we should not be surprised to encounter documentation that indicates considerable ingenuity and skill in their creation. The purpose and function of special effects in the English medieval theater were essentially no different from those that exist in the theater today. Although electricity is used frequently in attempts to simulate flame, the immediacy, danger, and emotional response associated with the use of real flame ironically cannot be replaced even in the late twentieth century with its preoccupation with safety.

NOTES

1. *The Ancient Cornish Drama*, ed. Edwin Norris (1859; rpt. New York: Benjamin Blom, 1968), I, 219.

2. Folger Shakespeare Library MS. V.a.354, fol. 191ᵛ; *The Macro Plays*, ed. Mark Eccles, EETS, 262 (London, 1969), frontispiece, p. 1.

3. The conventions and techniques concerned with "being seen" and "not being seen" in relation to given *loci* and scaffolds were clearly important; see Mary Loubris Jones, "How the Seven Deadly Sins 'Dewoyde from the Woman' in the Digby Mary Magdalen," *American Notes and Queries*, 16, No. 8 (April 1978), 118–19, and "Sunlight and Sleight-of-Hand in Medieval Drama," *Theatre Notebook*, 32 (1978), 118–26; Alan C. Dessen, *Elizabethan Stage Conventions and Modern Interpreters* (Cambridge: Cambridge Univ. Press, 1984), chap. 7; Philip Butterworth, "Book Carriers: Medieval and Tudor Staging Conventions," *Theatre Notebook*, forthcoming.

4. *Coventry*, ed. R. W. Ingram, Records of Early English Drama (Toronto: Univ. of Toronto Press, 1981), *passim*; *York*, ed. Alexandra F. Johnston and Margaret Rogerson, Records of Early English Drama (Toronto: Univ. of Toronto Press, 1979), I, 55, 242.

5. *Coventry*, ed. Ingram, pp. 167, 242, 245, 256, 469, 472.

6. Ibid., p. 221.

7. Ibid., p. 224.

8. R. W. Ingram, "'To find the players and all that longeth therto': Notes on the Production of Medieval Drama in Coventry," *The Elizabethan Theatre V*, ed. G. R. Hibbard (Hamden, Conn.: Archon Books, 1975), p. 30, and the same author's "'Pleyng geire accustumed belongyng & necessarie': Guild Records and Pageant Production at Coventry," *Proceedings of the First Colloquium*, ed. JoAnna Dutka (Toronto: Records of Early English Drama, 1979), p. 78, and "The Coventry Pageant Waggon," *English Medieval Theatre*, 2 (1980), 11; *Coventry*, ed. Ingram, pp. 217, 221.

9. Cf. Peter Meredith, "The Development of the York Mercers' Pageant Waggon," *Medieval English Theatre*, 1 (1979), 10; and see also William Donald Young, "Devices and Feintes of the Medieval Religious Theatre in England and France," unpublished Ph.D. diss. (Stanford Univ., 1959), pp. 122–24.

10. Gustave Cohen, *Le livre de conduite du régisseur et Le compte des dépenses pour le Mystère de la passion joué a Mons en 1501* (Paris: Champion, 1925), p. 14; *The Staging of Religious Drama in Europe in the Later Middle Ages: Texts and Documents in English Translation*, ed. Peter Meredith and John E. Tailby, Early Drama, Art, and Music, Monograph Ser., 4 (Kalamazoo: Medieval Institute Publications, 1983), p. 150.

11. See Charles T. McInnes, *Accounts of the Treasurer of Scotland* (Edinburgh: HMSO, 1970), XII, 405–06; Anna J. Mill, *Mediaeval Plays in Scotland* (1924; rpt. New York: Benjamin Blom, 1969), p. 340; Philip Butterworth, "The Baptisme of Hir Hienes Darrest Sone in Stirviling," *Medieval English Theatre*, 10 (1988), 28, 45.

12. Albert Feuillerat, *Documents Relating to the Revels at Court in the Time of King Edward VI and Queen Mary, from the Loseley Manuscripts* (1914; rpt. New York: Kraus, 1963), p. 108; Ian Lancashire, *Dramatic Texts and Records of Britain: A Chronological Topography to 1558* (Toronto: Univ. of Toronto Press, 1984), p. 146.

13. *A Calendar of Dramatic Records in the Books of the Livery Companies of*

London, 1485–1640, ed. Jean Robertson and D. J. Gordon, Malone Soc. Collections, 3 (Oxford, 1954), p. 34; "him that kept fire" is named as "Thom's Palm'." See Albert Feuillerat, *Documents Relating to the Revels at Court in the Time of King Edward VI and Queen Mary*, p. 110, and *Documents Relating to the Office of the Revels in the Time of Queen Elizabeth*, (1908; rpt. New York: Kraus, 1963), p. 308.

14. See below, n. 104.

15. John Bate, *The Mysteryes of Natvre and Art* (London, 1634), p. 66. Bate provides the following directions for making "*water called* Aqua Ardens": "Take old red wine, put it into a glased vessell, and put into it of orpment one pound, quicke sulphur halfe a pound, quicke lime a quarter of a pound; mingle them very well, and afterwards distill them in a rosewater still: a cloth being wet in this water will burne like a candle, and will not be quenched with water." See also R. J. Forbes, *A Short History of the Art of Distillation* (Leiden: Brill, 1948), chap. 4.

16. *Coventry*, ed. Ingram, pp. 217, 221, 224.

17. Different statements would have been possible according to whether the audience witnessed the source, its effect, or both.

18. *Coventry*, ed. Ingram, pp. 221, 224, 237, 250, 256, 259, 264, 475, 478–79, 481, 506.

19. Vannoccio Biringuccio, *The Pirotechnia*, trans. C. S. Smith and M. T. Gnudi (1942; rpt. New York: Basic Books, 1959), p. 438; *Three Bookes of Colloqvies concerning the Arte of Shooting in great and small pieces of Artillerie . . . written in Italian, and dedicated by Nicholas Tartaglia . . . And now translated into English by CYPRIANLVCAR. . . . Also the said CRYPRIANLVCAR hath annexed . . . a Treatise named LUCARAPPENDIX* (London, 1588), pp. 83, 86; John Babington, *Pyrotechnia; or, a Discourse on Artificiall Fireworks* (London, 1635), pp. 55–56; Takeo Shimizu, *Fireworks: The Art, Science and Technique* (Tokyo: Maruzen, 1981), p. 114; McInnes, *Accounts of the Treasurer of Scotland*, XII, 404. See also n. 97, below.

20. *OED*, 'turpentine,' sb. 1, and n. 94, below.

21. Rosins and resins should not be confused; see Thomas Kentish, *The Pyro-*

technist's Treasury (London, 1878), p. 175; Shimizu, *Fireworks*, pp. 114–15.

22. Ronald Lancaster, *Fireworks: Principles and Practice* (New York: Chemical Publishing, 1972), p. 39.

23. E. K. Chambers, *The Mediaeval Stage* (London: Oxford Univ. Press, 1903), II, 23n, 393; Pamela Sheingorn, *The Easter Sepulchre in England*, Early Drama, Art, and Music, Reference Ser., 5 (Kalamazoo: Medieval Institute Publications, 1987), p. 90; Karl Young, *The Drama of the Medieval Church* (Oxford: Clarendon Press, 1933), I, 408.

24. *Newcastle-upon-Tyne*, ed. J. J. Anderson, Records of Early English Drama (Toronto: Univ. of Toronto Press, 1982), p. 55.

25. *Records of Plays and Players in Kent, 1450–1642*, ed. Giles E. Dawson, Malone Soc. Collections, 7 (Oxford, 1965), pp. 209–10.

26. *Coventry*, ed. Ingram, p. 478.

27. *OED*, 'keeping,' vbl. sb. 3, sb. 4.

28. See Glynne Wickham, *Shakespeare's Dramatic Heritage* (New York: Barnes and Noble, 1969), pp. 214–31.

29. *Records of Plays and Players in Lincolnshire, 1300–1585*, ed. Stanley J. Kahrl, Malone Soc. Collections, 8 (Oxford, 1974), p. 67; see also M. D. Anderson, *Drama and Imagery in English Medieval Churches* (Cambridge: Cambridge Univ. Press, 1963), p. 127, and Peter Meredith, "Putting on Plays in the Fifteenth Century," in *Acting Medieval Plays*, Lincoln Cathedral Library Publications (Lincoln: Honywood Press, 1985), p. 26.

30. *The Creacion of the World*, ed. Paula Neuss (New York: Garland, 1983), p. 20.

31. Glynne Wickham, *Early English Stages, 1300 to 1660* (London: Routledge and Kegan Paul, 1959), I, 166, 377n.

32. Cohen, *Le livre de conduit du régisseur*, p. 507 (translation by Daphne Hale).

33. Ibid., p. 513.

34. *The Staging of Religious Drama*, ed. Meredith and Tailby, p. 90.

35. Ibid., but see also the paper by Pamela Sheingorn in the present volume. The use of polished steel plates or dishes to represent eyes on hell mouth, dragons, and devils appears to have been common. See Feuillerat, *Documents Relating to the Office of the Revels in the Time of Queen Elizabeth*, pp. 140, 241; *Norwich 1540–1642*, ed. David Galloway, Records of Early English Drama (Toronto: Univ. of Toronto Press, 1984), p. 195; Samuel Harsnet, *A Declaration of Egregious Popish Impostures* (London, 1603), p. 134; Henry Harrod, "A Few Particulars Concerning Early Norwich Pageants," *Norfolk Archaeology*, 3 (1852), 12–13; Thomas Sharp, *A Dissertation on the Pageants or Dramatic Mysteries Anciently Performed at Coventry* (1825; rpt. Wakefield: EP, 1973), p. 61.

36. See Cohen, *Le livre de conduit du régisseur*, p. 169; *The Staging of Religious Drama*, ed. Meredith and Tailby, p. 151.

37. See Allardyce Nicoll, *The Development of the Theatre*, 5th ed. (London: George G. Harrap, 1970), p. 62; Young, "Devices and Feintes," p. 82.

38. A difference in style is indicated by the Cappers' records concerning their devils: they carried clubs and not fireworks. None of the York Mercers' documents record the use of pyrotechnics.

39. See *The Chester Mystery Cycle*, ed. R. M. Lumiansky and David Mills, EETS, s.s. 3 (London, 1974), I, 325.

40. Chambers, *The Mediaeval Stage*, II, 425; Harrod, "A Few Particulars Concerning Early Norwich Pageants," p. 8.

41. Translation by Peter Meredith.

42. See *The Middle English Harrowing of Hell and the Gospel of Nicodemus*, ed. W. H. Hulme, EETS, e.s. 100 (London, 1908), pp. 96–99. For iconographic evidence, see M. D. Anderson, *The Imagery of British Churches* (London: John Murray, 1955), p. 125, and her *History and Imagery in British Churches* (London: John Murray, 1971), p. 123.

43. *The Life of Saint Meriasek*, ed. and trans. Whitley Stokes (London: Trübner, 1872), pp. 104–05; *The Staging of Religious Drama*, ed. Meredith and Tailby, pp. 102, 114.

44. For the text, see Tony Harrison, *The Mysteries* (London: Faber and Faber, 1985); divided into three promenade productions—*The Nativity*, *The Passion*, and *Doomsday*—which opened at the Cottesloe Theatre on 19 January 1985 and at the Lyceum on 18 May 1985.

45. Biringuccio, *The Pyrotechnia*, pp. 385–87; A. C. Crombie, *Robert Grosseteste and the Origins of Experimental Science, 1100–1700* (Oxford: Clarendon Press, 1953), pp. 218–19.

46. Lynn White, Jr., *Medieval Religion and Technology* (Berkeley and Los Angeles: Univ. of California Press, 1978), p. 127, and *Medieval Technology and Social Change* (London: Oxford Univ. Press, 1962), pp. 89–90.

47. *The Staging of Religious Drama*, ed. Meredith and Tailby, p. 114.

48. Sebastiano Serlio, *The Book of Architecture*, introd. A. E. Santaniello (1611; facs. rpt. New York: Benjamin Blom, 1970), Book II, fol. 26ᵛ; see also *The Renaissance Stage: Documents of Serlio, Sabbatini and Furtenbach*, ed. Barnard Hewitt (Coral Gables: Univ. of Miami Press, 1958), p. 34.

49. *Antiquarian Repertory*, ed. F. Grose and T. Astle (London, 1807), I, 172. The account, taken from Holinshed, refers to "Robert Sutton," not "Robert Dudley"; "Donhage," not "The Hague"; "Leidon," not "Leiden"; and "January 1585," not "January 1586."

50. White, *Medieval Religion and Technology*, pp. 87–88, 127.

51. Hugh Platte, *The Jewell House of Art and Nature* (London, 1594), pp. 31–32. John Bate, *The Mysteryes of Natvre and Art* (London, 1634), p. 157, copies Platte's account without acknowledgment. See Raymond Toole Stott, *A Bibliography of English Conjuring, 1581–1876* (Derby: Harpur and Sons, 1976), p. 189; and also Trevor H. Hall, *A Bibliography of Books on Conjuring in English from 1580 to 1850* (Lepton: Palmyra Press, 1957), p. 70, who, however, does not mention Platte's 1594 edition.

52. Platte, *The Jewell House*, p. 32.

53. Serlio, *The Book of Architecture*, II, fol. 26ᵛ. The technique that Serlio suggests is likely to be the one adopted and referred to in the Lincoln Cordwainers' inventory concerning their "pageant of Bethelem": "Item a great hed gildyd sett

w^t vii Beamez & vii glassez for ye sam And on long beame for ye mouthe of ye said hed" (*Records of Plays and Players in Lincolnshire*, ed. Kahrl, p. 96). I think the "Beamez" are painted beams, on wood or pasteboard with spaces left for the "glassez" near the point at which the "Beamez" converge, i.e., the "gret hed." The light sources would be placed behind the "glassez" in such a way as to produce an actual beam of light to coincide with one of the painted "Beamez." See also Hardin Craig, "The Lincoln Cordwainers' Pageant," *PMLA*, 32 (1917), 605–15, and Meredith, "Putting on Plays in the Fifteenth Century," in *Acting Medieval Plays*, p. 25.

54. I possess one of these lace-maker's lamps. The base is made of Canadian maple and is eight inches high; the globe is four inches in diameter. The total height is thus twelve inches.

55. Platte, *The Jewell House*, p. 32.

56. The same principle operates in a modern Fresnel lantern where the smoothness of the reflector is broken up into many different facets.

57. *Non-Cycle Plays and Fragments*, ed. Norman Davis, EETS, s.s. 1 (London, 1970), pp. 58–59.

58. Anderson, *Drama and Imagery*, pp. 128–29.

59. See Robert Bartlett, *Trial by Fire and Water: The Medieval Judicial Ordeal* (Oxford: Clarendon Press, 1986).

60. Other examples include *The Ancient Cornish Drama*, ed. Norris, I, 201 (l. 2628); *Two Coventry Corpus Christi Plays*, 2nd ed., ed. Hardin Craig, EETS, e.s. 87 (London, 1957), p. 42 (Weavers' Pageant, l. 292*sd*); *Chester* II.80*sd* (MS. H), IV.420, V.168.

61. *The Staging of Religious Drama*, ed. Meredith and Tailby, *passim*.

62. See ibid., pp. 268–70, for similar appreciation of this concern in a description of the Modena Corpus Christi play (1556).

63. William Tydeman, *English Medieval Theatre, 1400–1500* (London: Routledge and Kegan Paul, 1986), pp. 53–77; see also Darryll Grantley, "Producing Miracles," in *Aspects of Early English Drama*, ed. Paula Neuss (Cambridge: D. S.

Brewer, 1983), pp. 85–86, who suggests the use of a fountain to create the effect.

64. Sir James Balfour Paul, *Accounts of the Lord High Treasurer of Scotland* (Edinburgh, 1907), VII, 357; J. R. Partington, *A History of Greek Fire and Gunpowder* (Cambridge: W. Heffer and Sons, 1960), pp. 84, 214.

65. Tenney L. Davis, *The Chemistry of Powder and Explosives* (1941–43; rpt. Hollywood: Angriff Press, 1970), p. 122.

66. *The Staging of Religious Drama*, ed. Meredith and Tailby, p. 107; see also N. D. Shergold, *A History of the Spanish Stage from Medieval Times until the End of the Seventeenth Century* (Oxford: Clarendon Press, 1967), pp. 63–64.

67. *The Staging of Religious Drama*, ed. Meredith and Tailby, p. 106.

68. Lucar, *Appendix*, pp. 79–81; Bate, *The Mysteryes of Natvre and Art*, p. 63; Babington, *Pyrotechnia*, pp. 55–58.

69. Bate, *The Mysteryes of Natvre and Art*, p. 63; Butterworth, "The Baptisme of Hir Hienes Darrest Sone," p. 37.

70. See *The Staging of Religious Drama*, ed. Meredith and Tailby, pp. 236, 238, and, for further use of smoke, *Le Mystère d'Adam*, ed. Paul Studer (Manchester: Manchester Univ. Press, 1928), p. 29; Nicoll, *The Development of the Theatre*, p. 53; Cohen, *Le Livre de Conduite du Régisseur*, pp. 179–80, 184; and *The Staging of Religious Drama*, ed. Meredith and Tailby, pp. 96–97.

71. *The Late Medieval Religious Plays of Bodleian MSS Digby 133 and E Museo 160*, ed. Donald C. Baker, John L. Murphy, and Louis B. Hall, Jr., EETS, 283 (London, 1982), pp. 1–23.

72. Ibid., pp. xvi–xvii, xxix.

73. Ibid., p. 15 (*sd* following cancelled passage). See Young, "Devices and Feintes," pp. 82-83; *Chief Pre-Shakespearean Dramas*, ed. J. Q. Adams (Boston: Houghton Mifflin, 1924), p. 221n.

74. Henry Machyn, *The Diary*, ed. John Gough Nichols, Camden Soc., 42 (London, 1848), pp. 13, 47, 73, 196.

75. *Newcastle*, ed. Anderson, p. 55.

76. *A Calendar of Dramatic Records in the Livery Companies of London*, ed. Robertson and Gordon, pp. 38–39, 45; John Nicholl, *Some Account of the Worshipful Company of Ironmongers*, 2nd ed. (London, 1866), pp. 84–85; *Cambridge*, ed. Alan H. Nelson, Records of Early English Drama (Toronto: Univ. of Toronto Press, 1989), I, 199; R. T. D. Sayle, *Lord Mayor's Pageants of the Merchant Taylors' Company in the 15th, 16th and 17th Centuries* (London, 1931), pp. 22, 26, 36.

77. Sayle, *Lord Mayor's Pageants*, p. 2.

78. Ibid., p. 48.

79. Machyn, *The Diary*, p. 125.

80. Lancaster, *Fireworks*, p. 163.

81. Different terms were sometimes used to describe firework cases. See Peter Whitehorne, *Certaine wayes for the ordering of Soldiours in battleray* (London, 1573), who refers to cases as 'trunckes'; and Thomas [sic] Malthus, *A Treatise of Artificial Fire-Works Both for Warres and Recreation* (London, 1629), who used the term 'cartoush.' Bate and Babington called them 'coffins.'

82. Bate, *The Mysteryes of Natvre and Art*, p. 72.

83. See the following for methods of production: Lucar, *Appendix*, p. 83; Malthus, *A Treatise*, pp. 74–80; Bate, *The Mysteryes of Natvre and Art*, pp. 72–73; Kentish, *The Pyrotechnist's Treasury*, pp. 91–97.

84. *Macro Plays*, ed. Eccles, frontispiece, p. 1; see Philip Butterworth, "Gunnepowdyr, Fyre and Thondyr," *Medieval English Theatre*, 7 (1985), 68–76.

85. Bate, *The Mysteryes of Natvre and Art*, p. 73; Malthus, *A Treatise*, pp. 81–82; Lancaster, *Fireworks*, p. 162.

86. The technique seems to have been known in Italy; see Giovanni Battista Isacchi, *Inventioni . . . nelle quali si manifestano varij Secreti, & vtili auisi a persone de gverra, e per i tempi di piacere* (Parma, 1579), pp. 123–25; John Eliot Hodgkin, *Rariora* (London: S. Low, Marston, 1902), III, 8; E. and G. S.

Battisti, *Le macchine cifrate di Giovanni Fontana* (Milan: Arcadia, 1984); C. Walter Hodges, *The Globe Restored* (London: Ernest Benn, 1953), pp. 116–17, fig. 54.

87. *The Staging of Religious Drama*, ed. Meredith and Tailby, p. 266; Young, "Devices and Feintes," pp. 83–84.

88. Butterworth, "Gunnepowdyr, Fyre and Thondyr," pp. 72–73.

89. *The Staging of Religious Drama*, ed. Meredith and Tailby, p. 261; see also the paper by Barbara Palmer in the present volume.

90. *Il quaderno di segreti d'un regista provenzale del Medioevo: Note per la messa in scena d'una Passione*, ed. Alessandro Vitale-Brovarone (Alexandria: Dell'Orso, 1984), p. 36. For an account of this sort of trick in Spain, see *The Staging of Religious Drama*, ed. Meredith and Tailby, p. 121; Shergold, *A History of the Spanish Stage*, p. 125 and n. 1. The translation offered here by Arthur Pritchard is from the Italian translation provided by Vitale-Brovarone.

91. See n. 15, above.

92. Protective clothing seems to have been made for those helping to create the hell effects at Mons; see Cohen, *Le Livre de Conduite du Régisseur*, p. 516; *The Staging of Religious Drama*, ed. Meredith and Tailby, p. 150. Another method of protecting the skin is suggested in *The Book of Secrets of Albertus Magnus*, ed. Michael R. Best and Frank H. Brightman (Oxford: Clarendon Press, 1973), pp. 109–10; see also Partington, *A History of Greek Fire and Gunpowder*, p. 53.

93. *The Chronicles of Froissart*, trans. Sir John Bourchier (Lord Berners) (London, 1903), VI, 96–100; Glynne Wickham, *Early English Stages*, I, 397, Pl. XXII (fig. 32).

94. When turpentine, a sticky resin, is distilled with water it produces a rosin known as colophone or Greek Pitch.

95. *Il quaderno*, ed. Vitale-Brovarone, pp. 50–53 (translation by Lynette Muir). For "aqua ardens," see n. 15, above.

96. See *The Staging of Religious Drama*, ed. Meredith and Tailby, p. 90.

97. The technique is noted by Albertus Magnus, although he substitutes the rosin colophone for the sulphur. Partington (*A History of Greek Fire and Gunpowder*, p. 54) translates as follows: "'Take colophonium and pitch, grind to a very fine powder and project this by a tube [blowpipe] into a fire or into a candle flame.' This reading . . . gives a method of producing a cloud of fire . . . and is produced in theatres by lycopodium dust." The translation should not, however, read "colophonium and pitch" but "colophonium or pitch." Best and Brightman (*The Book of Secrets*, pp. 109–10) correctly translate "pitch" as "Greek Pitch." See also n. 94, above.

98. Plaster was used to build up hell at Mons, and hair was incorporated into the mix in order to take paint (Cohen, *Le Livre de Conduite du Régisseur*, pp. 498–99).

99. I have in mind something resembling the fireproof hood worn underneath the helmet by modern racing drivers.

100. The same requirement seems to have been made by the Modane Antichrist play. See *The Staging of Religious Drama*, ed. Meredith and Tailby, p. 105.

101. The problem of timing such an effect is also presented by the well-known stage direction concerning the vice in John Heywood's *A Play of Love* (*Four Tudor Interludes*, ed. J. A. B. Somerset [London: Athlone Press, 1974], p. 88).

102. *The Staging of Religious Drama*, ed. Meredith and Tailby, pp. 91, 102, 157, 256–57.

103. This is a topic that I am addressing in current research toward a publication tentatively entitled *Royal Firework Drama*.

104. *The Life of Saint Meriasek*, ed. and trans. Stokes, p. 228; John G. Nichols, *Literary Remains of King Edward the Sixth* (London: Roxburghe Club, 1857), I, 287; Robert Withington, *English Pageantry* (Cambridge: Harvard Univ. Press, 1918), I, 161, 186, 205; Edward Hall, *Hall's Chronicle; Containing the History of England during the Reign of Henry the Fourth . . . to the End of the Reign of Henry the Eighth*, ed. Henry Ellis (London: J. Johnson, 1809), pp. 638, 799; *Letters and Papers, Foreign and Domestic of the Reign of Henry VIII*, ed. James Gairdner (London, 1882), VI, 276–78; John Leland, *Collecteana*, 2nd ed. (London, 1774), IV, 218; John J. Nichols, *The Progresses and Public Processions of Queen Elizabeth* (London, 1823), I, 319–20; Bate, *The Mysteryes of Natvre and*

Art, pp. 79–80; Babington, *Pyrotechnia*, pp. 36–41; Butterworth, "The Baptisme of Hir Hienes Darrest Sone," pp. 46–50.

The Sounds of Hell

Richard Rastall

In *Mankind* the vices Nought, New Guise, and Nowadays play a trick on the audience in the course of teaching them a song (ll. 331–43).[1] Nought apparently sings a line at a time, each being repeated by New Guise and Nowadays leading the audience. This method of teaching a song by ear is quick and efficient and no doubt had a long tradition of use: the technique is now associated mainly with a pantomime act, but was formerly much used in psalmody, where it was known as "lining out."[2] In the context of the drama, there is an obvious parallel with the scene in the Chester cycle[3] where Garcius leads the audience and the other shepherds in a "merry song" (VII.447*sd*).[4] But the whole event in *Mankind* is set up to deceive the audience, and it is in this that the three vices show their allegiance to the forces of hell.

The substantial difference lies in the text itself (*Mankind*, ll. 335–43), which is obscene enough to be shocking to many of the audience and to make a vivid contrast with the earlier part of the play. Some minor indecencies have indeed already been heard: but the vices have been careful to present themselves as good fellows who mean no real harm—rough diamonds at worst—and have even quoted from the Psalms (ll. 324–26) to echo the kind of language and sentiments expressed by Mankind himself in lines 310–22. Mention of the Devil (l. 325) as the author of the psalm in question is only one of several indications of the vices' true allegiance, but it is easily overlooked, perhaps, in view of their cheerful promise of a "Christmas song" in which the audience is invited to join "wyth a mery chere" (l. 334). In these circumstances, even the first line of the song, "Yt ys wretyn wyth a colle," will seem innocuous. Only in retrospect is "colle" (also

102

"coll," "cole") significant as symbolic of hellish business. Whether it means "coal" in the modern sense or (as seems more likely) "charcoal," its blackness and association with fire is clearly a deliberate allusion.

At the time, however, the gross indecencies of the second and subsequent lines come as a shock. In performance the audience's sense of being shamefully duped is very strong. Cajoled into singing the (apparently harmless) first line, the members of the audience are committed to singing the song by the time they are asked to repeat the scatological second line: "He þat schytyth wyth hys hoyll." It is a brilliant dramatic stroke, an audience "set-up" of the most telling kind.

The deceit of this event is paramount. Since mortals' songs of praise are in imitation of angelic song, the vices' promise of a "Christmas song" would have borne precisely that implication. Thus the event nicely exemplifies the dangers discussed by Walter Hilton in his late-fourteenth-century treatise *Of Angels' Song*. In that work Hilton describes angelic singing mainly in order to warn his readers against music that might seem angelic but is not.[5] Some people, he says, come so close to perfection that their souls are gladdened and strengthened by all created things (ll. 26–66, 108–12). "Neuer-þe-latter," he warns, "sum men er desayued be þar awn ymaginacioun, or be illusioun of þe enemy in þis mater" (ll. 112–14). Even when, by God's Grace, the soul has come so far, then, it is not out of danger: indeed, the danger is greater than ever. Hilton states that if at this stage a man relinquishes God's guidance and relies too much on his own intellect, his brain may be turned to the extent that he imagines heavenly sounds when there are none (ll. 114–24); and then, like a man in a frenzy, he "thynk þat he heres & sese þat nan oþer man dos, & al es bot a uanite & a fantasy of þe heued, or els it es be wirkyng of þe enemy þat feynes swylk soun in his herying" (ll. 126–29). In this last situation, when the Devil "entyrs man be fals illuminaciouns, & fals sownes, & swetnes" he "desayues a mans saule" (ll. 130–35); and the result will be that

of þis fals ground springes errours & heresys,
fals prophecies, presumpciouns, & fals roysyngs,
blasphemes, & sclaunderyngs, & many other myscheues.
(Hilton, ll. 136–38)

This passage not only warns of the danger to the individual soul—which is the immediate message of any morality play, too—but suggests also the wider implications of the work of the Devil and of the coming of Antichrist.[6]

It would be a mistake, then, to underestimate the connection between the Devil's deceit and that of his agents. The fact is underlined by the Devil's own deceit in the Fall of Man sequences of the Cornish plays. When the Devil comes to Eve "like a serpent" in the first day of the *Ordinalia* (I.148*sd*),[7] he tells her that he came from heaven (I.165) to better her position by persuading her to eat the forbidden fruit. Eve is afraid that he is deceiving her (I.196) but later tells Adam that he was an angel and that he sang to her (I.215, 229). Whether Eve really believes this or not is beside the point: the fact is that it is at worst a possible excuse for plucking the fruit. Adam contradicts her, saying that "he was an evil bird/ Whom thou didst hear singing" (*Ordinalia* I.223–24). But the possibility of a singing angel is powerful—again, it does not matter whether Adam really believes it or not—and Adam eats the fruit. As in the biblical account, he accuses Eve of deceiving him.

We are not told what the "angel" sings to Eve, so we have information only on the Devil's general deceit in making Eve think that she has heard angelic song. In *The Creacion of the World*[8] the deceit is more comprehensively specified. Lucifer not only dresses up like a "sweet angel" (l. 538) but changes his voice to sound like that of a girl (ll. 531–32). Moreover, Eve is impressed by the beauty of the "angel's" face (ll. 563–64). The visual and vocal transformation, then, is a radical one. The Devil is not half-hearted in deceit: the rewards are too important. No song-text is given, but Lucifer presumably sang flattering praises of Eve's beauty, "many fair words" (l. 1016). Eve gives these "fair words" as a reason for thinking that Lucifer was an angel from heaven (ll. 1017–19), so possibly they were in the form of a song of praise such as those addressed to the Blessed Virgin.[9] Certainly the playwright has set up a context in which such a parody would be possible, for the angels have already praised God in song (at l. 78), providing a direct model against which a parody could be understood.

Deceit of a different kind is found in the Chester play of the Flood. Mrs. Noah wants her gossips to join the family in the Ark and tells Noah that if he will not let them in he can sail off without her (*Chester* III.201–08). The deceit may be partly self-deceit, for Mrs. Noah's statement that her gossips "loved me full well, by Christe" (III.205) is not quite borne out by the events that follow. In a speech (or song) by a single gossip, Mrs. Noah is asked to "lett us drawe nere."[10] But immediately (and perhaps because Mrs. Noah is obviously willing) a different suggestion is put forward by the gossip(s): that Noah can wait while they drink a quart each— indeed, the drink is poured out by the start of the third stanza (omitted from MS. H):

Here is a pottell full of malnesaye good and stronge;
yt will rejoyse both harte and tonge.
Though Noe thinke us never soe longe,
yett wee wyll drinke atyte.

(*Chester* III.225–36)

That the apparent anxiety of the gossip(s) should give way to delaying tactics such as this is symptomatic of a standard deceit. Knowingly or not, the gossips are being used by the Devil to keep Mrs. Noah out of the Ark—typologically, to prevent her salvation. That music should be used as an aid to this process was a well-known phenomenon.

As always, the text is the feature that identifies this song as being from the Devil. It is clearly a drinking song, but at the same time line 234 is close enough to descriptions of the effects of heavenly music to introduce an element of parody into it: "It will rejoice [the] heart" is very much the language of holy rejoicing, including that brought on by music. Drink is thus being equated with (among other things) heavenly music. Clearly these people are not to be trusted. In addition, this is not a pre-existent drinking-song, for the text is to the immediate purpose: this, too, shows that it is no ordinary drinking party. The song therefore must be sung so that the words can be clearly heard.

Text audibility apart, it would be appropriate if the Gossips' song were badly sung. There is no information on that point, however,[11] although we shall return to the type of performance that music receives when it is used deceitfully by the Devil and his agents. In those plays where music is clearly seen as coming from God, the general principle that music is characteristic of God's servants has an important corollary—namely, that an unmusical man is a servant of the Devil. Thus the singing of a lullaby by Mak, the sheep stealer in the Towneley Second Shepherds' Play, is denigrated as "clere out of toyne" by the First Shepherd (*Towneley* XIII.477). Mak's wife, Gyll, is groaning at the same time in the aftermath of "childbirth," and the Third Shepherd cannot distinguish the singing of the one from the groaning of the other—or so he pretends (XIII.476). Similar musical deficiency characterizes the priest and his boy in the Digby *Mary Magdalene*.[12] Their singing of the service is prefaced by the priest's injunction to the boy to clear his throat ("Cowff vp þi brest," l. 1224) and the boy's amateurish assurance "I home and I hast, I do þat I may" (l. 1226). Despite these preparations the music breaks down: the boy makes the performance go badly wrong, and the priest is evidently too incompetent musically to retrieve the situation. Their unmusicality probably results in singing that is both out of tune and out of time.

This "service" is presumably a real one—or at least a recognizable parody of a real one. Liturgical parody is another characteristic of the Devil's agents because it makes fun of some of the most sacred aspects of the life of the playwright and audience alike. Thus Herod gives a parody blessing in the York play of the Trial before Herod (*York* XXXI.370),[13] and a left-handed blessing by Titivillus in *Mankind* (l. 522) is deliberately identified as a curse; the Coventry Herod misquotes the liturgical text *Qui statis in domo domini* (Pageant of the Shearmen and Taylors, l. 486) as a statement of his own importance;[14] and Mak's "prayer" before sleep—"Manus tuas commendo,/ poncio pilato" (*Towneley* XIII. 266–67)—is a jumble from at least two liturgical or biblical sources, all the more telling for having its own perfectly clear but perverted meaning: "I commend your hands to Pontius Pilate."[15] Another example occurs in the Chester Antichrist play when Antichrist performs a blasphemous parody of the giving of the Holy Spirit (which occurs two plays earlier) by sending his spirit to the four kings with the words "Dabo vobis cor novum et spiritum novum in medio vestri" (*Chester* XXIII.196sd). Lumiansky and Mills identify this text in their notes (*Chester*, II, 338) as a modified version of *Ezechiel* 36.26 ("Et dabo vobis cor novum et spiritum novum ponam in medio vestri") and quote the Authorized Version: "A new heart also will I give you, and a new spirit will I put within you"). Although I cannot find this as a liturgical item, Antichrist's use of it is clearly a parody of the same type.

The most concentrated and far-reaching example of this technique is found in the Digby *Mary Magdalene*, where the boy's reading of the "*Leccyo mahowndys, viri fortissimi sarasenorum*" ("*Lesson of Mahomet, the very great man of the Saracens*") is a monstrous parody filled with blasphemous and obscene allusions (ll. 1186–97). Here, too, there are reversed blessings. The boy gives one in the concluding versicle of the lesson, naming two demons ("Ragnell and Roffyn . . ./ Gravntt yow grace to dye on þe galows," ll. 1200–01); and the priest's final blessing is a more extended parody of the same type:

> Lorddys and ladyys, old and ynge,
> Golyas so good, to blysse may yow bryng,
>   Mahownd þe holy and Dragon þe dere,
> Wyth Belyall in blysse ewyrlastyng,
> Þat ye may þer in joy syng
> Before þat comly kyng
>   Þat is ower god in fere.
>   (*Mary Magdalene*, ll. 1242–48)

On a slightly different plane, the priest's business with the relics is as disgraceful as the failure to sing the service properly.

The problem for the playwright is to portray pagans effectively and to make some valid distinction between them. In this scene he shows the relationship between worship of Mohamet and that of the Devil. Such gross blasphemies as we hear in this play mark out the priest and his boy as true devil worshippers. The King and Queen of Marseilles, on the other hand, can be understood as merely misguided since they take no active part in these parodies.

The Devil's agents on earth, and demons themselves, are quite capable of quoting Latin texts when it suits them. As noted earlier, in *Mankind* New Guise even quotes a psalm correctly and attributes it to the Devil (ll. 325–26). Many of the plays show the forces of hell speaking Latin, ranging from two words in the middle of an English sentence, through two-line legal or scriptural tags, to passages of several lines. These characters' competence with Latin varies a good deal, as we have already seen. While it is sometimes to the Devil's advantage to quote Latin correctly, this is not usually the case. Because Latin is the language of all intellectual activity (including liturgy), it is the Devil's work to make nonsense of it. That is presumably why the vices in *Mankind* use nonsense mock-Latin to upset Mercy and Mankind—they even use garbled vernacular words with Latin endings (for instance l. 57, Mischief's "Corn seruit bredibus, chaffe horsibus, straw fyrybusque")—and why Tutivillus uses a similar technique in the Towneley Doomsday play (e.g., *Towneley* XXX.251: "ffragmina verborum/ tutiuillus colligit horum/ Belzabub algorum/ belial belium doliorum"). In *Mankind* the vices go further and use Latin for verbal indecencies, baiting Mercy both by challenging him to translate an indecent couplet (ll. 129–34; see below) and by translating an indecent expression themselves (l. 142: "Osculare fundamentum" = "Kiss [my] arse").

It may be surprising to find such characters speaking Latin, and indeed the dramatists' rationale for using the language is not entirely obvious. But two results of the use of Latin in these plays are inescapable: first, that a flexible use of Latin fulfills a number of dramatic functions concerned with both characterization and the articulation of action; and second, that it provides a context for matters such as parody.

Another matter raised by this discussion is that of scatological speech. Indecent language is also a mark of the Devil and his agents, and a brief study of it may help in the understanding of hellish attitudes to music and other sounds. Some examples from *Mankind* have already been mentioned in relation to their use of Latin, but this was only one of the vices' ploys in trying to upset Mercy. Nought tries to shock him with the line "Yf ȝe wyll putt yowr nose in hys wyffys sokett" (l. 145), which Mercy describes as "ydyll language." By this he presumably means the kind of loose speech warned against by St. Paul—speech that is symptomatic of an unclean mind and negative, undirected thinking.[16] It is partly with this destructive attitude in mind that variants of the ancient insult "Kiss my arse" should be read. There are two occurrences in *The Castle of Perseverance*, both spoken contemptuously by the Bad Angel to the Good Angel:

> Þerfore, goode boy, cum blow
> At my neþer ende!
> (ll. 813–14)
> Goode syre, cum blowe myn hol behynde.
> (l. 1276)

Cain's opening remark to Abel in the Towneley cycle is just as direct: "Com kis myne ars" (*Towneley* II.59); and, in the same speech, "Com nar, . . ./ and kys the dwillis toute" ("the Devil's arse," ll. 62–63). Further examples occur at II.266 ("Yei, kys the dwills ars behynde") and at II.287 ("Com kys the dwill right in the ars"), while his dismissive command "Go grese thi shepe vnder the toute" (II.64) is closely related.

Such ideas are part of a common stock of insult and threat, the very gratuitousness of which is indicative of hell's influence. It is in this light that we should view the lewdness of the priest's boy in the Digby *Mary Magdalene*—for instance at line 1149—and of the shipman's boy in the same play. Both are beaten for their vulgarity. In the latter case the boy uses an expression—"I ly and wryng tyll I pysse" (l. 1409)—that belongs to a strong scatological tradition. *Mankind* uses this tradition more concentratedly than other plays, and in the couplet offered to Mercy for translation in fact expresses an idea discussed by Karl P. Wentersdorf:[17] "I haue etun a dyschfull of curdys,/ Ande I haue schetun yowr mowth full of turdys" (ll. 131–32). A distinction must be drawn, however, between the behavior itself and the mention of it. The active nature of the lines from *Mankind*, like the imperative "Kiss my arse," demonstrates hellish allegiance; and Caiaphas' reference to Christ as "pewee-ars" (*Chester* XVIA.150)[18] does so too. However, one similar usage evidently works the other way, the hoydenish language of one of the Chester mothers of the Innocents apparently being an accurate characterization of the soldier she is addressing and striking:

> Have thou this . . .
>   . . .
> . . . and thou this,
> though thou both shyte and pisse!
>   (*Chester* X.353, 357–58)

Here the indecency is a true reference to the nature of the person addressed and does not indicate hellish allegiance in the person speaking. A more difficult example is Colle's description in the *Play of the Sacrament*[19] of his master as "Þe most famous phesy-cyan/ Þat euer sawe vryne" (ll. 535–36). This certainly indicates the allegiance of the doctor. That of the boy is less obvious, but is likely to be the same.

This discussion explains something that otherwise might remain obscure: Lucifer's farting in the first pageant of the N-town cycle.[20] Lucifer, as an angel, must originally have been musical, but when pride overtakes him he stands aloof from the angels' singing of praise to the Creator (*N-town* I.40). Subsequently deprived of "merth and joye," he is presumably deprived of music also (I.71). His statement "Ffor fere of fyre a fart I crake" (I.81) therefore emphasizes his fall from grace: he now cracks a fart, whereas he formerly cracked musical notes.[21] This is not a parody of angelic music but a substitution for it, and it becomes a normal reaction of demons under stress. When Satan fails to tempt Christ, he too will "let a crakke" (*N-town* XXIII.195). This textual evidence of farting is too thin to allow much speculation on its own, but it is possible that farting was a not unimportant feature of the devils' stage business. On the basis of a wide range of iconographic and literary evidence, Wentersdorf came to the conclusion that devils were depicted as breaking wind as part of their technique in attacking angelic virtues or humanity.[22]

This behavior is funny to a modern audience and may have been so to a contemporary one.[23] Its main effect was perhaps threatening, however, and it is backed up by other noise-making expedients. Perhaps undirected energy is itself hellish. Hell is certainly a noisy place, as various directions for thunder and shouting indicate. Thunder occurs in the Digby *Mary Magdalene* (l. 691*sd*) at the Bad Angel's entry into hell; a devil enters with thunder and fire in the Digby *Conversion of St. Paul* (l. 411*sd*); the devil Mercury enters "*wyth a fyeryng*" in the same play (l. 432*sd*), and, again in that play, Belyal and Mercury vanish together "*wyth a fyrye flame, and a tempest*" (l. 501*sd*). The three examples from *The Conversion of St. Paul*, which have already been noted by Philip Butterworth in his paper on hellfire in the present volume, all come from the mid-sixteenth-century section of the play, but the ideas must be much older, and the tempest of the last-cited is presumably staged with the sound of thunder. Wentersdorf's review of the use of farting and the ancient insult "Kiss my arse" also convincingly associates this general picture with the use of fireworks by demons in the plays.[24]

Stage directions for and text references to the shouting of demons hardly need to be listed here. It is, however, worth pointing out that this shouting is semantically meaningless. A direction such as "*clamant*" does not imply the transmission of a message by the devils but, rather, loud undirected noise-making.[25] This is, of course, the opposite, the total negation, of the angelic use of suitable texts.

The direction for shouting at Christ's coming in the Chester Harrowing of Hell play introduces another noise-making expedient (*Chester* XVII.152*sd*): "Tunc venit Jesus et fiat clamor, vel sonitus magnus materialis" ("Then Jesus comes and there shall be shouting, or a great 'material' noise"; translation by David Mills). The "material noise"[26] is an alternative to the shouting, then; it may signify thunder, but what can this wording mean? The Harrowing of Hell play at Chester was performed by the Cooks, and it seems likely that this direction indicates how the Cooks made the necessary noise—by banging on pots and pans.[27] There is a whole area here, I suspect, that we understand only imperfectly: the idea of hell as a kitchen; marginal grotesques in manuscripts playing a pair of bellows like a stringed instrument, with a pair of tongs as a bow; and the famous misericord in Great Malvern Priory in which a monk gets his own back on the Devil by sticking a bellows in his backside and pumping.[28] There is a practical side, too, of course: the Cooks were the right people to make and control fire and therefore to play hellish scenes successfully and safely. The noise-making of "material" might also explain the payment for a rattle in the play accounts of the Coventry Cappers for 1544, as the Cappers seem to have played (among other episodes) the Harrowing of Hell.[29]

As these uses of unstructured noise would suggest, the Devil and his agents often dislike music, for they find it annoying or distressing. In the Towneley Harrowing of Hell the demon Rybald hears the singing of *Salvator mundi* by the souls in Limbo and describes it first as a "dyn" (*Towneley* XXV.90) and then as an "vggely noyse" (*York* XXXVII.101, *Towneley* XXV.95: the plays run in parallel here). It is perhaps the text rather than the music itself that is so offensive to the demons, for Rybald complains that the Prophets "crie on Criste full faste/ And sais he schal þame saue" (*York* XXXVII.107–08, *Towneley* XXV.101–02). The offensive message need not be verbal: in the Towneley Judgment play the devil Tutivillus shows a strong aversion to church bells calling the faithful to worship:

> Then deffys hym with dyn/ the bellys of the kyrke,
>   When thai clatter;
> he wishys the clerke hanged
> ffor that he rang it.
>   (*Towneley* XXX.344–47)

This aversion to meaning, whether expressed verbally or otherwise, also shows itself in Caiaphas' slighting references to singing the services in the Towneley Buffeting play. "As euer syng I mes" is not an oath that we should expect from a priest (*Towneley* XXI.159), while there is a positive anti-liturgical thrust to his curse on the man "that fyrst made me clerk/ and taght me my lare,/ On bookys for to barke" (*Towneley* XXI.307–08). In these circumstances it is hardly surprising that Christ's hell-shattering cry of "Attollite portas" is described as calling "hydously" (*York* XXXVII.138, *Towneley* XXV.119).

We have seen that music can be a part of the armory of the Devil and his agents: but on what principles, precisely, do the plays use song, minstrelsy, and dancing to characterize the forces of evil? From what has gone before, two clear positions can be identified:

(1) The Devil and his agents use music—even good music—to beguile a potential victim. This might be called the "seduction" or "deceit" position.
(2) The antithesis of meaning and directed communication is used: loud unstructured noise, etc. In this case, which might be called the "force of arms" position, the corollary is that the forces of hell actually dislike order and clarity of structure— and therefore they hate music.

There are positions between these, but they are not easily identified. The Chester gossips, for instance, might belong to the first position as far as we can tell from the evidence; but it is unlikely that their drinking song would be given a fine musical performance if only because it is a drinking song and the deceit involved in its use by the gossips depends on its acceptance as "normal" of its type. Thus the position of the gossips is presumably nearer to (1) than to (2) but definitely somewhere between them. I accept, of course, that in practice *all* performances resulting from position (1) will be less than perfect. In discussing the philosophical position it seems to me clear, nevertheless, that the Chester gossips do not sing with the same intention as, say, the Serpent in the Cornish Fall sequences discussed above.

It will be useful to examine the position adopted by most of the Church Fathers: namely, that however good music may be in itself as a *speculum* of Divine Order, it is harmful to the soul if one gives way to an appreciation of its beauties at a purely sensual level. Here it becomes not a gateway to understanding of the Eternal but the path to carnal vice.[30] There is a particular danger that the sensuous enjoyment of music may take the place of spiritual exercises, of which church attendance is the one most easily identified. This is the message of Robert Mannyng's warnings against minstrelsy:

> entyrludes, or syngynge,
> Or tabure bete, or oþer pypynge,
> Alle swyche þyng forbodyn es,
> Whyle þe prest stondeþ at messe.[31]

Elsewhere it is clear that Mannyng views dancing in the same light.[32] This warning against such entertainments in the time of Mass is echoed by Accidia (Sloth) in *The Castle of Perseverance*, who describes his followers as men

> Þat had leuere syttyn at þe ale
> Thre mens songys to syngen lowde
> Þanne toward þe chyrche for to crowde.
>
> (ll. 2234–36)

In *Wisdom* the vices put this into practice, celebrating their vicious powers by singing a song in three parts—presumably a three-men's song (1. 620*sd*). As with all vocal music, in performance the text itself no doubt underlined the difference between godly and ungodly mirth.

The dangers of misuse are seen in the realm of minstrelsy also. The Reynes *Delight* fragment[33] associates "swet musyciauns in dyuers melody" with dangerous worldly pleasures (ll. 49–54), and this is clearly the allusion intended when in *Wisdom* Will tells a group of carnal sins that their accompanying minstrel is "a hornepype mete/ Þat fowll ys in hymselff but to þe erys swete" (ll. 757–58). In particular, sweet music was associated with seduction, a connection that is common enough in iconography and to which we shall return with respect to dancing. It is not inappropriate, either, that Nought should play a pipe to bring out Titivillus, the devil responsible for collecting all "idle words" spoken for presentation at the Judgment (*Mankind*, 1. 453).[34]

The ambivalent attitude to music shown by the Church Fathers and retained throughout the Middle Ages was inherent in the dichotomy between the nature of *musica instrumentalis* (i.e., sounded music, the third type of music in the Boethian triad) and the place that music held in society.[35] As the audible result of musical philosophy, *musica instrumentalis* ("music" in the modern sense) descended directly from *musica mundana* (the Music of the Spheres) through *musica humana* (the smaller-scale order of the universe) and could therefore be regarded as the practical expression of the Divine Order that these represented; and, more precisely, it was the mortal equivalent of *musica caelestis*, the music of the heavenly host.[36] On the other hand, as the only kind of music that could be manipulated by Man, *musica instrumentalis* could be used badly or even misused deliberately. In other words, *musica instrumentalis* was the only kind of music open to perversion. This caused a problem for dramatists: the distinction between *musica caelestis* and *musica instrumentalis* could not be shown in the plays, where the former must be represented by the latter. The anomaly in Lucifer declining to sing at *N-town* I.39*sd* but singing to Eve in the Cornish *Ordinalia* I.148*sd* and *The Creacion of the World*, l. 538*sd*, is thus a practical one only: there is no *philosophical* anomaly. Lucifer's pride makes him ineligible to join in *musica caelestis*, but as the Serpent he can use *musica instrumentalis* in any way he chooses in the cause of Evil.

The dangers of music are entirely reliant on the uses to which humans can put it, therefore, and the confusion in St. Augustine's thoughts about it stem not only from the subjective nature of his assessment[37] but also, presumably, from the difficulties attendant on self-analysis. Commentators in the later Middle Ages were really no more successful in finding an objective viewpoint, and the result was some controversy and no single clear direction to those who needed it. On the one hand monks and others welcomed the recreation offered by "minstrels of honor" who would sing the deeds of the saints; on the other, the authorities were always aware that minstrels could be vicious and highly undesirable socially. Thomas of Chabham's well-known categorization of minstrels is simply an attempt to make sense of a difficult situation. In the same way the larger churches used music as an embellishment of the services in praise of God, yet there were many warnings against the dangers of polyphony and musical instruments in church and even against the antics and morals of lay singers.[38]

This philosophical position makes it unnecessary to look for technical characteristics of hellish music other than out-of-tuneness or a lack of rhythmic precision. Several commentators have suggested a direct technical means of portraying hellish music, however, and a brief diversion is necessary here to examine the possibilities. The best discussion of the matter is Dutka's in her *Music in the English Mystery Plays*: she starts by making out a good case for the use of out-of-tune music, citing Act II of Marston's *The Malcontent* as evidence. From there she moves on to suggest that the use of the tritone (the interval of the augmented fourth) and of the "imperfecting of perfect consonances" were "equally available and would just as effectively grate on medieval ears."[39] This is perfectly correct, as is her summary statement connecting consonance and harmony with the divine order of heaven.[40] Her conclu-

sion that the music of hell is real but distorted music is surely
correct also, therefore; but it does not follow that out-of-tune music and dissonant music are equally valid as manifestations of
hellish activity. In the first place, there is a world of difference
between out-of-tune performance and the deliberate *composition* of
music using dissonant intervals irregularly. It is the difference
between the distortion of music and the distortion of Music. The
effects are not dissimilar since the result is dissonant to the ear in
either case, albeit in different ways: so it is doubtful if the considerable time and energy needed to compose the latter kind of music
would be worthwhile. It may be argued that the distortion of Music itself—the composition of a new hellish kind of dissonant
music—is intellectually closer to (indeed, a part of) the cosmic
perversion that is the Devil's activity in the universe. But the
Devil's attacks in the plays are not, in general, of an intellectual
cast. His purpose is immediate deceit through the most easily
available means: subversion of the World Order is unnecessary if
he can win individual humans to himself in a series of small and
winnable contests. Thus the perversion of musical *performance* is
much more useful than the distortion of Music. And in the context
of the drama it is more immediately effective, is easier for the
performers to accomplish, and requires no special composition.

Most important of all, from an intellectual standpoint, deliberately dissonant music would be hardly less ordered than "heavenly" music. Indeed, it is a necessary condition of such music that its
structure at all levels must be very carefully ordered: it is less
ordered only in the sense that it uses fewer of the simple mathe-
matical proportions on which the universe was supposedly
founded, and this is a concept that we comprehend through the
intellect, not through our ears. If deliberately dissonant music is
not carefully ordered the whole thing breaks down into chaotic
sounds anyway, and the result is unordered—the reverse of what
was originally intended at a musical level. As we have already
noted, a dramatically clear way of indicating hellish activity is the
unordered and incoherent noise of shouting and banging.[41]

To sum up, then: in dealing with humans, composed dissonance would be an inefficient way to further the kind of deceit which is the Devil's aim in using the "seduction/deceit" method, while the sounds of hell itself in the "force of arms" category are disordered noise. Thus the kind of technically analogous music suggested would become a rather heavy-handed type of perversion of very limited effect either aurally or intellectually.

It is also unnecessary to suppose that music showing an evil character's social position was automatically subject to the type of conditions governing singing by one of those characters. Mak, Mrs. Noah's gossips, or the priest's boy must show their allegiance through unmusicality; but a social position entitling a character to music is itself a situation susceptible to perversion, and the music which identifies the position does not need to be badly performed. In fact, the position itself is partly identified by the *high* quality of the performance. That is, it is part of Herod's dangerousness that his position is marked by *good* minstrelsy. Of course, it is perfectly possible to portray Herod as an unsuccessful ruler through low quality minstrelsy, and then he becomes a sort of "force-of-arms" agent of Evil—a legitimate way of playing him in some of the plays.

Several plays apparently use good minstrelsy to show real power. Mundus uses the showy music of worldly pomp in *The Castle of Perseverance*, for instance (ll. 455*sd*, 574*sd*). He expects to be served at table with "mynstralsye and bemys blo" (ll. 616–17) and holds out this style of life as a temptation to Mankind. Herod has this style of life, too, and misuses the power that goes with it: his demand for the minstrels to "blowe up a good blast/ Whyll I go to chawmere and chaunge myn array" (*N-town* XVIII.19–20) not only emphasizes the essential shallowness of his way of life but also serves as a showy event intended to impress the Magi at their arrival. The frivolousness and waste are there also in the Coventry cycle, where Herod orders "Trompettis, viallis, and othur armone" when he goes to rest (*Pageant of the Shearmen and Taylors*, l. 538). The misuse of power is put in close proximity with Herod's music in the N-town Massacre play, in which Herod orders minstrelsy for the banquet that immediately follows the killing of the Innocents (XX.153–54); and later in the same play the minstrelsy emphasizes the empty show of his life by taking place at the moment when Herod and his soldiers are killed (XX.232*sd*).

In *The Castle of Perseverance* trumpets are used both at Detraccio's crying of his message (l. 646*sd*), an event that parodies the beginning of the banns for the play itself, and on three occasions for an attack on the castle (ll. 1898, 2198, 2377). This is again the showy music of worldly pomp—specifically, of those who can afford to make war.

Dancing in the plays is governed by the same philosophical considerations as music: indeed, that is bound to be at least partly the case, since dancing is accompanied by music. The dancing of the vices in *Mankind* is the equivalent of their "idle talk"; Mercy is moved to protest at it (l. 81*sd*) and then declines to dance himself (ll. 90–97). Curiosity's dancing with Mary Magdalene is the beginning of his seduction of her (Digby *Mary Magdalene*, l. 533), a well-known connection of dance and lust echoed in *Everyman* when Kindred's description of a "nyse" (i.e., wanton) girl includes her love for feasting and dancing (ll. 360–62).[42] Magdalene's dancing with Curiosity would fall into the same category as music resulting from the first philosophical position discussed earlier—that is, it is a "seduction/deceit" situation, and the dancing is a real social dance, properly done. The iconography of the occasion shows this to be the case.[43] In *Wisdom* dancing is made into a special feature—the forces of evil at *Wisdom*, line 685, the Devil's dance at lines 700–08, and dancing by the Quest of Holborn ("an euyll entyrecte") at lines 730–34. Here, too, we must assume (for want of precise information) that this dancing and the music accompanying it constitute a good performance with no deliberate hint of incompetence. These uses of dancing by the forces of hell are clear enough to suggest that the metaphorical phrase "dance in þe devil way" in the York cycle (*York* VII.52, XXIX.395, and XXXI.423, for instance) is intended to show the speaker's allegiance to the forces of hell.[44]

A more difficult matter is the direction in the N-town Passion

Play for the executioners to dance around the Cross: *"here xule þei leve of and dawncyn a-bowte þe cros shortly"* (XXXI.753*sd*). There are two basic possibilities here. First, it could be an actual dance, with or without music of some kind. In this case it might have some ritual purpose (now unknown to us) or it could be an occasion of mockery. Second, the direction could refer metaphorically to an informal capering having mockery and humiliation of Christ as its sole or main purpose. Dutka regards it as an actual dance, as does Meredith: and the latter notes that the executioners' dancing relates to all the "game" implications of the torturers' treatment of Christ, both in drama and in iconography.[45] This direction does separate the nailing of Christ to the cross from the scene of mocking that follows, so it may well be correct to see the dancing as an extension of the "game" element rather than as a mere letting-off of high spirits. If this is so, the dance is an ordered event with its own structure.

Dutka attempted to make sense of this dance by showing a tradition of such dancing by the torturers at the Crucifixion.[46] Her evidence does seem to suggest that a tradition of some sort existed, although it perhaps relates more to the Mocking and Scourging than to the Crucifixion itself: (a) an English alabaster carving of the Scourging in which one of the torturers wears a rope of bells round his waist; (b) morris dancers wear bells; (c) Hugh Gillam, a noted morris dancer, was paid by the Chester Coopers for appearing in their play, and may therefore have played one of the executioners; (d) in Matthias Grünewald's *Christ Mocked* of 1503, one of the onlookers plays pipe-and-tabor; and (e) three dances are performed by the virgins in *The Killing of the Children* in the Digby manuscript. This last item is difficult to use as evidence and ultimately can be no help. The virgins are not evil characters and, as I have tried to show above, there is a clear relationship between music/dancing that is good in itself and that which is perverted. Item (a) is of considerable interest, since the illustration cited does seem to show bells.[47] The Grünewald painting (item d) does not seem to connect with this, however, for there is no hint that anyone is dancing: the torturers are going about their usual violent business, and the onlookers behind them are apparently fairly static. The minstrel could be explained, anyway, by the fact that executions (though not torturings) were occasions of public spectacle at which minstrelsy was usual.[48] Whatever the painter's reason for including a taborer in his composition, there is no necessary connection with the Crucifixion and its dramatization in the N-town plays.

Items (b) and (c) require further consideration. Morris dancers did indeed wear bells: at least, some depictions of the *moresca* show bells on the dancers' costumes.[49] There may therefore be some connection between the *moresca* and the torturer in the Hildburgh alabaster. The connection apparently cannot be demonstrated by reference to Hugh Gillam, however, for the Chester records show only that Gillam was paid for dancing on occasions unrelated to the plays. Moreover, Gillam probably played the doubled roles of Herod and Pilate, not a torturer, in the Coopers' pageant of the Trial and Flagellation.[50] There is, of course, the possibility that Herod and/or Pilate danced in the Coopers' pageant as part of the tradition for which we are searching, but there is no evidence for that.

In all, the evidence does not support a case for regarding the N-town stage direction as belonging to a tradition of dancing at the Crucifixion. This is not to say that the N-town direction cannot be taken as an indication of real dancing in that particular play, that dancing did not take place in any other Crucifixion play, or that there is no possibility of evil characters dancing in any one of several other episodes in the Passion sequence. But what the tradition and the precise significance of the evidence might be, we are really in no position to discover at present.[51]

As with singing, it is worth asking if any observable characteristics distinguish the dancing of evil characters from that of the good. Ingrid Brainard has suggested two features that would characterize dancing by these two categories.[52] First, good characters will perform social dances, whereas evil characters will dance the *moresca*. Social dancing, certainly, would be a deliberate and observable *speculum* of *musica humana* in showing an ordered relationship between the individual and society, while the *moresca* had connotations of anarchy and pagan power. It is nevertheless notable that it is precisely the former category that would be perverted, and that Mary Magdalene and Curiosity perform a social dance before her seduction (see above) because that is a vital element in the deceit of the situation. The perversion is all on the part of Curiosity, of course: Mary Magdalene is not an agent of the Devil. Second, dancing by good characters will proceed clockwise, that by evil characters anti-clockwise (*widdershins*).

The musical and aural representation of evil in the plays was clearly not the result of a single unified view by the dramatists. On the contrary, the philosophical and social contexts were far too complex for the playwrights to take any simple approach to the problems of characterizing the inmates and agents of hell aurally, even in a single play. It is no doubt true that characterization was effected primarily—and is now understood primarily—through iconographic and literary traditions: but there obviously were some widely-understood aural conventions too, and clearly these have to be taken into account when the characterization of evil roles is discussed.

It may be somewhat unrealistic to summarize a discussion that has resulted in so few firm conclusions, but even a provisional summary can be useful in pointing the way for further enquiry. That enquiry should probably take account of the following points:

(1) We can identify a position in which a good musical performance is used by the Devil or his agent as part of a stratagem to ensnare a human by deceit or seduction. The quality of the performance is of course dependent upon circumstances, but it will probably be the best that the performing body can obtain. The Devil's singing to Eve in the Cornish plays is of this type, and Herod's minstrelsy in the N-town and Coventry cycles is likely to be as well.[53]

(2) An analogous position may be held by dancing. The dancing of Mary and Curiosity in *Mary Magdalene* is an example.

(3)   A rather lower level of performance quality will obtain if the deceit does not depend on it. The gossips' song in *Chester* III must be recognizable as a drinking song and should therefore be quite different in performance style from the Cornish Devil's wooing of Eve, for example—but the words need to be heard. Similar arguments would obtain for the "Christmas song" of the vices in *Mankind.*

(4)   The liturgical parodies must be performed well enough for the texts to be effective. Where the textual parody is specific (Mak's "prayer" before sleep, for instance, or the boy's parody lesson in *Mary Magdalene*) it is again important that the words be heard. On the other hand, this is not true of a liturgical parody that needs to be understood as such only in the general sense. In the "service" of *Mary Magdalene* (l. 1227*sd*) no text is given. Evidently the important points are: (a) that it *is* a liturgical parody (and therefore must be recognizably, if risibly, in Latin), and (b) that it breaks down. The texts could be those of an actual service, complete nonsense (albeit in Latin forms), or something between—it is actually immaterial as long as the parody is entertaining and the two points are made.

   These two types of liturgical parody seem to coincide with speaking and singing, respectively. It is true that the evidence is partly negative, that the distinction does not allow for intermediate performance styles such as recitation on a monotone (which would be liturgically appropriate for the reciting of a lesson), and that matters of both text and performance method would be at the director's discretion—but this apparent coincidence demands further consideration.

(5)   It is sometimes the case that a really bad performance is used to characterize an agent of hell. Mak is the obvious example (*Towneley* XIII). This is analogous to, and probably identical with, the second type of liturgical parody noted above. Here, too, the text is not given, and we can assume that the dramatist did not envisage that the actor would choose to sing words of any importance for the audience.

(6) The Devil sometimes uses the complete negation of verbal communication—the unordered sound of shouting, banging, and "thunder," perhaps associated with fireworks. This is what I have called the "force of arms" position.

(7) Another association of (6), above, is with obscenity of various kinds.

But perhaps the most important conclusion of all is that music in the plays is not an isolated phenomenon but one that connects with liturgy, dramatic performance styles, linguistic register, disordered noise, fireworks, and other matters of interest to students of drama.

NOTES

1. For *Mankind*, see *The Macro Plays*, ed. Mark Eccles, EETS, 262 (London, 1969); subsequent citations of this play as well as the other Macro moralities (*The Castle of Perseverance* and *Wisdom*) will hereafter be cited in parentheses in my text.

2. See "Lining Out" and Nicholas Temperley, "Psalms, Metrical" (sec. III.1 [iv]), in *The New Grove Dictionary of Music and Musicians*, ed. Stanley Sadie (London: Macmillan, 1980), XI, 7, and XV, 362. Although Temperley cites a work of 1644 as the first evidence of lining out, he comments that the method "may have existed earlier." Given the example in *Mankind*, it must have been in use, at least in secular practice, as early as the 1460's.

3. *The Chester Mystery Cycle*, ed. R. M. Lumiansky and David Mills, EETS, s.s. 3, 9 (London, 1974–86), 2 vols.; subsequent references to Vol. I will appear in parentheses in my text as *Chester*, followed by the number of the play being cited and the line number(s).

4. "Hilare carmen" in MS. H; "Troly loly loly lo" in HmARB; for the *sigla* of the various Chester manuscripts, see *Chester*, ed. Lumiansky and Mills, I, ix–xxvii. On the Christmas song and its effects, see Paula Neuss, "Active and Idle Language: Dramatic Images in *Mankind*," in *Medieval Drama*, ed. Neville Denny, Stratford-upon-Avon Studies, 16 (London: Edward Arnold, 1973), pp. 54–55.

5. See Walter Hilton, *Two Minor Works*, ed. Fumio Kuriyagawa and Toshiyuki Takamiya (Tokyo, 1980); citations to Hilton's *Of Angels' Song* in my text will be by line number. This work, formerly believed to be by Richard Rolle of Hampole, has not been easily available, and is in fact not generally known to either musicologists or students of early English drama.

6. See *Revelations* 19.20, for instance, concerning the false prophet's deceitful miracles. In relation to the Devil's deceit, note that in the Towneley Judgment play (XXX.285–86) Tutivillus actually quotes the saying "Diabolus est mendax/ Et pater eius" ("The Devil is a liar, and the father [of lies]"); see B. J. Whiting, *Proverbs, Sentences, and Proverbial Phrases from English Writings Mainly before 1500* (Cambridge: Harvard Univ. Press, 1968), p. 129 (D186). Quotations from the Towneley plays are from *The Towneley Plays*, ed. George England and Alfred W. Pollard, EETS, e.s. 71 (1897; rpt. New York: Kraus, 1978); subsequent references in my text will appear in parentheses along with the number of the play and the line number(s).

7. Citations are to *The Ancient Cornish Drama*, ed. Edwin Norris (London: Oxford Univ. Press, 1859), 2 vols.; subsequent references to the Cornish *Ordinalia* appear in parentheses in my text.

8. *The Creacion of the World*, ed. Paula Neuss (New York: Garland, 1983).

9. I suggest this because Eve is the typological forerunner of the Blessed Virgin, and a Marian text (perhaps changing "Maria" to "Eva" as necessary) would be understood in this way by a medieval audience.

10. I discuss the textual problems of this song in "Music in the Cycle," in *The Chester Mystery Cycle: Essays and Documents* (Chapel Hill: Univ. of North Carolina Press, 1983), pp. 156–57. It seems to me that there are several gossips, that a single gossip sings at ll. 225–32, and that all the gossips sing at ll. 233–36. However, these last four lines do not appear in MS. H, in which the speech heading shows that ll. 225–32 are spoken; hence MS. H seems to transmit a version in which the gossips are not required to sing.

11. Rastall, "Music in the Cycle," p. 119; Richard Rastall, "Music in the Cycle Plays," in *Contexts for Early English Drama*, ed. Marianne Briscoe and John C. Coldewey (Bloomington: Indiana Univ. Press, 1989), p. 210.

12. For the Digby plays, see *The Late Religious Plays of Bodleian MSS Digby*

133 and E Museo 160, ed. Donald C. Baker, John L. Murphy, and Louis B. Hall, Jr., EETS, 283 (London, 1982).

13. For the York Corpus Christi plays, see *The York Plays*, ed. Richard Beadle (London: Edward Arnold, 1982); hereafter cited in parentheses in my text as *York*.

14. For the extant Coventry plays, see *Two Coventry Corpus Christi Plays*, revised ed., ed. Hardin Craig, EETS, e.s. 87 (London, 1957).

15. *In manus tuas Domine commendo spiritum meum* is a short responsory at Sunday Compline (*Antiphonale Romanum*, pp. 62–63; *Liber Usualis*, pp. 269–70), based on *Luke* 23.46: "Pater, in manus tuas commendo spiritum meum." "Pontio Pilato" is from the Nicene Creed, recited at Mass on greater feasts. On the popular use of Christ's words, see Richard Proudfoot, "The Virtue of Perseverance," in *Aspects of Early English Drama*, ed. Paula Neuss (Cambridge: D. S. Brewer, 1983), p. 93.

16. See, for example, *Colossians* 3.8: "But now put you also all away: . . . filthy speech out of your mouth" (Douay); also n. 27, below. This subject is fully discussed by Neuss, "Active and Idle Language," pp. 41–67.

17. Karl P. Wentersdorf, "The Symbolic Significance of *Figurae Scatologicae* in Gothic Manuscripts," in *Word, Picture, and Spectacle*, ed. Clifford Davidson, Early Drama, Art, and Music, Monograph Ser., 5 (Kalamazoo: Medieval Institute Publications, 1984), pp. 10–12.

18. Glossed as "pissy-arse" in *Chester*, ed. Lumiansky and Mills, II, 250.

19. For the text of this play, see *Non-Cycle Plays and Fragments*, ed. Norman Davis, EETS, s.s. 1 (London, 1970), pp. 58–89.

20. For the N-town plays, see *Ludus Coventriae*, ed. K. S. Block, EETS, s.s. 120 (London, 1922); references to this edition in my text will be designated *N-town* and will indicate the number of the play and the line number(s).

21. See H. H. Carter, *A Dictionary of Middle English Musical Terms* (1961; rpt. New York: Kraus, 1980), p. 102; *OED*, s.v. *crack*. The implication of loud, sudden noise would make the word relevant to ceremonial and laudatory music, such as the angels would sing to God. There is also a possibility that "cracking"

notes had a meaning close to "hack" in a musical context—i.e., splitting long notes into shorter ones, and hence singing difficult, florid music—but this is not certain; see JoAnna Dutka, *Music in the English Mystery Plays*, Early Drama, Art, and Music, Reference Ser., 2 (Kalamazoo: Medieval Institute Publications, 1980), p. 110.

22. Wentersdorf, "The Symbolic Significance of *Figurae Scatologicae*," p. 8.

23. Among other factors, there is a long history of farting as entertainment. In *The City of God* XIV.24, St. Augustine mentions entertainers who could "make musical notes issue from the rear of their anatomy, so that you would think they were singing" (*The City of God*, ed. Gerald G. Walsh and Grace Monahan, Fathers of the Church, 14 [Washington: Catholic Univ. of America Press, 1952], p. 403). One Roland le Pettour, later also called "le Fartere," was rewarded by Henry II for his service, apparently a special trick of his, of making "a leap, a whistle and a fart" (*saltum, siffletum et pettum*) before the king on Christmas day (John Southworth, *The English Medieval Minstrel* [Woodbridge: Boydell Press, 1989], p. 47). Although this sounds like an isolated instance, farting as entertainment was certainly known elsewhere in the later Middle Ages, for it is one of the minstrels' accomplishments listed by Haukyn in *Piers Plowman*; see John Andrew Taylor, "Narrative Minstrelsy in Late Medieval England," unpublished Ph.D. diss. (Univ. of Toronto, 1988), pp. 138–40. Finally, "Le Petomane" (Joseph Pujol, 1857–1945) appeared at the Moulin Rouge in 1892–94 and elsewhere in Paris until 1914 with an extraordinary farting act (Jean Nohain and F. Caradec, *The Master Farter*, trans. Warren Tute [London: New English Library, 1981]).

24. Wentersdorf, "The Symbolic Significance of the *Figurae Scatologiae*," pp. 8–11.

25. Martin Stevens expresses this idea well in his discussion of musicality and the "vice" figure Mak in the Towneley *Secunda Pastorum*; see his *Four Middle English Mystery Cycles* (Princeton: Princeton Univ. Press, 1987), pp. 177–78. Although he confuses the issue by using 'discord' in a non-technical sense, Stevens clearly contrasts the shepherds' musicality and the unordered and meaningless shouting that results from Mak's behavior toward them.

26. David Mills' unpublished translation for the 1983 performance at Leeds treats 'materiale' as an adjective, and hence his quotation marks. In *The Medieval Latin Word-List*, ed. J. H. Baxter and Charles Johnson (London: Oxford Univ. Press,

1934), p. 260, it is given as a noun, however, so that "a great sound of material" should be a possible translation. It has occasionally been suggested that the sound to which reference has been made is the noise of hell-gate breaking down, but this cannot be correct, since Christ has not yet declaimed the *Attollite portas* text. I take it that shouting and "material" noise are likely to occur together.

27. John Stevens, "Music in Mediaeval Drama," *Proceedings of the Royal Musical Association*, 84 (1958), 85n. Stevens cites the more specific stage direction in the Anglo-Norman *Adam* at the entry of Adam and Eve to hell, which requires the banging of "caldaria et lebentes" (i.e., cauldrons and pans); see *Le Jeu d'Adam*, ed. Willem Noomen (Paris: Champion, 1971), p. 54.

28. For the grotesques playing bellows and tongs, see Mary Remnant, *English Bowed Instruments from Anglo-Saxon to Tudor Times* (Oxford: Clarendon Press, 1986), pp. 71, 114. The Great Malvern misericord is rather coyly described by Vera L. Edminson, *Ancient Misericords in the Priory Church of St. Mary and St. Michael, Great Malvern* (Worcester: Ebenezer Baylis and Son, n.d.), p. 15, and not illustrated; it is on the south side of the chancel, back row, the fourth stall from the east.

29. *Coventry*, ed. R. W. Ingram, Records of Early English Drama (Toronto: Univ. of Toronto Press, 1981), p. 167.

30. For St. Augustine's views in this matter, see Herbert M. Schueller, *The Idea of Music*, Early Drama, Art, and Music, Monograph Ser., 9 (Kalamazoo: Medieval Institute Publications, 1988), pp. 255–56.

31. Robert Mannyng of Brunne, *Handlyng Synne*, ed. F. J. Furnivall, EETS, o.s. 119, 123 (London, 1901–03), II, 283 (ll. 8991–94).

32. Ibid., I, 36, 156–57, and especially II, 283ff (l. 8987).

33. *Non-Cycle Plays and Fragments*, ed. Davis, pp. 121–22.

34. For Titivillus (spelled *Tutivillus* in *Towneley* XXX), see Neuss, "Active and Idle Language," pp. 55–56, and especially Clifford Davidson, *Visualizing the Moral Life* (New York: AMS Press, 1989), pp. 35ff. Gail McMurray Gibson points out that in *Mankind* the vices' indecent play on the idea of Christ as "head" involves parodic references to the penis (*The Theater of Devotion* [Chicago: Univ. of Chicago Press, 1989], p. 111): so "playing on the flute" might well

have an indecent meaning at this stage of the play.

35. See Richard Rastall, "Minstrelsy, Church and Clergy in Late Medieval England," *Proceedings of the Royal Musical Association*, 97 (1971), 83–98, and "Music in the Cycle Plays," in *Contexts*, ed. Briscoe and Coldewey, pp. 194–95, 197–98.

36. *Musica instrumentalis* included vocal music, not merely "instrumental" music as we now understand it. *Musica mundana* is treated by many authorities, perhaps the most useful being Kathi Meyer-Baer, *Music of the Spheres and the Dance of Death* (1970; rpt. New York: Da Capo Press, 1984); Patrick L. Little, "The Place of Music in the Medieval World-System," unpublished diss. (Univ. of Otago, Dunedin, New Zealand, 1975); Joyce L. Irwin, "The Mystical Music of Jean Gerson," *Early Music History*, 1 (1981), 187–201; and Schueller, *The Idea of Music, passim*. Little treats matters untouched by other commentators; for his section on *musica mundana*, see pp. 45–91.

I have formerly followed John Stevens ("Music in Mediaeval Drama," p. 82) in assuming that the significance of the music around the throne of God was somehow derived from *musica mundana*; see my "Music in the Cycle," in *The Chester Mystery Cycle: Essays and Documents*, pp. 114–16, and "Music in the Cycle Plays," in *Contexts*, ed. Briscoe and Coldewey, pp. 194–95. It is, however, clear that the problem must be solved by reference to *musica caelestis*, which Little, pp. 125–62, is the only authority to explain (although Irwin does mention it). Little makes it clear that *musica caelestis*, which Jacobus Leodensis regarded as a structure separate from that of the Boethian triad (*musica mundana, humana, and instrumentalis*), is probably best understood as being in a different dimension (i.e., spiritual, rather than physical) from the triad.

37. Schueller, *The Idea of Music*, pp. 255–56.

38. For Thomas of Chabham's categories, see William Tydeman, *The Theatre in the Middle Ages* (Cambridge: Cambridge Univ. Press, 1978), pp. 187–88; further on this matter, see my discussion in "Music in the Cycle Plays," in *Contexts*, ed. Briscoe and Coldewey, p. 197.

39. Dutka, *Music in the English Mystery Plays*, pp. 11–12. The reason for the suggestion of the tritone's use is that it was known as the "devil in music"; however, F. Joseph Smith points out, in his *Jacobi Leodensis Speculum Musicae II: A Commentary* (New York: Institute of Medieval Music, n.d.), p. 116, that no medieval theorist used the term *diabolus in musica* for the tritone, the eighteenth-

century theorist J. J. Fux being the first to do so.

40. Dutka, *Music in the English Mystery Plays*, p. 12.

41. Thus I do not agree with Dutka's comment that the banging of pots and pans is a naive way of expressing hell; see my comments concerning this matter above.

42. *Everyman*, ed. A. C. Cawley (1961; rpt. Manchester: Manchester Univ. Press, 1981).

43. See H. Colin Slim, "Mary Magdalene, Musician and Dancer," *Early Music*, 8 (1980), 460–73, esp. figs. 4 and 5a on pp. 463–64.

44. For proverbial sayings concerning the dancing of the Devil, see Whiting, *Proverbs, Sentences, and Proverbial Phrases*, pp. 129–30 (D191).

45. Dutka, *Music in the English Mystery Plays*, p. 151. Meredith discusses the nature of such games as "Hot Cockles" and relates it to the text of the play; see *The Passion Play from the N.Town Manuscript*, ed. Peter Meredith (London: Longman, 1990), pp. 197, 208–09. In this context it is easy to see the dance as being in the nature of a *ritual*, like a children's game being played according to strict procedures.

46. Dutka, *Music in the English Mystery Plays*, p. 151.

47. The alabaster is illustrated in W. L. Hildburgh, "English Alabaster Carvings as Records of the Medieval Religious Drama," *Archaeologia*, 93 (1949), Pl. 17b. Since the alabaster is considerably damaged, it is impossible to be certain of some details.

48. Grünewald's painting has been frequently reproduced; see, for example, Nikolaus Pevsner and Michael Meier, *Grünewald* (London: Thames and Hudson, 1958), Pl. 43; and, for a color reproduction, Giovanni Testori and Piero Bianconi, *Grünewald* (Milan: Rizzoli Editore, 1972), Pl. 1. The picture was no doubt a political statement by the painter; but reference to fifteenth-century politics does not alter the fact that Christ, having been tried by civil authority, was tortured and executed, as a criminal of Grünewald's day would be. Only the method of execution was different.

49. See Alan Brown, "Moresca," in *The New Grove*, XII, 572–73.

50. *Chester*, ed. Lawrence M. Clopper, Records of Early English Drama (Toronto: Univ. of Toronto Press, 1979), pp. 70, 74, 96; John Marshall, "Players of the Coopers' Pageant from the Chester Plays in 1572 and 1575," *Theatre Notebook*, 33 (1979), 21.

51. Dutka's general thesis could indeed be supported by the evidence of the twelfth-century Anglo-Norman *Adam*; there, when Adam and Eve are taken to hell (see n. 27, above), the demons welcome them with *magnum tripudium*, which just might indicate dancing. I think, however, that the more general meaning of the term is probably correct; "Adam, a Twelfth-Century Play," trans. Lynette R. Muir, *Proceedings of the Leeds Philosophical and Literary Society*, Literary and Historical Section, 13, No. 5 (1970), 183, renders it as "noisy rejoicings," and other translations do similarly.

52. In comments made at the Twenty-fourth International Congress on Medieval Studies on 5 May 1989.

53. In the case of Herod the element of specific deceit is minimal; it is present, however, when Herod attempts to show the Magi that he is a just and competent ruler.

Filth and Stench as Aspects
of the Iconography of Hell

Thomas H. Seiler

Philippe Braunstein has asserted that "unbearable odors define the limits of civilization and give grounds for xenophobia,"[1] and if this is true it is not so difficult to imagine why, in their efforts to portray hell as the antithesis of all that was civilized, desirable, and good, apocalyptic writers should employ images of filth and stench to describe the place of eternal punishment. Again and again, the Edenic, paradisiacal garden with its calm, its flowers, its light, its sweet smells is counterpoised by a chaotic and cacophonous place that is dark, dirty, and offensively smelly. The contrast appears in the earliest stages of the Bible where the calm and order of *Genesis* 1.1 is counterbalanced by the disorder and babble of *Genesis* 11 and the fire and odoriferous brimstone that devastate the Cities of the Plain in *Genesis* 19.24, and it is a contrast that consistently appears throughout the Middle Ages. In sacred texts and sermons, in poetry and drama, evil and the punishment of evil, hell and damnation are always represented by sights, sounds, and scents designed to be abhorrent to *all* our senses.

More often than not the images used to stress the unattractive, undesirable, offensive nature of sin and punishment are generic, no more specific than the "tristo fiato" ("the vile breath") that prompts the pilgrim Dante to delay his descent into the inferno.[2] In the *Apocalypse of St. Paul* from the second century of the common era, for example, an angel is reported to announce of a sinful soul: "Let his soul be taken away out of our midst, for since it came in its stench has passed up to us angels";[3] and the Monk of Evesham reports of the third place of punishment: "I neither saw nor recognized many in that place, because I was overcome with horror by the enormity of the torments and obscenity, and by the filthy stench, so that it was offensive to me beyond measure either to stop for a moment or to look at what was being done."[4]

But writers are wont to give "to aery nothing/ A local habitation and a name,"[5] to seek to evoke the atmosphere of which they speak in quite specific images chosen to engage the auditor's sensory memory, and thus we find, throughout the Middle Ages, that certain categories of images, drawn from the realities of people's lives, are used to characterize damnation and—the writers no doubt hoped—to persuade to holiness by making the alternative profoundly repulsive.

The least complex image is one that depends on associations which people might have with sulphur or pitch. It is "sulphur et ignem" that had rained down to punish Sodom and Gomorrah. In the fourth- or early fifth-century *Apocalypse of Zephaniah*, the visionary reports: "I saw a great sea. I thought it was a sea of water. I found it was a sea of fire and slime that threw off much fire, whose waves glowed with sulphur and pitch."[6] In the fourteenth century John Bromyard warns of evil men and sinners: "Their soul shall have, instead of palace and hall and chamber, the deep lake of hell, with those that go down into the depth thereof. In place of scented baths, their body shall have a narrow pit in the earth; and there they shall have a bath more black and foul than any bath of pitch and sulphur."[7]

A more complex variation on this image includes references to various smelting processes. In the vision known as *St. Patrick's Purgatory*, Christ's soldier sees "numerous large cauldrons, which were full of pitch, sulphur, and melted metals,"[8] and the Monk of Evesham reports of the souls in hell that "Some were roasted before fire; others were fired in pans; red hot nails were driven into some to their bones; others were tortured with a horrid stench in baths of pitch and sulphur mixed with molten lead, brass and other kinds of metal; immense worms with poisonous teeth gnawed some; others were fastened one by one on stakes with fiery thorns."[9]

Geographically hell was depicted as beneath, down, under, or within. It was a boglike place, or a pit, or a well. "The Sheol in which the Hebrew Bible places the dead to lead their shadow existence," according to Martha Himmelfarb, "is often conceived as a pit or bog. . . . Mire and mud are important for the ideas about Hades associated with Orphism. They provide a sort of measure-for-measure punishment: the impure wallow in impurity."[10] In the *Apocalypse of St. Paul*, the visionary who has been given power to see all the torments of hell is brought to the edge of a well and warned: "Stand far off so that you will be able to endure the stench of this place." He then reports: "When the well was opened . . . a hard and very evil stench immediately arose there out of it. It surpassed all the other torments."[11] St. Gregory the Great reports standing on a bridge in his vision, and under the bridge was "a black and smokey river that had a filthy and intolerable smell,"[12] while the Monk of Evesham reports of the second place of punishment in hell that "The bottom of the valley itself contained a body of water, whether flowing or stagnant I know not, very wide and dreadful because of its stinking water, which continually sent forth a vapor of intolerable odor."[13]

The "vapor of intolerable odor" often results from putrefaction, as in the eighth chapter of the Ethiopic version of the *Apocalypse of Peter* in which women punished for abortion "stand up to their necks in a pit of refuse,"[14] or in the third place of punishment witnessed by the Monk of Evesham where the stench that pervades everything is caused by "Dead vipers torn in pieces [that] were collected in heaps beneath the wretches."[15] The most notable image of this type, however, might be that which Dante employs to communicate the atmosphere of the last cloister of Malebolge:

Qual dolor fora, se de li spedali
    di Valdichiana tra'l luglio e'l settembre
    e di Maremma e di Sardigna i mali
fossero in una fossa tutti 'nsembre,
    tal era quivi, e tal puzzo n'usciva

qual suol venir de marcite membre.

(Such suffering as there would be if, between July and
September, the sick from the hospitals of Valdichiana
and of Maremma and of Sardinia were all in one ditch
together, such was there here; and such a stench issued
thence as is wont to come from festering limbs.)[16]

Dante's image, rooted as it is in realities of medieval Italian
life, is one of many efforts he makes in his *Commedia* to stress
that, despite the "otherness" of the hell, purgatory, and paradise
which he reports seeing, there are definite affinities between the
afterlife and this one. His hell bears an unsettling geographic re-
semblance to Italy in general and the Valley of the Arno and Florence in particular, and the plague-stricken Florence Boccaccio
describes in his *Decameron* bears an ominous similarity to the hell
depicted in the vision literature. During the "sore affliction and
misery of our city," Boccaccio reports, "the reverend authority of
the laws, both divine and human, was all in a manner dissolved
and fallen into decay," and some people "went about, carrying in
their hands, some flowers, some odoriferous herbs, and various
other kinds of aromatic drugs which they often held to their noses,
accounting it an excellent thing to fortify the brain with such
odors, since the air seemed all heavy and tainted with the stench of
the dead bodies and that of the sick and of the remedies used."[17]

What we know of urban centers during the Middle Ages indicates that, with or without the plague, life could be distinctly
unlovely, especially for those who could not afford to surround
themselves with open space or to execute ways to dispose of animal and human wastes. Speaking of fifteenth-century York, B. P.
Johnson, after noting the beauties of the city and its setting, notes
also that "hygiene was non-existent, plague and sickness rampant,
and the whole place stank to high heavens!"[18] And Madeline Pelner Cosman's description of the river Thames oozing past "bearing
such Swiftian trophies as sweepings from butcher's stalls, dung,
guts, blood, drowned puppies, stinking sprats, all drenched in mud,

dead cats, and turnip tops tumbling down the sluggish flood,"[19] could as well be of a river in hell.

It is possible—even likely—that the general discomfort of medieval urban life was intensified and focused in particular areas; that "stench was indelibly associated with certain professions and certain parts of cities; [that] whole segments of the population were made pariahs by their smell."[20] In the dyeing process, for example, the extraction of some colors often included the addition of such substances as "table salt, natron, vegetable and fruit juices, urine, vitriol, or alum,"[21] and the preparation of hides for tanning could include "immersion in either a cold infusion of pigeon or hen dung or a warm infusion of dog dung."[22] Both processes involved pits and steeping for various lengths of time, and both involved the odorous accumulation of raw materials on the one hand, and the even more odorous disposal of leftovers on the other. So little as a generation ago in African cities bordering the Sahara where the crafts of dyeing and tanning were still carried on in traditional ways, one could see and smell the dyeing and tanning pits, could see and smell the foetid, slime-covered run-off ponds, could see and smell the discolored hands and forearms of those who had dedicated their lives to their crafts. It must have been so in medieval cities.

If it was so, it raises interesting possibilities for the representations of hell and the satanic in medieval drama. Eileen Gardiner notes of medieval visionary literature that, although it was primarily visual in its appeal, "great emphasis [was] often put on the visionary's experience of the otherworld through his other senses, such as smell, hearing and even taste,"[23] and a similar variety applied to dramatic representation in the Middle Ages, as is evident from the essays by Butterworth and Rastall above, from civic records, from the accounts of contemporary witnesses, and from the texts of the plays themselves. Sometimes an effect is reported, as it is, for example, in the York Barkers' play of the Fall of the Angels where a devil declares "All oure fode is but filth,"[24] or in the Cornish *Ordinalia* where Lucifer says: "Push, O riffraff, strain, blast your tripes! Or else you will get it hot and heavy since the plain truth is, he [Jesus] robs us of our power each passing instant and will leave us, I am convinced, without the strength even to break wind."[25] At other times effects are more immediate. The explosions and fires that so frequently accompany the representations of hell surely left hovering in the air an after-smell of burning sulphur, as in Paris in 1419, for example, where "in one of the sections the Anima Christi shall cast out the devils, and from the other shall come forth flaming sulphur, cannon-fire, thunder, and other fearful sounds."[26]

To engineer such special effects it may have been, as some scholars have suggested, that the nature of the play a guild sponsored and performed was somehow connected to the profession of the guild. Christopher Fitz-Simon mentions, for example, that, in Dublin, guilds "were deputed to enact stories which had some relevance to their own members' craft or trade,"[27] and Alan Justice long ago proposed that "the importance of trade symbolism to both the text and the performance of the York cycle suggests that the relationship was deeper and more intimate that has hitherto been thought."[28] He suggested, for instance, that the play of the Harrowing of Hell was appropriate for the Glaziers because of their association with light and for the Saddlers and Fuystours because of the military connotations of their professions;[29] that the Mercer's Guild appropriately mounted the final play, Doomsday, because of its association with weights and weighing;[30] and that the performing of Play I, the Fall of the Angels, by the Tanner's Guild was particularly appropriate. The Tanners performed the play on this subject in York and Chester,[31] and Justice points out that "The equipment used in the tanning process included large pits in which raw hides were put to soak in noxious, caustic solutions. In the pageant, when Lucifer falls from heaven, he tumbles into a pit of filth, the nature of which may be surmised: dung was sometimes used as an ingredient in the tanning process. An analogy between the tanner's pit and the pit of hell is not difficult to make."[32]

Analogy does not constitute proof, of course, and it does appear that—in York, at least—practitioners of the same trade were less concentrated in one area of the city than they tended to be in London, Paris, and Bruges.[33] Still, a man's work marks a man, or at least it did when most work was performed by man's body rather than his brain. If in some cases the very nature of a man's work and the discolorations and smells associated with it made the man conspicuous in his society, it is not unimaginable that those otherwise negative effects of his labors could be put to positive use by assigning him an appropriate role to play in the public ritual that celebrated at one and the same time virtues of the community and the glory of God.

NOTES

1. Philippe Braunstein, "Toward Intimacy: The Fourteenth and Fifteenth Centuries," in A History of Private Life, II: Revelations of the Medieval World, ed. Georges Duby, trans. Arthur Goldhammer (Cambridge: Harvard Univ. Press, 1988), p. 614.

2. Citations of the Commedia are from Dante Alighieri, The Divine Comedy, trans. Charles S. Singleton, Bollingen Series, 80 (Princeton: Princeton Univ. Press, 1970–75), 6 vols.

3. Visions of Heaven and Hell Before Dante, ed. Eileen Gardiner (New York: Italica Press, 1989), p. 23.

4. Ibid., p. 210.

5. A Midsummer Night's Dream V.i.16–17; citation to The Riverside Shakespeare, ed. G. Blakemore Evans (Boston: Houghton-Mifflin, 1974).

6. The Apocalypse of Zephaniah, quoted in Martha Himmelfarb, Tours of Hell: An Apocalyptic Form in Jewish and Christian Literature (Philadelphia: Univ. of Pennsylvania Press, 1983), p. 153.

7. Quoted in G. R. Owst, Literature and Pulpit in Medieval England, 2nd ed. (Oxford: Basil Blackwell, 1966), pp. 293–94.

8. Visions of Heaven and Hell, ed. Gardiner, p. 141.

9. Ibid., p. 205.

10. Himmelfarb, *Tours of Hell*, p. 107.

11. *Visions of Heaven and Hell*, ed. Gardiner, p. 43.

12. Ibid., p. 48.

13. Ibid., p. 206.

14. The Ethiopic Version of the *Apocalypse of Peter*, quoted in Himmelfarb, *Tours of Hell*, p. 97.

15. *Visions of Heaven and Hell*, ed. Gardiner, p. 210.

16. *Inferno* XXIX.46–51.

17. Giovanni Boccaccio, *Decameron*, trans. John Payne, revised Charles S. Singleton (Berkeley, Los Angeles, London: Univ. of California Press, 1982), I, 11 (Day 1).

18. B. P. Johnson, "The Gilds of York," in *The Noble City of York*, ed. Alberic Stacpoole *et al.* (York: Cerialis Press, 1972), p. 535.

19. Madeline Pelner Cosman, *Fabulous Feasts: Medieval Cookery and Ceremony* (New York: George Braziller, 1976), p. 97.

20. Braunstein, "Towards Intimacy," p. 614.

21. Robert P. Multhauf, "Dyes and Dyeing," in *The Dictionary of the Middle Ages*, ed. Joseph R. Strayer (New York: Charles Scribner's Sons, 1982–), IV, 326.

22. Victoria Gabbitas, "Leather and Leatherworking," in *The Dictionary of the Middle Ages*, VII, 531.

23. Gardiner, ed., *Visions of Heaven and Hell*, p. xxi.

24. *The York Plays*, ed. Richard Beadle (London: Edward Arnold, 1982), p. 52 (l. 106).

25. *The Cornish Ordinalia,* trans Markham Harris (Washington, D.C.: Catholic Univ. of America Press, 1969), p. 171. The breaking of wind is both comic and unpleasant and is frequently referred to in the context of hell. See Dante, *Inferno* XXI.136–39 where a devil "made a trumpet of his arse."

26. *The Staging of Religious Drama in Europe in the Later Middle Ages: Texts and Documents in English Translation,* ed. Peter Meredith and John E. Tailby, Early Drama, Art, and Music, Monograph Ser., 4 (Kalamazoo: Medieval Institute Publications, 1983), p. 90.

27. Christopher Fitz-Simon, *The Irish Theatre* (London: Thames and Hudson, 1983), p. 10.

28. Alan David Justice, "Trade Symbolism in the York Cycle," *Theatre Journal,* 31 (1979), 58.

29. Ibid.," 55. The Fuystours, or makers of saddle trees, apparently represented a contributory guild; see the *Ordo Paginarum* of 1415 and also a record dated 23 May 1551 which assigns "the thridd part of chardges of settyng forth the pagiant" to the Saddlers and a third to the Glaziers and identifies these two guilds as responsible for the production in the past (Alexandra F. Johnson and Margaret Rogerson, *York,* Records of Early English Drama [Toronto: Univ. of Toronto Press, 1979], I, 22, 297–98).

30. Justice, "Trade Symbolism in the York Cycle," p. 56.

31. Ibid., p. 47; Ian Lancashire, *Dramatic Texts and Records of Britain: A Chronological Topography to 1558* (Toronto: Univ. of Toronto Press, 1984), pp. 109, 294. Justice had also included Beverley and Wakefield in his list, but recent records research has confirmed that the Tanners were not involved at these locations.

32. Justice, "Trade Symbolism in the York Cycle," p. 56.

33. On medieval York, see especially Angelo Raine, *Mediaeval York* (London: John Murray, 1955), *passim.*

The Harrowing of Hell at Barking Abbey and in Modern Production

Ann Faulkner

The representation of hell without a formal hell mouth in a liturgical drama could involve the temporary designation of a chapel as infernal space. Such was the case at Barking Abbey, where the staging of the Harrowing, which is the focus of this paper, deserves careful attention as a scholarly problem but also involves sufficient evidence concerning performance to merit an attempt at re-creation of the dramatic event, as in fact was done when the Chicago Medieval Players presented a reconstruction of the play in 1989 (see fig. 22).

At Easter, sometime between 1358 and 1377, Lady Katherine of Sutton, Abbess of Barking,[1] grew alarmed at the *accidia* among those committed to her spiritual care.[2] Lady Katherine, "desiring to get rid of the said torpor completely, the more to excite the devotion of the faithful to such a renowned celebration . . . caused to be written" certain liturgical plays, including a *Descensus* or Harrowing. What would have informed Katherine of Sutton's "iconography of memory"[3] as she staged this play? And, how can one best realize her vision today? This essay offers some tentative answers, but first it is necessary to attempt to place the Barking Harrowing in its historical context before there can be discussion of modern performance.

Founded in the late seventh century, Barking Abbey remained an important women's monastery until its dissolution in 1539. Barking was a Royal foundation and its abbess a baroness in her own right with precedence over all other abbesses in the Realm.[4] The abbess did not live in poverty during our period: her personal

141

household included chaplains, a full-time legal counsel, various lay gentlemen and women, and a multitude of servants. Barking took in children to educate in the social graces, while lay elderly retired there and others came to recuperate from long illnesses or simply to find a respite from daily stresses.[5] Indeed, in the mid-fourteenth century when this play was written, Barking Abbey thrived as a most powerful and wealthy house.

The Abbey must have been a lively place in the fourteenth century. In 1308, Bishop Baldock of London complained of regular wrestling matches in the abbey church along with wild games and "inappropriate dancing."[6] In 1311 similar charges were brought.[7] In 1346, the then Abbess was convicted of diverting funds from a leper hospital to her own use.[8] Certainly by the time Katherine of Sutton was elected abbess in 1358, Barking nunnery was a prime candidate for spiritual reform.

The only extant manuscript containing the Barking plays dates from the early fifteenth century. Currently in the possession of University College, Oxford (MS. 169, pp. 119–24), it is an *ordinarium* copied by order of Sibille Felton, abbess from 1394 to 1419, and presented to the convent in 1404.[9] The exact author of the plays remains unknown, although Lady Katherine is clearly indicated as supervising their creation. The lack of musical notation in the manuscript has frustrated musicologists and potential performers alike because many of the items are unique to this manuscript and identified only by incipits.[10] Fortunately, in spite of the difficulties involved, the music of the Harrowing can be adapted with reasonable accuracy from other sources, primarily the thirteenth-century Worcester Antiphonal.[11]

The *Descensus* or Harrowing of Hell play is particularly interesting in that it is integrally attached to the following *Elevatio* and *Visitatio*, and indeed a non-specialist observer would view all three as one dramatic work. The Harrowing text draws partially on the account in *Matthew* 27.51–53:

> the earth quaked, and the rocks were rent. And the graves were opened: and many bodies of the saints that had slept arose, And com-

ing out of the tombs after his resurrection, came into the holy city, and appeared to many.[12]

However, it is based more substantially on the *Gospel of Nicodemus*, which enjoyed widespread popularity throughout England during the Middle Ages, especially in the fourteenth century, since the story had been made available in Middle English verse.[13] The account of the *Descensus Christi ad inferos* which makes up the second section of the *Gospel of Nicodemus* contains a vivid, dramatic description of three events: (1) The breaking down of the gates of hell by Christ sometime after his death on Good Friday; (2) his binding of Satan; and (3) the deliverance or leading-out of the prophets and patriarchs.[14] The narrative is related by two of the delivered. It is, of course, a variation on a theme common in the mythology of many religions.

The binding of Satan need not concern us here since this scene is not contained in the Barking play—nor, for that matter, should we expect it to be since the practicalities of staging would have presented insurmountable problems of decorum: a priest binding up an actor of either sex in a side-chapel of the abbey church obviously could not have suited Lady Katherine's stated moral and spiritual purposes! On the other hand, the two remaining events, the breaking down of the gates and the deliverance of the saints, form the basis for the Barking plot, unfolded mostly in the words of Scripture and the liturgy.

The architectural setting for the performances in the fourteenth century was the abbey church. This church, as Katherine Sutton knew it, was dedicated 11 October 1215 and enlarged with the Lady Chapel about one hundred years later. Unfortunately, the evidence for its interior plan remains meager; as Elliot Stock, Bishop of Barking, commented in 1913, the abbey church "has been so utterly swept away that it has passed into oblivion."[15] Almost completely destroyed in 1540–41, the few remaining walls of the Abbey foundation were excavated in 1910.[16] The Royal Commission on Historical Monuments notes that only six portions of the original structures remain: the Lady Chapel, the Saints'

Chapel, the side aisle of the presbytery, the south transept with an
eastern chapel, the south aisle of the nave, and the Southwest tower.[17] The slight amount of published architectural material includes only some highly suspect floor plans[18] and descriptions of
the ruins. However, a few inferences may be drawn from the minimal solid evidence that remains, including a tentative floor plan
for the areas of the abbey church with which we need be concerned (fig. D).

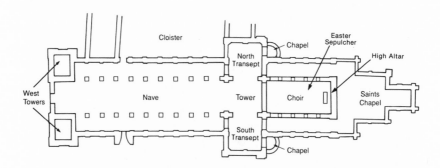

D. The Abbey Church at Barking. Diagram showing the choir with
the high altar and probable location of the temporary Easter Sepulcher set up at the north side of the altar for the play, small chapels
(one of which was used for the Harrowing), transepts, nave, and
westwork.

The role of memory as iconography, which has been noted
above, is related to the expectations we bring to a performance—
expectations that include our total acculturative experience but particularly that portion involving symbolic relationships. While in
modern drama a director has much interpretive freedom, in plays
such as the Barking Harrowing the author already has crafted the
interpretation into the text. To ignore this intrinsic symbolism is to
doom any production, but to make careful use of it is to breathe
life into the story. Therefore, our discussion of the Barking Harrowing of Hell script must be predicated on the symbolism that informed both Lady Katherine's staging decisions and the expectations of her audience. The only concessions in this regard can be

those necessitated by differing architecture.

The Harrowing begins immediately following the third responsory of Easter Matins. The nuns and any attendant clergy are in their stalls. A congregation of lay convent residents and townsfolk doubtless attended as well, since English practice allowed laity to witness the Easter *Depositio, Descensus*, and *Elevatio* ceremonies,[19] with distinguished personages presumably joining the community in the choir and others probably witnessing them in the nave.

The Harrowing play opens with the following rubric: "First the lady abbess shall go with all the convent and with certain priests and clerks dressed in copes, and with each priest and clerk carrying in his hand a palm and an unlighted candle. They shall enter the chapel of St. Mary Magdalene, signifying [figurantes] the souls of the holy Fathers descending into hell before the coming of Christ; and they shall shut the door of the aforesaid chapel on themselves." The order of the procession is easily determinable if the Benedictine nuns of Barking followed the Sarum practice during Holy Week and the Easter Octave. In this instance, however, a reverse order was presumably used, a common symbolism for events connected with hell or Satan. Thus, the Mother Abbess, who normally would have followed at the end of the procession, here would have led the procession to the side chapel; she would have been followed in turn by her nuns in order of precedence, the attendant clergy in order of precedence (again, the reverse of the normal order). Remaining behind and apart from the procession were the hebdomadary priest, a crucifer, a thurifer, and other clergy as well as acolytes. As in Sarum practice, a verger may have preceded the nuns to clear the way although he formed no part of the actual procession itself.[20] The nuns should walk, surely but sedately, to the chapel. No chants are indicated, for traditionally hell was associated with cacophony and noise, and hence ecclesiastical singing would be highly inappropriate.[21] On the other hand, secular instrumental music, usually flute and drum (or fife and tabor), traditionally appeared to lure souls to the Devil; hence the processions could not impossibly have been accompanied by drum, flute, or even a small portative organ (using, for example, a 4′ flute stop). Any such music should cease as the gates to the chapel clang shut.

The procession moved from the choir towards the westwork as such processions always did. The westwork symbolized everything non-spiritual, and at churches in other locations Harrowings were represented there. But where did the procession go next? The north transept contained the altar of the Resurrection, hardly an appropriate placement for hell. The Saints' Chapel behind the high altar was dedicated to St. Ethelburga and St. Mary the Virgin—also inappropriate. This leaves the small chapel in the south transept which some authorities label "SS. Peter and Paul," although such a dedication cannot be confirmed in the fourteenth century at the time these ceremonies were being introduced. Assuming the use of this chapel, the procession then would have gone down from the choir, turning left into the south transept and left again into the small chapel. The symbolism of going *down* and turning *left* (not once but twice) cannot be overestimated, for only the devil and his associates oriented their movements in that direction.[22] The carrying of unlighted candles is similarly symbolic, corresponding to the snuffed candle of exorcism and burial. The psychological effect of carrying a candle which cannot be lighted far outweighs that of a mere empty hand.

The presumed space is about right for the maximum of thirty-seven nuns in residence and their attendants when we consider that claustrophobia was a desired effect. There being no room for the laity, such persons probably remained standing in the main area of the south transept. In modern performance, staging adjustments are often required at this point, mainly to accommodate sight-line considerations. Present-day edifices are often without side chapels, especially ones with closable gates, and they usually present the additional problem of immovable congregational seating. Thus, this director chose to stage the entire scene at the westwork and to use portable gates.

The play continues:

Then the officiating priest [sacerdos ebdomodarius], dressed in an alb and cope, coming to the said chapel with two deacons, one carrying a cross with the Lord's banner hanging from the top, the other carrying a censer in his hand, and with other priests and clerks with two boys carrying lighted candles approaching the door of the said chapel, shall begin three times this antiphon: *Tollite portas*. This priest indeed shall represent [representabit] the person of Christ about to descend to hell and break down the gates of hell. And the aforesaid antiphon shall be begun at each repetition in a higher or louder voice [altiori uoce], which the clerks repeat the same number of times, and at the beginning each time he shall beat with the cross at the aforesaid door, signifying [figurans] the breaking down of the gates of hell. And at the third knock, the door shall open. Then he shall go in with his ministers.

In contemporary visual representations of this scene, Christ is almost always reaching out in a very strong and determined way. Positioned at the gates of hell, he usually holds a cross staff with a banner. The Barking script calls for the cross to be carried to the Magdalene chapel by a deacon and to be taken in hand at the gates by the priest representing Christ before he begins the *Tollite portas*.

The *Tollite portas* lines ("Lift up your gates, O ye princes") appear in several other places in addition to the regular *rota* of daily psalmody: (1) in ceremonies for the opening of the city gates, (2) at the church door in the Palm Sunday procession, (3) at the ceremony of dedication for a church building, (4) during Advent as a gradual for the third Sunday, and (5) at Mass for the day preceding Christmas. The common theme of these occasions is the grand entry of Christ into a particular situation: an edifice, Jerusalem, hell, the world at his Nativity. The text, itself taken from the last four verses of Psalm 23 (24), would have sounded a familiar note of triumph to all who heard it. This is a royal warrior's command, not a polite request or an invitation to negotiations. It demands to be delivered accordingly: the voice strong, the pace brisk (Example I).

Example I

Tóllite portas príncipes vestras, * et elevámini portae æternáles,   allelúia.
[Lift up your heads, O ye gates; and be ye lift up, ye everlasting doors, alleluia.]

The Prophets' and Patriarchs' response follows: "Meanwhile a certain priest being inside the chapel shall begin the antiphon *A porta inferi*, which the cantrix shall take up, with the whole convent: *Erue domine [animam meam]* ("From the gates of hell deliver my soul, O Lord"]. It is interesting to note that those inside are crying for delivery *after* the gates have been opened. This is not inconsistent with medieval literary notions of time; events adjacent were often perceived as events juxtaposed.[23] Nor has it been the writer's experience that modern audiences are confused by such treatment. Certainly, it would be impossible for the *Tollite portas* to be heard by an audience over the din of hell. Moreover, most Harrowing illustrations that include the Prophets and Patriarchs show them responding plaintively rather than confidently. The text of the antiphon *A porta inferi, erue domine animam meam* and its music reflect this—twenty-two notes to cry "help," and these twenty-two notes must be sung as one cry (Example II).

Example II

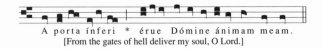

A porta ínferi * érue Dómine ánimam meam.
[From the gates of hell deliver my soul, O Lord.]

Immediately, the mood changes as we hear another antiphon: *Domine abstraxisti ab inferis animam meam* ("Lord you have brought my soul out of hell"). The music sketches a picture strong and victorious, grateful, but not a passive sound of mere relief. In performance, it must contrast absolutely with the previous line, for this dissimilarity signals a shift not only in mood but in time as well—from a reiteration of a long-standing lament to the ecstasy of the here and now (Example III).

Example III

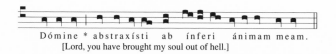

Dómine * abstraxísti   ab   ínferi   ánimam meam.
[Lord, you have brought my soul out of hell.]

Here the manuscript reads: "Then the officiating priest shall lead out all those who were inside the aforesaid chapel, and in the meantime the priest shall begin the antiphon *Domine abstraxisti*, and the cantrix shall follow: *Ab inferis*. Then all shall go out from the chapel, that is, from the Limbo of the Fathers, and the priests and clerks shall sing the antiphon *Cum rex glorie* in a procession through the middle of the choir to the sepulcher, each one carrying a palm and a candle, signifying [designantes] victory recovered from the enemy, with the lady abbess, the prioress, and all the convent following, as if they are the early Fathers [sicut sunt priores]." Careful reading shows another example of the medieval attitude towards time: the script indicates the nuns being led out twice, once before and once after the antiphon *Domine abstraxisti*. Whether or not this is merely a scribal error, a choice must be made between the two directions. Here is where a modern production can inform scholarship, for it immediately becomes obvious that the time elapsed in singing the antiphon provides the time necessary to begin distributing palms and lighting candles. Thus the dramatic change in the musical effect and the opening of the gates are combined with a sudden burst of light, the holding aloft of branches, and the swinging of the newly lighted censer as the faithful turn twice to the *right* and process *up* into the chancel. In short, participants at once are presented with a deafening array of godly symbolism.

The "palms" borne in procession carried the symbolic meaning of glory or victory. The term *palma* is used generically to refer to any branches but in England especially willows[24]—many illustrations show such branches or flowered ones—although it is not totally impossible that Barking may have had access to actual palms. While the script is ambiguous with regard to giving either palms or candles to the nuns, Barking Abbey surely could have afforded them, and they would have served a needed symbolic purpose in the drama. We may imagine that in the closeness of the St. Mary Magdalene Chapel safety may have been a concern, but a modern director would be mistaken not to provide candles for all, especially if this portion were to be staged at the westwork. It is hard to imagine any lack of candles at Barking Abbey in the fourteenth century, and problems of staging with regard to these candles are solved quite simply, as we shall see.

The *Cum rex glorie*[25] which follows at first appears redundant, and in textual terms alone it is:

> Cum rex glorie Christus infernum debellaturus intraret et chorus angelicus ante faciem eius portas principum tolli preciperet. Sanctorum populus qui tenebatur in morte captivus voce lacrimabili clamaverunt: advenisti desiderabilis quem expectabamus in tenebris ut educeres hac nocte vinculatos de claustris. Te nostra vocabant suspira. Te larga requirebant lamenta. Tu factus es spes desolatis magna consolatio in tormentis. Alleluia.

> (When Christ the king of glory victoriously entered the netherworld, the angelic chorus commanded the princes to lift up their gates before his face. The people of saints who had been held captive by death cried out in woeful voice: You have come, the desired one, for whom we have waited in the darkness, that you might this night lead the fettered ones out of prison. We called to you with our sighs. We sought you with abundant laments. You are made the hope of the desolate, the great consolation in torment. Alleluia.)

However, in theatrical terms this apparent redundancy makes perfect sense. Many candles need to be lighted. This cannot be done in crowded conditions. Thus they must be lighted singly as their bearers leave the chapel. Then all must process to the Sepulcher.

This takes time, and no good playwright would try to advance the plot and change the scene at the same time. Therefore, considering the number of persons involved, the distance to be travelled—to the middle of the choir facing the Easter Sepulcher in its usual place on the north side of the chancel[26]—and the tasks to be completed, the length and content of *Cum rex gloriae* are both necessary and appropriate. Logistics dictate this approach as well, since Sarum custom concerning "in procession" meant "stations"[27]—thus the men sing while the women walk, then the women sing *Consurgit Christus* while the men come to join them in front of the Sepulcher on the last verse.

The mode of the triumphal return procession was very likely some form of dance. While the procession to hell involved neither singing nor dancing but only the instrumental music that bespoke a change of scene to a medieval audience, the procession back from the font represented praise and celebration—and hence was in my view almost certainly danced. Indeed, there is considerable evidence that all processions were originally line dances, which included the rhythmic swinging of censers and involved flowers, or at least flower petals.[28] While a word of caution is of course necessary here, it is nevertheless proper symbolically to view the procession from hell to the chancel in terms of Christ leading souls with music and dance to heaven, where they will join the dance of the Saints. In fact, from the earliest times there has been an iconographic tradition of souls being led upwards to heaven or otherwise liberated, and seldom do they travel alone.[29]

The evidence for dance is strong and continuing; fourteenth-century hymn writers made frequent references to liturgical dancing. A verse from a Continental dance-song c.1360 describes such an event:

> Before the eyes of the nuns
> Stands in purple splendour,
> Deeply and devoutly honoured,
> The Bishop, guiding the cult.
> Numerous hands join and clasp in dance;

This broad and joyous path
Gives ample space for the chain of dancers.

. . .

All these festive gestures
Intend the gift of inward joy.[30]

An account of the 1478 Easter ceremony at Hildesheim illustrates the symbolism of the Easter dance:

> Hereafter comes the solemn procession in memory of the procession which Christ . . . solemnized when he returned from the underworld, leading out those he had delivered into the paradise of ecstasy, dancing and hopping. He introduces both music and dance in consideration of the liberation of so many souls. He sings to them a song which none should utter except to God's immortal Son after his wondrous triumph. And we all, happy and adorned with spiritual perfection, follow our highest master, who himself leads the solemn ring dance.[31]

A frequently used dance was the *tripudia,* a term derived from a military victory dance but later used to designate religious dance;[32] it seems to have involved a pattern of three steps forward and one backward.[33] It and other dances are often mentioned in the fourteenth century. In some places a maze was danced during the return procession.[34] Though known to be popular in contemporary edifices, there is no evidence concerning a maze at Barking. The maze represents hell from which the line-dance leads lost souls.

The Harrowing now lacks only its finale: "And when they have reached the Sepulcher, the officiating priest shall cense and enter the Sepulcher, beginning the verse *Consurgit.* Then the cantrix shall follow with *Christus tumulo*; the verse *Quesumus auctor*; the verse *Gloria tibi Domine.*" Certainly the music of the *Consurgit Christus* found in the Worcester Antiphonal (Example IV) cries out for physical motion. Unique for England in its early use of colored notation, it is at once a fitting conclusion to the Harrowing and a proper prelude to the *Elevatio* which follows without pause.

Example IV

Con - sur - git Chris - tus tu - mu - lo   *   Vic - tor re - dit de ba - ra - thro,
[Christ rises from the tomb. He returns from Hell a victor.]

Ty - ran - num tru - dens vin - cu - lo, Et par - a - dis - um re - ser - ans.
[thrusting the tyrant into chains, and opening paradise.]

Que - su - mus, Auc - tor om - ni - um,   In hoc pas - chal - i gau - di - o,
[Author of all things, we pray, in this Paschal joy:]

Ab om - ni mor - tis im - pe - tu Tu - um de - fen - de po - pu - lum.
[defend thy people from every assault of death.]

Glo - ri - a ti - bi Do - mi - ne,   Qui sur - rex - is - ti a mor - tu - is,
[Glory be to you, Lord, who has risen from the dead.]

Cum Patre et Sanc - to Spir- i - tu, In sem - pi - ter - na sae - cu - la. A - men.
[With the Father and the Holy Spirit, unto eternal ages.]

Some important conclusions can now be drawn. Perhaps most important is the point that although contemporary theologians may have argued that Christ entered hell in the spirit as *Anima Christi,* the Barking playwright clearly envisioned an embodied Christus and a staging informed by physicality. Thus, modern productions must guard against the well-intentioned intrusion of modern notions of decorum and appropriateness. Indeed, the most problematic moments in the Chicago Medieval Players' production arose when certain cast members were forced to accommodate just such fantasies to historical reality. The dramatic vitality that inspired the Barking Harrowing must inform its modern performance as well.

Finally, one must address the efficacy of Lady Katherine's designs. Did enacting this play have any real effect on the spirituality of the residents of Barking Abbey? If a modern production can serve as evidence, the verdict must be affirmative. The Chicago Medieval Players' production of the Barking Harrowing of Hell, rehearsed over six weeks and then performed over a period of a month, involved a company of actors who brought to their task a professional training that did not allow undisciplined emotional involvement. As the work progressed, the value of the work nevertheless became increasingly apparent to the members of the cast. Perhaps our experience corroborates the success of the Harrowing for the ladies of Barking since we came to feel that they inevitably would have found the effect of the play to be salutary and an antidote to *accidia*.

NOTES

1. The election of Katherine of Sutton received the royal assent on 15 March 1358 (Pat. 32 Edward III, Pt. 1, m. 24); her death occurred in 1377 sometime before 16 April when the license was granted to elect her successor (Pat. 51 Edward III, m. 24). The motive for the plays is explained in the *Ordinale and Customary of the Benedictine Nuns of Barking*, ed. J. B. L. Tolhurst, Henry Bradshaw Society, 66 (London, 1927), I, 107. For a brief notice, see Nancy Cotton, *Women Playwrights in English, c.1363–1750* (Lewisburg: Bucknell Univ. Press, 1980), pp. 27–28, 213n.

2. For a discussion of *accidia*—a blend of boredom, apathy, and sometimes depression that was endemic to monastic life—see Eileen Power, *Medieval English Nunneries* (New York: Biblo and Tannen, 1964), pp. 293ff.

3. The term 'iconography of memory' and its application here draw on the work of Jody Enders, particularly her article, "Visions with Voices," *Comparative Drama*, 24 (1990), 34–54.

4. As a woman, however, she did not sit in Parliament, although she was bound to send men to do her knight's service.

5. "Receyved of my Lord of Oxeforde for the Comons of my Lorde Bullebith for a moneth. iiij li xvs. Receyved for the comens of Mr. Smyth's two doughters for the xvj wekes every of them paying by the weke. xxxijs" (Mins. Acc. 929, Pt. 2, fol. 7, as quoted by James E. Oxley, *A History of Barking* [Barking, 1935], p. 20).

6. Bishop Baldock's Register, fol. 15ᵛ, as cited by Oxley, *History of Barking*, p. 14.

7. Bishop Baldock's Register, fol. 29ᵛ, as cited by Oxley, *History of Barking*, p. 13.

8. Ibid., p. 13.

9. Facsimile in Pamela Sheingorn, *The Easter Sepulchre in England*, Early Drama, Art, and Music, Reference Ser., 5 (Kalamazoo: Medieval Institute Publications, 1987), figs. 12–17; for transcription of the text, see ibid., pp. 132–37, and *The Ordinale and Customary of the Benedictine Nuns of Barking Abbey*, ed. Tolhurst, pp. 107–09, and also Karl Young, *The Drama of the Medieval Church* (Oxford: Clarendon Press, 1933), I, 165–66. My quotations from the Barking text are from Tolhurst's edition, and for English translations I have used Evelyn Kaehler's unpublished performing edition as prepared for the Chicago Medieval Players.

10. Susan Rankin, whose Cambridge University dissertation addresses the music of English medieval music-dramas (recently published as *The Music of the Medieval Liturgical Drama in France and England* [New York: Garland, 1989]), has indicated in a private letter her doubts concerning the possibility of reconstructing of the Barking *Visitatio*, which follows the Harrowing in the manuscript.

11. Worcester Cathedral Library, MS. f 160; for a facsimile, see *Antiphonaire monastique, XIIIᵉ siècle: Codex F. 160 de la Bibliothèque de la Cathédrale de Worcester*, Paléographie musicale, 12 (Tournai, 1922).

12. Biblical citations are to the Douay-Rheims translation of the Vulgate.

13. See *The Middle-English Harrowing of Hell and Gospel of Nicodemus*, ed. William Henry Hulme, EETS, e.s. 100 (London, 1907).

14. Ibid., pp. 96–119.

15. Foreword, in Walter A. Locks, *Barking Abbey in the Middle Ages* (London: Elliot Stock, 1913) [unpaginated]. For a summary account of the destruction of the abbey, see James E. Oxley, *The Reformation in Essex to the Death of Mary* (Man-

chester: Manchester Univ. Press, 1965), p. 130.

16. "Notes and Reviews," *The Essex Review*, 23 (1914), 116–17.

17. Royal Commission on Historical Monuments, *An Inventory of the Historical Monuments in Essex* (London: HMSO, 1916–26), II, 7–9.

18. See Daniel Lysons, *The Environs of London* (London: Cadell, 1792–96), facing p. 615, and *An Inventory of the Monuments in Essex*, II, 8. The latter plan can claim greater accuracy as it depends upon more recent excavations.

19. See Sheingorn, *The Easter Sepulchre in England*, pp. 29–30.

20. Christopher Wordsworth, *Ceremonies and Processions of the Cathedral Church of Salisbury* (Cambridge: Cambridge Univ. Press, 1901), *passim*.

21. Kathi Meyer-Baer, *Music of the Spheres and the Dance of Death* (Princeton: Princeton Univ. Press, 1970), pp. 284, 288. See also, however, the paper by Richard Rastall in the present volume.

22. Clifford Davidson, "Space and Time in Medieval Drama: Meditations on Orientation in the Early Theater," in *Word, Picture, and Spectacle*, ed. Clifford Davidson, Early Drama, Art, and Music, Monograph Ser., 5 (Kalamazoo: Medieval Institute Publications, 1984), pp. 40–46.

23. Ibid., pp. 46–58.

24. See R. E. Latham, *Revised Medieval Latin Word-List* (London: British Academy, 1965), *s.v.* palma (2).

25. On *Cum rex glorie* and the Harrowing of Hell theme, see Audrey Ekdahl Davidson, *Holy Week and Easter Ceremonies and Dramas in Medieval Sweden*, Early Drama, Art, and Music, Monograph Ser., 13 (Kalamazoo: Medieval Institute Publications, 1990), pp. 9–11.

26. The Sepulcher used for the *Depositio, Elevatio*, and, though less frequently performed, the *Visitatio Sepulchri* in England often was a temporary one rather than the Sepulcher in the North Wall of the chancel; the location of the temporary structure was, in English practice, normally on the north side of the chancel or choir. See Sheingorn, *The Easter Sepulchre in England, passim*.

27. In Sarum usage, "in procession" denoted any portion of the service conducted outside the choir area, usually in stations. A soloist might actually sing as the procession moved along, but, as a group, the usual practice was to stand still to sing. See also Terence Bailey, *The Processions of Sarum and the Western Church* (Toronto: Pontifical Institute of Mediaeval Studies, 1971), *passim.*

28. See E. Louis Backman, *Religious Dances in the Christian Church and in Popular Medicine* (London: George Allen and Unwin, 1952), pp. 85–88.

29. Meyer-Baer, *Music of the Spheres and the Dance of Death,* p. 291.

30. *Analecta Hymnica Medii Aevi,* XX, 135–36 (No. 178), trans. in part by Margaret Fisk Taylor, *A Time to Dance: Symbolic Movement in Worship* (Philadelphia: United Church Press, 1967), p. 96.

31. Karl Bartsch, *Mittelniederdeutsche Osterlieder* (1880), p. 49, as quoted in translation by Taylor, *A Time To Dance,* p. 94.

32. As in the designation *tripudiare,* indicated in connection with *Stella splendens* in the fourteenth-century *Llibre Vermell.*

33. Taylor, *A Time to Dance,* p. 94.

34. See ibid., pp. 92–93.

The Iconography of Hell
in the English Cycles:
A Practical Perspective

Peter Meredith

The search for hell in the English cycle plays[1] must inevitably center on the pageants dramatizing the Creation, Harrowing of Hell, and Last Judgment. It is only in these episodes that hell regularly appears as a central element. Of these the Harrowing and the Last Judgment have the strongest recurring pictorial traditions. The Creation, involving the fall of the rebel angels, has a less fixed iconography.[2] Since, therefore, I shall be partly interested in the relationship between pictorial and theatrical representation in the paper that follows, I shall concentrate on the Harrowing and the Judgment. For these two episodes it is possible to conjure up what we might call a common late-medieval form.[3] In the Harrowing, the principal character, Christ, would have appeared—naked but for a cloth draped around his hips and over his shoulders, with a cross banner in his hand—treading on the fallen gates of hell. Out of the gaping mouth of hell issue the souls, while devils threaten and blow horns on the battlements which surround it. The Last Judgment conjures up a Christ, again appearing naked except for a cloth draped around him, seated on a rainbow and displaying his wounds while angels circling him carry the instruments of the Passion. The resurrection of the dead is pictured below him, with on his left the damned being coerced into hell. Frequently Mary and John the Baptist kneel at Christ's feet, and sometimes the apostles and the hosts of heaven sit in serried ranks below and on either side of him while, below, St. Michael may weigh the souls in his scales. The Harrowing differs from the Judgment inasmuch as hell is the centerpiece of the scene. In the Judgment, hell is merely a picturesque dustbin for sinful humanity. It is part of the central image but only as a point of reference—where the damned will end up. Obviously both of these are generalized pictures, and I am not claiming them as fixed images; they very clearly vary in individual representations in many details, but they serve as a general pictorial background against which to place the theatrical representation.[4]

The Harrowing of Hell. The York-Towneley and Chester cycles[5] take the Harrowing as a separate episode and devote a single pageant to it so that it is, as in the pictorial versions, the central focus. A single pageant and a single picture, however, are, as has often been said, very different things. At the most basic level, in one the action is revealed sequentially and in the other simultaneously. In a picture, past and future elements of the episode can be included or implied, but all coexist. Christ's foot on the gates of hell implies the breaking down of the gates, the release of the souls implies their imprisonment, the warlike posture of the devils implies their defense of their domain, but the whole exists as a single image. One of the first requirements of the English pageant seems to have been sequential representation. All the cycle pageants begin with a scene of the imprisoned souls in hell —in the case of York-Towneley after an initial speech by Christ. Hell must be seen as closed, yet to be broken into by Christ, while at the same time the souls within must be both visible and audible. Pictorial imagery is no real help here since no Harrowing as far as I know presents the episodes in a series of such sequential details. If a director were to start with the traditional scene in mind, he would very soon find himself coerced by theatrical necessity into adjusting it. Furthermore, each pageant begins, as in the *Gospel of Nicodemus*, with another narrative element: light as a harbinger of Christ.[6] This must at first seem like compounding the problem, the triumph of narrative over drama, since it immediately involves a further difficulty for the director. How do you provide an intense divine light *aureus solis calor purpureaque lux* ("a golden heat of the sun and a purple royal light")[7] on a pageant wagon in a city street in broad daylight within a closed hell? The Paris Resurrection stage direction gives an answer to both problems. For the first,

> Limbo . . . should be made like a tall square tower surrounded by nets so that through the said nets one can see from the audience the souls who are inside when the Anima Christi has forced his way inside there. But before his coming the said tower shall be provided with black cloth curtains all round which will cover the said nets and prevent [the souls] from being seen until the entrance of Anima Christi, and then the said curtains shall be cunningly pulled aside on small rings so that the people in the audience can see inside the said tower through the said nets.[8]

The Paris Resurrection direction is for a fixed stage, not a pageant wagon, but it provides a viable solution to the first problem, the enclosed hell. It also deals with the second problem, the coming of divine light: "And in addition at the coming of the Anima Christi there shall be in the said tower several torches and lanterns or great burning flambeaux."[9] Such use of flame may perhaps be an alarming prospect on an enclosed wagon, but it does provide a possible solution to the two problems at once: the seen, yet imprisoned souls and the glowing light. Or, rather, it perhaps shows that the inclusion of one (the light) helps to solve the other (the visibility of the imprisoned souls).

Another element to bear in mind in considering the relationship between pictorial and theatrical representations of this episode is the focus or emphasis. The pictorial image focuses on the falling of the gates and the simultaneous release of the souls. Despite the additional detail that any picture may have, it is a fixed focus. Though this moment (or rather these moments) occurs in all the pageants, the emphasis is considerably altered. To call this *the* iconographic moment of the pageant, the point at which pictorial and theatrical images coalesce, would certainly be misleading. In York-Towneley the focus is particularly on the debate between Christ and Satan, about the justice of Christ's action in breaking the power of hell, which forms a long section between the fall of the gates (presumably around ll. 195 and 207) and the release of the souls (at ll. 348 and 357–58). In Chester the focus shifts among the debate of the devils in hell, the freeing of the souls, the series of meetings as they are led to paradise, and the ale-wife scene with which the pageant concludes. These elements shape the audience's perception of hell. In York-Towneley hell is the dominant image at first and perhaps until the fall of the gates, but the debate reduces its dominance to the point where at the actual moment of the release of the souls the focus is more on the human reaction to Christ's mercy than the release from hell. The traditional pictorial image is therefore seriously obscured.

In Chester the debate among the devils means that before the fall of the gates the inside of hell must in some sense be visible (space, presumably, apart from where the souls are) and must contain Satan's throne (l. 96*sd*). I have tried to give some idea of possible arrangements in the accompanying sketches.[10] Fig. E incorporates a hell mouth with collapsing gates, a netted enclosure for the souls (about 12′ by 4′), a space at the front of the wagon for Satan's throne (about 3′ 6″ deep), and a ramp for entry onto the wagon. I imagine devils outside the wagon on street level at their first appearance (ll. 97ff) and using the upper battlements during Christ's "attack." The *cathedra* is perhaps unnecessarily large and awkwardly placed if, as I suspect, Satan's "entry" stage direction is actually a "discovery" one (l. 96*sd*). This sketch, for which it should be stressed there is no record evidence beyond the text, is not one which would spring naturally out of the traditional Harrowing of Hell image. It uses broadly medieval elements to piece together a multiple scene. It is ironic that though the action is sequential the set is necessarily a fixed amalgam, designed to cope with a series of different narrative elements, in this case the souls in hell, the debating devils, the "attack" of Christ, the fall of the defenses of hell, the leading forth of the souls, the journey to paradise, and the final scene with the ale-wife. It still differs from the pictorial iconography, however, because it is tied to a narrative sequence. This layout, though it can cope with most of these narrative elements, has one considerable drawback. The facing hell

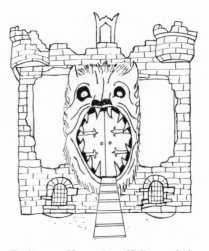

E. Chester Harrowing. Hell mouth with ramp and gates. Satan's throne is placed in front of the net enclosure for the souls, from which the back curtains have been drawn back.

F. Chester Harrowing. Hell mouth in center of wagon. Satan's throne has been moved to roof; the net enclosure is not shown.

G. Chester Harrowing. "End-on" hell mouth; net enclosure not shown.

mouth obscures from a large section of the audience much of the recessed hell where the souls are placed. Moving the hell mouth to the center (as in fig. F) does not solve the problem of visibility and means that Satan's *cathedra* would almost certainly have to be placed on the roof of the wagon—though this in itself is by no means an impossible position.

My main reason for placing the hell mouth in this dominant position, however, is the existence of the traditional pictorial version. Far more satisfactory in many ways would be the placing of the hell mouth on the end of the wagon (as in fig. G), but then only a very small proportion of the audience would see the traditional iconographic moment of the fall of the gates. Even more satisfactory from the point of view of visibility would be the solution used at the performance of the York Harrowing in Toronto in 1977, where a wide mouth framed the superstructure of the wagon (as in fig. H). This layout, however, moves even further from a traditional view. It is unlikely that any gates could cover so large an opening, certainly not if they were to fall in anything like the commonly pictured way. There are, of course, ways of suggesting a defended building by the use of a form of collapsible portcullis (fig. I), lowered by the devils, to fill the space and collapsing on itself at the *Attolite portas.* But it is worth noting, in relation to Chester, that there is no actual mention by the devils of defenses of any kind. Are we, therefore, even in expecting hell gates, depending too much on a traditional view? Chester relies closely on the *Gospel of Nicodemus* which certainly has a number of references to gates and bars, prison and chains, and also treats Satan's resistance as warfare. All this is omitted in the Chester pageant except Christ's words (ll. 152*sd*, 153, and 193) and David's confirmation (l. 191). Comparison of this with York and Towneley reveals just how different is the approach. In York there is a clear setting-up of the defenses in the early section of the pageant: "Spere our ȝates" (l. 139); "sette furthe watches on þe wall" (l. 140); "Our baill is brokynne/ And brosten are alle oure bandis of bras" (ll. 195–96). There is also in both a much clearer perception of the souls in a separate place: "they are sperde in speciall space"

H. Chester Harrowing. "Wide-mouthed" hell mouth with throne on roof and steps for ascent to wagon. Based on PLS production of York Harrowing at Toronto in 1977.

(l. 110); "þes lurdans þat in Limbo dwelle" (l. 102). Towneley retains these references and develops them even further in its adaptation of York: "Thou must com help to spar,/ we ar beseged abowte" (ll. 146–47); "Oure yates I trow will last,/ thay are so strong I weyn:/ Bot if our barres brast,/ ffor the they shall not twyn" (ll. 201–04); "harro! oure yates begyn to crak!/ In sonder, I trow, they go" (ll. 209–10). The specificity of Towneley regarding the nature of the effects of Christ's attack on hell goes beyond even York. This suggests, perhaps, that York and Towneley require something along the lines of the sketches I have made, but it is possible that Chester used a rather different set-up. Only Towneley seems to require action which approaches the traditional iconography, and even there the focus moves to the debate between Christ and Satan before the souls are released.

I have up to now limited my discussion of the Harrowing episode to the cycle texts which survive. As it happens, however, one of the large surviving runs of craft accounts from Coventry relates to a Harrowing pageant. Unlike the York-Towneley and Chester versions, however, the Cappers' pageant at Coventry included not simply the Harrowing but a number of surrounding episodes as well. The cast paid by the craft suggests that they were responsible for the Setting of the Watch, the Harrowing, the Resurrection, and the Visit of the Maries to the Sepulcher as well as probably the Appearances to Mary Magdalene and to the Virgin Mary. There is no evidence for more than a single wagon, though there is an isolated reference in 1543 to "settyng vpp ye foreparte of ye pageant" and, starting in the same year, a series of references to "ye skaffolde."[11] If there was a single set, how were these rather different episodes staged? And what kind of a theatrical iconography might have been produced from this combination of episodes? Pilate's "court" requires no more that a canopied seat (if that), but

I. Chester Harrowing. As in fig. H but with collapsible porticullis.

the Harrowing must surely have a hell and the Resurrection a sepulcher. One possible arrangement would be that suggested for Chester by Glynne Wickham many years ago, the drawing-up of the scaffold in the front of the wagon.[12] In the accompanying diagram (fig. J) I have also included a possible arrangement for the "foreparte" of the pageant. If these positions were adopted a number of problems and possibilities arise. The wagon could contain a hell mouth curtained off until needed. Pilate's "court" could occupy the forepart and scaffold, around the sepulcher, if the setting of the watch involved Pilate, Annas, and Caiaphas *at* the sepulcher, as in the sealing of the tomb in the N-town *Passion II* (ll. 1280–1311),[13] rather than at the "court" in a preliminary scene. If there were a preliminary scene, then the sepulcher might be sunk into the scaffold, flush with the floor, and raised at the appropriate moment (see figs. K and L). This is not so fanciful as it might seem, bearing in mind the regular appearance of a "wynde" or windlass in the accounts. It is never specified what the "wynde" is for, and at least one possibility is raising something up to scaffold-floor level.

The "spret of god" or *Anima Christi*, released at Christ's death, might then enter through the audience at street level beyond the scaffold and face the hell now revealed on the pageant wagon for the *Attollite portas*. After the Harrowing the "spret" can return to the sepulcher, the two angels can raise the table-top stone of the sepulcher, and Christ can arise. This would produce some interestingly layered scenes, but it must be confessed that it seems rather a wasteful use of the available acting areas—especially if the Harrowing was as simple as it appears it was. It must also be borne in mind that the existence of a separate scaffold may well imply the existence of two quite separate acting areas—and of the possible permutations of the use of the areas, wagon and "foreparte" on the one hand and scaffold on the other.

The cast list raises interesting questions about the relative importance of the episodes. There are no souls mentioned at all and only one devil. How is it possible to perform a Harrowing with no souls to release and only a single devil to defend hell?

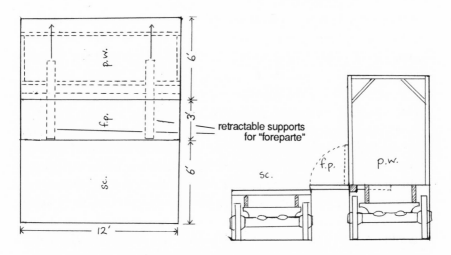

J. Coventry Harrowing, etc. Diagrams of a possible arrangement of pageant wagon, "forepart," and scaffold. The "forepart" is shown hinged to the wagon (see also figs. K and L).

K. Coventry Harrowing, etc. Pageant wagon, "forepart," and scaffold with enclosed hell mouth and sepulcher lowered flush with the floor.

L. Coventry Harrowing, etc. As in fig. K but with sepulcher raised. No means of ascent onto the wagon or scaffold is shown in either sketch.

There are, it is true, hints of the existence of souls; three "folles' hedes" in an antiquarian copy of the Cappers' 1567 inventory could be wigs for souls.[14] In the same inventory there are a "dystaff & aspayde," perhaps for Adam and Eve. It seems unlikely, however, if they did exist, that they spoke, since they would almost certainly have been paid and have appeared in the craft accounts. There is no additional evidence for extra devils. We are left with a considerable puzzle. It is perfectly possible to create various layouts for the "stages" of the Cappers, but it is very difficult to envisage what kind of a Harrowing of Hell they performed. In addition to this there is the large amount paid to Pilate each year (3s 8d, rising to 4s 4d) and the still unexplained leather balls supplied to him. Whatever is happening here it must surely mean that the pageant was dominated by a Pilate "act," perhaps to the detriment of other parts of the pageant, in particular the Harrowing. The Coventry Cappers' evidence seems to me important because it suggests a situation that does not appear in the surviving texts—and one which is again dictated by theatrical demands.

It should also be noted with regard to the Cappers that they did possess a hell mouth. In 1543 they spent 2d on mending it and 3d on painting it.[15] In the following year it was again painted, together with a number of other items, for a total of 16d.[16] In 1568, over twenty years later, it was made new at a cost of 21d.[17] None of these transactions suggests an elaborate stage property— 21d for making hell mouth new, especially, looks small when compared with the 2s 4d spent on "makynge and coloringe the ij myters" in the same year. The fact that there is no other mention of hell mouth in the forty-five years of pageant activity covered by the Cappers' accounts supports this. The hell mouth finally appears in the 1591 inventory. It is kept in the underchamber of the craft along with various costumes, masks, curtains, banners, and props. Nothing appears to be very large. It is difficult to square the familiar Harrowing of Hell with its battles, tumbling gates, escaping souls, and transcendent spirit with all this.

The Last Judgment. In turning to the Last Judgment pageant we come to a very much more familiar area and to one very much better documented. There are three surviving pageants: York, Towneley (in this case better treated as a separate pageant even though in part identical with York), and Chester. There are the extensive records of the Mercers' company in York, which was responsible for the York Doomsday Play,[18] and the extensive Drapers' records from Coventry, which also relate to a Judgment pageant.

We thus have four pageants for which there is some evidence. The York pageant, performed by the Mercers, has a complete late fifteenth-century text with a very few stage directions, none relating to hell: a full set of accounts stretching with gaps over the whole period of the play but, as far as the pageant is concerned, giving primary evidence from 1433 until 1526. The Chester pageant, performed by the Weavers, has complete text (late sixteenth-century) with a number of stage directions, but no records. Towneley has a text (?early sixteenth-century) with the beginning missing, minimal stage directions, and no records. Coventry has no text, but the records of the Drapers, who performed the pageant, certainly exist from 1561 and probably from 1539.[19] The evidence from York is, therefore, the only set based on text *and* records and the only strictly medieval evidence which exists.

A good deal of miscellaneous information about the staging of the Last Judgment can be gleaned from the two sets of records. The York Mercers in 1433 have a pageant with an elaborately decorated heaven made of iron containing a raising mechanism. It is closed off at the back with colorful curtaining and adorned with angels. The only information about hell is unfortunately brief and uninformative—"helle mouthe."[20] In 1463 one wagon becomes two with the addition of the "now [new] pagond yat was mayd for ye sallys [souls] to ryse owt of."[21] Then in 1501–07 the main wagon was scrapped and a new one made under the direction of the noted York carver Thomas Drawswerd.[22] From Coventry the information is of a very varied kind. Apart from cast lists and payments, there is evidence for music, props, costumes, face paint, machinery, and staging business, some of which relates directly to the presentation of hell.

The actions of the pageants for which texts survive are best shown in the comparative chart included here on pages 170–71.

COMPARATIVE CHART OF THE ACTIONS
OF THE THREE SURVIVING TEXTS
OF LAST JUDGMENT PAGEANTS

Chester		York		Towneley	
GOD's solo speech	24	GOD's solo speech (tells angels to divide souls to right and left)	80	?	
ANGELS (2) [Angels blow trumpets; all dead arise]	16	ANGELS (2)	16	?	
SAVED SOULS (4) individually designated	132	GOOD SOULS (2)	16	?	
DAMNED SOULS (6) individually designated	184	EVIL SOULS (2)	56	EVIL SOULS (4)	72
		ANGEL (+1) divides souls right and left	8	ANGEL divides souls right and left	8
[Jesus descends, in cloud if possible; Instruments of Passion shown]		GOD's descent + APOSTLES (2)	29 11	JESUS' descent	8
		[To Judgment seat with angels' singing]			
		DEVILS (3)	12	DEVILS (3)	297

Chester		York		Towneley	
JESUS' address [Blood comes from side]	80	GOD's address	48	*JESUS' address* [Shows wounds]	48
SAVED SOULS	16				
Judgment of SAVED	48	Judgment of GOOD	40	*Judgment of GOOD*	40
ANGELS [Angels sing as they pick out saved souls]	8				
DEVILS (2)	96				
Judgment of DAMNED	72	Judgment of EVIL	48	*Judgment of EVIL*	50
		GOOD welcomed	4	*GOOD welcomed*	4
		EVIL dismissed	4	*EVIL dismissed*	4
DEVILS [Devils carry off damned]	32			DEVILS	81
EVANGELISTS	32	GOD's conclusion	8	Conclusion of GOOD SOUL	8
		[Make an end with music of angels passing from place to place]			

(Characters' names are in capitals, stage directions are in square brackets. Where Towneley overlaps with York the action is in italic.)

These brief summaries demonstrate that the pageants contain considerable differences. Looked at in terms of the spoken word, Chester is dominated by the souls (348 lines out of 708), York by God (245 out of 380), and Towneley by the devils (378 out of 620). I am not suggesting that speech is everything in a play, however, and this needs to be weighed against spectacle and simple presence. When looked at in this way, God, at Chester, acquires more prominence, not only opening and controlling the pageant but also being the center of the only spectacular moments, the descent "in the clouds if it may be," and the letting of blood, while the devils become even less significant, apparently not even appearing until after line 508. Their prominence is also to some extent affected by where they come from and where they go to. Without any record evidence it is impossible to prove the existence of a hell. The late banns state that each pageant was provided with a carriage.[23] Since God's position as Judge is essential to the pageant, it seems certain that the Weaver's carriage contained a heaven and a place for the Judgment. It perhaps seems impossible to us that there should not also be a hell to receive the damned after Judgment, but there is no *theatrical* reason why the devils at Chester should not have made use of the natural terrain of the streets. In the Harrowing of Hell, Enoch and Elijah and the Saved Thief should be, according to the *Gospel of Nicodemus*, in paradise already when they meet the souls released from hell, but the meetings in Chester surely take place in some unspecified location on the way. Similarly, in the Judgment there is no theatrical reason for the existence of a paradise for the souls, and if the existence of paradise in uncertain, that of hell is doubly so. The devils *exportabunt eos* ("carry them off"). Few things are more effective in a darkening street than figures moving away slowly and orderedly led by angels and in the other direction figures at random trying to escape from pursuing devils.

It may seem to be working against the words of the text to claim that there is no paradise in the Chester Judgment play. God tells his angels to divide the saved from the damned and "bringe them unto blysse./ On my right hand they shall be sett" (ll. 496–97), and the first angel replies, "Lord, we shall never blynne [cease]/ tyll we have brought them blys within." (ll. 501–02). It seems likely that the angels pick out the saved and lead them individually, singing as they come and go, up to the wagon. But this is not paradise, only *in aere prope terram* ("in the air near earth," l. 356*sd*), and the journey to paradise where Christ will be already sitting is yet to come. Or to look at it another way, it is the opposite of Marlowe's Mephostophilis' situation: to be near where God is, is to be in paradise. It seems to me very possible that there was no visible paradise in the Chester pageant.

The situation in York is clearly different. The existence of a "helle mouthe" is proved by the 1433 indenture. But it is interesting that there is no further mention of it until the 1526 list—if, that is, it is to be equated with the "hell dure" that occurs there.[24] That there is no reference does not prove that it was out of use, but at the same time the introduction of the souls' pageant in 1463[25] could have changed the layout of the staging and in turn altered the form that the hell mouth took. I have suggested elsewhere that it could have been attached to the front of the wagon.[26] This still seems to me to be possible, though it is also possible that it was an entirely separate structure. Certainly if the souls' pageant was placed immediately in front of the wagon, the hell mouth must have been elsewhere. I must say I find it much more odd, if it was a separate structure, that there is no mention of it at all in nearly a hundred years, and also that it should at the last be called "hell dure." The rest of the wording of the 1526 list is very prosaic, and it may be that "hell dure" means what it says. In which case it may be all that was left of a once more elaborate structure, now out of use, or, on the other hand, that it was the form that hell took then as an adjunct to the main pageant wagon. The 1526 list contains no reference to the wagon itself, however, and the argument could be made that the hell mouth was a similarly large item excluded from the list by its size.

In relation to the text of the pageant, the devils play a very small part indeed. Attempts to give them a larger part seem to me often to be merely distracting. There is no doubt that the pageant is dominated by God in words and spectacle. The elaboration of the heavens in the 1433 indenture merely underlines the space devoted to God in the text.

Little can be said about Towneley. It will be apparent from the summary chart that the pageant is overwhelmed by the devils. There is no proof that they enter from hell at the beginning, and no sense that they enter hell mouth at the end. As with Chester the street seems as likely a destination for all the souls as any stage location. This is borne out in a way by the ending of the Good Soul, "Therfor full boldly may we syng/ On oure way as we trus [go];/ Make we all myrth and louyng [praise]/ With te deum laudamus" (ll. 617–20). How the devils take over from God is shown by the way in which the York text used by Towneley is transformed. In York at line 179 God makes known his intention of descending to earth to judge mankind. He summons his apostles and at line 216 leads them to the judgment seat. The devils speak for the first time (12 lines), and then God resumes with his final address to man at line 229. In Towneley Jesus' announcement of his descent to earth (York, l. 179; Towneley l. 83) is not followed by the summoning of the apostles, who play no part in this pageant, but instead, at the end of the stanza, by 297 lines of devils' speeches. Jesus' final address, which in York begins fifty lines after the announcing of his descent, in Towneley follows 304 lines later (York, l. 229, Towneley, l. 386). Such is the presence of the devils that there seems to be no need of a hell.

The final Last Judgment pageant to be examined is that of the Drapers of Coventry. Like the Cappers' Harrowing of Hell, though not for the same reasons, this presents a rather different picture from those of Chester, York, and Towneley. Its well-known specialty is the burning world, and this certainly must have dictated a theatrical iconography of a very individual kind,[27] but there are a number of other recurrent items in the Drapers' accounts—hell mouth, a "wynde," and an earthquake—which add further details to an impression of the staging. The first appearance of the burning world is in [1558], but the hell mouth recurs with considerable regularity from [1538], together with the "wynde" or windlass from [1539],[28] and presumably represents an earlier stage of the pageant's development. From [1558], in addition to worlds, there is the earthquake, "the yorthe quake." Unlike the Cappers' pageant, there is no sign of an additional scaffold or even a forepart to the pageant. The pageant involves a trumpeter (to start with, earning as much as God and occasionally more), presumably for the playing of the last trump, regals, and singing men, presumably for the music of heaven, from 1561 onwards,[29] as well as the expected elements like the three white and three black souls (their coats are mentioned in [1538]), three demons, four angels, three Patriarchs, and God, all from [1539]. Only the two spirits or "wormes of Conscyence" and the prologue are added later. References to hell mouth (or hell head) and the "wynde" are frequently to "kepying" them—that is, looking after, being in charge of, or operating them. It is the "wynde" that is problematic. What is it used for? It could be for a descent by God to the Judgment, it could be for hoisting the worlds onto their decorated "pen" or pin for their spectacular burning,[30] or it could be for operating the jaws of hell. Quite frequently, though not by any means invariably, "kepying the wynde" and "kepying hell mowth" occur together or next to each other.[31] This may mean no more than that the same person was responsible for both—though that, taken a step further, might imply that the two jobs were close enough together to be done by a single person. The other collocation is keeping hell mouth and setting the worlds on fire, which implies probably that both involved the theatrical use of fire.[32] In relation to the presentation of hell two possibilities emerge, neither canceling the other out, that hell mouth had moving jaws and that it spouted fire and smoke. Figs. M and N are an indication of a possible portable hell mouth with moving jaws.

If we can use wages in the absence of text as some indication of importance of role, then like York the pageant is dominated by God. With wages at their highest, God receives 3s 4d (his wages never change), the devils and the souls 1s 8d each, the worms 9d, and the Patriarchs and angels 6d. In the earliest records the white souls receive 6d each, the black 8d, and the devils 1s, a sign, perhaps, that over the years the depiction of the saving and damning had changed. The introduction of the "worms," too, suggests greater play with the souls, since they must be the inward accusers of man drawn ultimately from Innocent's *De Contemptu Mundi*.[33] The rise in the wages of devils and souls and the addition of the worms of conscience taken with the fixed wage of God perhaps suggest a shift in their relative importance in the pageant.

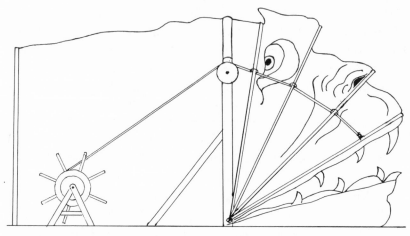

M. Coventry Last Judgment. A "transparent" view of a portable hell mouth showing the "wynde" and raising mechanism.

N (below). The same hell mouth but with jaw opened.

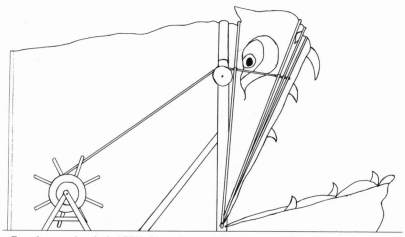

Based on a sketch (c.1700) for a dragon in the National Museum, Stockholm, Tessin Coll., S7, fol. 218, reproduced in Bamber Gascoigne, *World Theatre: An Illustrated History* (Boston, 1968), p. 207.

When we put all this together we again have an iconography which is theatrically determined. The burning worlds, as a nighttime culmination of the whole Corpus Christi play, is obviously effective. So too are the fires of hell and the moving jaws, letting out hairy devils and presumably smoke (and perhaps flame), and taking in and holding damned souls—theatrically damned, that is, black in costume (coats and hose) and face. What is very difficult to conceive is that this all took place on a single pageant wagon.

I have looked up to now at what seem to me to be some of the implications for the presentation of hell in the texts and records which survive for the English cycle pageants. This makes up what I have called the "theatrical iconography." It will be clear by now that by that phrase I do not mean what might simply be called the scenic design, where theater may well have many elements in common with painting and sculpture, but the whole presentation of an episode in words, costume, movement, and sound and visual effects. One aspect of the theatrical iconography that I have not really touched on at all is the natural setting of the city street. The iconography of a pageant is obviously affected by the kind of context within which it is performed, and I should like finally to look at just one element of that background.

Accepting Margaret Dorrell's calculations as a working basis,[34] the Harrowing of Hell pageant in York would have been in performance roughly between three o'clock in the afternoon and ten in the evening of Corpus Christi day. In the course of this the wagon would start in a roughly southwest-northeast alignment in Micklegate, swing 90 degrees to roughly southeast-northwest at the Spurriergate end of Coney Street; swing almost back to southwest-northeast at the beginning of Stonegate and roughly round to northwest-southeast at Petergate, ending at northeast-southwest on the Pavement. During this time the sun will have moved from high in the sky and slightly to the west of south at the beginning, to low in the sky and in the west by the end, and the light will have changed from broad daylight to (with luck) a bright twilight (see fig. O).[35]

Taking the earliest (21 May) and the latest (24 June) for Corpus Christi day,[36] the sun would set always during the performance

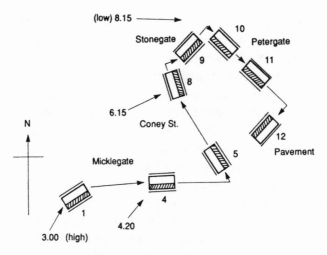

O (a). Position of the Harrowing pageant wagon in York in relation to the sun: relation of the sun and "side-on" pageant wagon.

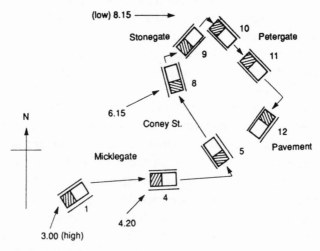

O (b). Position of the Harrowing pageant wagon in York in relation to the sun: relation of the sun and "end-on" pageant wagon.

at the tenth station in Petergate. Whether the performance was "end-on" or "side-on," the wagon's relation to direct light would change radically in the course of the twelve performances. Furthermore, by the last three performances the light might, depending on the weather conditions, need artificial boosting, particularly in Petergate which was relatively narrow. The extent to which direct sunlight could be used at all would depend on the orientation of the wagon, the nature of the superstructure, the width of the street, and the height of the buildings lining the route.

My sketches are an attempt to give some idea of where the sun would be coming from during the performance of the Harrowing of Hell at York. The place were the sun would be of most use is probably in Micklegate, especially for reflecting back into the interior of the wagon whether playing on "side-on" or "end-on." The sun could have provided a particular effect before the Common Hall gates (Station 8), where it would probably have been shining directly into a "side-on" wagon, but the buildings at the entrance to the Common Hall lane might well have got in the way. In Stonegate, side-lighting is a likelihood for a "side-on" pageant, and for both "side-on" and "end-on." The sun could have provided a particular effect before the Common Hall gates (Station 8), where it would probably have been shining directly into a "side-on" wagon, but the buildings at the entrance to the Common Hall might well have got in the way. In Stonegate, side-lighting is a likelihood for a "side-on" pageant, and for both "side-on" and "end-on" it might, as in Micklegate, have been possible to reflect sunlight onto the inner part. Thereafter artificial lighting of some kind must have been used for "interior" scenes. Meg Twycross' "end-on" Doomsday pageant (fig. 23) of 1988, playing at the Minster Gates (Station 10) at about eight-thirty in the evening (i.e., 19.30 hours GMT) on a dullish day in early July, was quite dark underneath the roof though on top it was still reasonably well lighted.[37]

It may not immediately seem that this can by any stretch of the imagination be called iconographic variation, but its effects might well be. An enclosed pageant wagon with souls behind a netted curtain or simply within a box superstructure is, when the sun has set, in darkness. The necessity of the appearance to the souls of the redeeming light means either the lighting of torches (or of fireworks) within the pageant wagon—a procedure involving some considerable danger—or the reflection of a light, again torches or fireworks, into hell by means of a polished reflector.[38] Both these devices would affect the iconography of the scene. If the torches were used on the wagon they would almost certainly be visible sources of light within the main focus of the scene, in which case they might seem more like the fires of hell than the redeeming light of Christ. If they were behind some translucent screen at the back they might give the right effect but would inevitably split the focus of the scene into two, since the source of the light would be seen as part of the action, the sign of the approach of Christ, and instead of a simple scene in hell there would be a double one. In a way this split focus already exists in York-Towneley since Christ's introductory speech must be from outside hell, and the projected light would inevitably be seen as part of Christ's presence. This kind of double scene is not by any means unknown in pictorial versions. The Brueghel-Cock engraving has Christ's approach and hell as separate entities,[39] but here they are within the same focus. The street performance requires a separation, which further affects the iconography of the scene.

The changing patterns of light are just one part of the changing street background of the pageant. The background of buildings affects scale. A picture controls its own scale, a pageant is to some extent within the scale of the buildings before which it is performed—especially if, as seems to be the case in Chester, the buildings are used for some of the action.[40] The iconography is not therefore self-contained. There is also the effect of the everyday context. No medieval artist goes as far as the plays must inevitably go in placing the biblical story in the everyday life of the audience. No artist can, since the background of the pageant *is* the everyday world—transformed, maybe, by decoration and by receiving the transcendental into its midst, but still the world into which all must return in the morning.

David Bevington and Pamela Sheingorn, in their interesting article on the relationship between the visual arts and drama in the presentation of the Last Judgment, say that despite differences "a reading of Corpus Christi plays of Judgment in visual terms yields extensive and detailed resemblances in both iconography and compositional methods between dramatic conventions and those found in the pictorial arts."[41] In a way, I agree. It would be foolish not to look for ways of visualizing the pageants in the contemporary visual arts. I feel quite certain that the selection of elements for presenting the Harrowing or the Judgment pictorially would be similar to the selection of elements for a pageant on the same subjects. As I have tried to show, however, there are such fundamental differences between the two presentations that it is dangerous to assume that what we see in the surviving visual arts is, generally speaking, what we would have seen when attending a performance in the late Middle Ages. Even a still photograph of a modern production is in a way a lie about what was perceived at the moment of performance. It is not that one is sequential and one is not, or that one is spoken and one is not, but the ways of perceiving are different. Christ in the upper part of a painting of the Judgment is utterly different from Christ portrayed by a human actor towering over you on the roof of a pageant wagon in a city street. The latter is different also from Christ in a Doom over a chancel arch. It is not the height but the presence of the human actor that transforms the effect. In one sense it is the uncertainty, the lack of fixity, in this case, the precariousness, even. There is a tendency to see the pageants through the spectacles of medieval pictorial art. Again, obviously, the pictorial presentation of a scene must be a guide and an inspiration, and the more detailed information that we can gather about local presentation of scenes the better, but it must also be possible to reject it. If Christ at the Judgment is never pictured with a golden face, if the souls are never pictured black and white, then it is equally possible that other elements of the iconography of the theater are different from those of painting and sculpture.[42]

NOTES

1. I am using the terms 'cycle' and 'cycle plays' as convenient labels for the processionally staged York, Chester, and Coventry plays. I have also included Towneley because both the pageants under discussion are derived from York, but it

is a doubtful partner here because of the uncertainty about its staging. N-town is omitted because though it has elements of the cycle in it (it is in part a series of pageants) it is written for fixed staging.

2. See, however, Clifford Davidson and Nona Mason, "Staging the York *Creation, and Fall of Lucifer,*" *Theatre Survey,* 17 (1976), 162–78.

3. Pamela Sheingorn's paper in this volume has treated the traditional hell mouth as it appeared in the pictorial art of the Middle Ages in the Harrowing and Last Judgment scenes.

4. Pamela Sheingorn and David Bevington in their discussion of the Last Judgment use similar generalized pictorial versions, or rather individual pictures as models for differing approaches ("'Alle This Was Token Domysday to Drede': Visual Signs of Last Judgment in the Corpus Christi Cycles and in Late Gothic Art," in *Homo, Memento Finis: The Iconography of Just Judgment in Medieval Art and Drama,* Early Drama, Art, and Drama, Monograph Ser., 6 [Kalamazoo: Medieval Institute Publications, 1985], pp. 121–45). A glance at a collection of pictorial images, such as the illustrations of the Harrowing in Gertrud Schiller, *Ikonographie der christlichen Kunst* (Gütersloh: Gerd Mohn, 1971), III, Pls. 158–72, reveals just how varied even a collection of a relatively limited period can be.

5. References in my text are to *The Chester Mystery Cycle,* ed. R. M. Lumiansky and David Mills, EETS, s.s. 3, 9 (London, 1974–86); *The Towneley Plays,* ed. George England and Alfred W. Pollard, EETS, e.s. 71 (London, 1897); *The York Plays,* ed. Richard Beadle (London: Edward Arnold, 1982).

6. Though not a common pictorial feature, light is used in the restored wall painting of the Harrowing in the North Yorkshire church of Pickering where a sun with its beams appears behind Christ's head. On light in this scene in the York Harrowing, see also Clifford Davidson, *From Creation to Doom* (New York: AMS Press, 1984), pp. 136–37.

7. *Evangelia Apocrypha,* ed. Constantinus Tischendorff (Leipzig: 1853), p. 370; *Apocryphal Gospels: Acts and Revelations,* trans. Alexander Walker, Ante-Nicene Christian Library, 16 (Edinburgh, 1890), p. 199.

8. I have quoted but slightly adapted the translation of this stage direction from *The Staging of Religious Drama in Europe in the Later Middle Ages,* ed. Peter Meredith and John E. Tailby, Early Drama, Art, and Music, Monograph Ser., 4 (Kalamazoo:

Medieval Institute Publications, 1983), p. 91; for the original text of the stage direction, see p. 277.

9. Ibid., p. 91. For a description of the kind of technology that would focus light, see Philip Butterworth's paper in the present book, pp. 72–78, above.

10. The wagon in my sketch is roughly 17′ by 7′6″ and about 18′ high, perhaps rather large for Chester streets but not impossibly so. John Marshall calculates a size of 12′ by 7′6″ and 12′ high before any additional superstructure is added, but draws attention to the imprecise nature of the evidence. The narrowest point of the pageant route is only 8 feet. See John Marshall, "'The manner of these playes': The Chester Pageant Carriages and the Places Where They Played," in *Staging the Chester Cycle*, ed. David Mills, Leeds Texts and Monographs, n.s. 9 (Leeds, 1985), pp. 34, 41.

11. *Coventry*, ed. R. W. Ingram, Records of Early English Drama (Toronto: Univ. of Toronto Press, 1981), p. 162 and *passim*.

12. Glynne Wickham, *Early English Stages, 1300 to 1660* (London: Routledge and Kegan Paul, 1959), I, 173.

13. *The Passion Play from the N. town Manuscript*, ed. Peter Meredith (London: Longman, 1990), pp. 140–41.

14. *Coventry*, ed. Ingram, p. 240.

15. Ibid., p. 163.

16. Ibid., p. 167.

17. Ibid., p. 245.

18. For the records, see *York*, ed. Alexandra F. Johnston and Margaret Rogerson, Records of Early English Drama (Toronto: Univ. of Toronto Press, 1979); they are discussed, particularly in relation to the 1433 indenture, by the same authors in "The Doomsday Pageant of the York Mercers, 1433," *Leeds Studies in English*, n.s. 5 (1971), 29–34, and "The York Mercers and Their Pageant of Doomsday, 1433–1526," *Leeds Studies in English*, n.s. 6 (1972), 10–35; see also Peter Meredith, "The Development of the York Mercers' Pageant Waggon," *Medieval English Theatre*, 1 (1979), 5–18.

19. See *Coventry*, ed. Ingram, Appendix 2, pp. 455–81, for the complex situation regarding the undated accounts. I have placed all the dates given by Ingram for these accounts in square brackets. Ingram also discusses the accounts and the pageant in "'Pleyng geire accustumed belongyng & necessarie': Guild Records and Pageant Production at Coventry," in *Proceedings of the First Colloquium*, ed. JoAnna Dutka (Toronto: Records of Early English Drama, 1979), pp. 60–92.

20. *York*, ed. Johnston and Rogerson, I, 55–56.

21. Ibid., I, 95–96.

22. Ibid., I, 241–42.

23. F. M. Salter and W. W. Greg, *The Trial and Flagellation with Other Studies in the Chester Cycle*, Malone Soc. Studies (Oxford, 1935), p. 151: "ffor every pagiante a Cariage provided with all" (l. 132).

24. *York*, ed. Johnston and Rogerson, I, 55–56, 241–42.

25. Ibid., I, 95–96.

26. Meredith, "The Development of the York Mercers' Waggon," pp. 10, 14.

27. For a discussion of the Drapers' pageant in relation to local pictorial representations, see Clifford Davidson, "The Lost Coventry Drapers' Play of Doomsday and Its Iconographic Context," *Leeds Studies in English*, n.s. 17 (1986), pp. 141–58.

28. *Coventry*, ed. Ingram, pp. 465–66, 478.

29. The records dated 1561 appear in ibid., p. 217; however, those dated [1560] on pp. 480–81 are the same, apart from some differences in wording, and clearly relate to the 1561 performance.

30. See ibid., p. 242: "Itm pd for Cullern [coloring] apen [a pin] that beryth The worlds . . ." (Drapers' Accounts, 1567).

31. See ibid. for the Coventry Drapers' Accounts for 1561 (p. 217), 1563 (p. 224), 1567 (p. 242), 1571 (p. 257), and [1539] (p. 466), [1567] (p. 475), [1568] (p. 476), [1558] (p. 478), [1560] (p. 479), [1560] (p. 480).

32. It would be wrong to lay too much stress on the collocation of payments as evidence that the jobs to which they refer were combined. The 1561 accounts (ibid., p. 217), for example, have "Itm pd for kepyng of the wynde and of hell mowth xvj," while the copy of the same accounts on pp. 480–81 has "pd for kepyng the wynde viijd" and "pd for kepyng hell mowthe viij." The two have obviously been combined in what was probably a fair copy of draft accounts, and may well have been quite separate activities. See also, however, the comments of Philip Butterworth in his paper in the present volume.

33. "vermis conscientiae tripliciter lacerabit," *De miseria condicionis humanae* 3.2; the reference is taken from *The Riverside Chaucer*, ed. Larry Benson (Boston: Houghton Mifflin, 1988), note to the Physician's Tale, ll. 277–86, on p. 904.

34. Margaret Dorrell (now Rogerson), "Two Studies of the York Corpus Christi Play," *Leeds Studies in English*, n.s. 6 (1972), 77–111. The timing charts are on pp. 102–07, and the times of the Harrowing on p. 106. Though I would not wholly accept these timings, they do seem to me to provide a reasonable basis for discussing this element of staging.

35. The direction in which the pageant faces, whether "side-on" or "end-on," undergoes a 180 degree turn in the course of performances, from facing at first roughly west ("side-on") or north ("end-on"), through south or west, to facing roughly east or south.

36. The possible dates of Corpus Christi day are here given as they are found in C. R. Cheney, *Handbook of Dates* (London: Royal Historical Society, 1970), pp. 84–155. They are often given as 23 May–24 June; see, for example, Wickham, *Early English Stages*, I, 139, and Mills, *Staging the Chester Cycle*, p. 3. For the calculations of the time of sunset given below, I have added ten days to the present date to make up, relatively, for the changes in the calendar effected in 1752; see Cheney, *Handbook*, p. 10.

37. No full account of this exciting experimental production has, as far as I know, been published. Four pageants were performed—the Death, Assumption, and Coronation of Mary, and the Last Judgment—as a pendant to the York Festival of 1988 at three stations in Petergate: Minster Gates, Goodramgate head, and the beginning of Colliergate. All pageants were performed "end-on."

38. As at Revello in 1483; see *The Staging of Religious Drama*, ed. Meredith and Tailby, p. 114. For a discussion of the technology involved, see the paper by Philip

Butterworth in the present volume.

39. Reproduced in Robert Hughes, *Heaven and Hell in Western Art* (New York: Stein and Day, 1968), p. 194. The globe of light in which Christ travels gives perhaps some visual notion of the "tent of fine gauze" used for Christ at the Harrowing of Hell at Mons in 1501; see *The Staging of Religious Drama*, p. 113.

40. See Peter Meredith, "'Make the asse to speake' or Staging the Chester Plays," in *Staging the Chester Cycle*, ed. Mills, p. 67.

41. Sheingorn and Bevington, "Alle This was Token Domysday to Drede," p. 139.

42. Meg Twycross has some interesting general comments on the relation between pictorial and dramatic presentation in her "Beyond the Picture Theory: Image and Activity in Medieval Drama," *Word and Image*, 4 (1988), 589–617; see esp. p. 617.

"It circumscribes us here":
Hell on the Renaissance Stage

Cecile Williamson Cary

From Marlowe to Middleton, hell on the English stage is more a metaphorical than a literal state. Protestant iconoclasm resulted in the suppression of actual representations of divine mysteries,[1] and some Protestant thinkers entertained non-literal conceptions of hell. Though Reformation drama could not and does not represent much in the way of literal hell, there are metaphoric connections to medieval art and drama; there are also some surprisingly literal hellish manifestations early in Renaissance dramatic development.

As has been noted long ago by numerous critics, sixteenth-century moralities changed the focus of the genre from mercy to judgment. This is so much the case that the plays of R. B., Ulpian Fulwell, W. Wager, and George Wapull have been christened "homiletic tragedy,"[2] and their similarities to Last Judgment cycle plays in such matters as horizontal symmetry of good and evil figures, vertical indication of final dispensation, and assorted specific details have been noted.[3] These Protestant allegories (not literal representations) are influenced in detail by the increased late medieval artistic interest in depicting the torments of the damned and in focus by the pessimistic implications of Calvinist thought.[4] Such works might be described as medieval Last Judgment plays in morality form, the mixture a result of iconoclasm and Calvinism.

In addition to medieval heritage and Protestant theology, Elizabethan drama was stereotypically influenced by the burgeoning classicism that has given the Renaissance its very name. To illustrate a dramatic possibility tangential to the general argument

187

of this paper, Thomas Kyd's *The Spanish Tragedy* gives an unusually complete description of hell, but one determined by the classical Hades:[5]

> Where bloudy furies shakes their whips of steele,
> And poor *Ixion* turnes an endles wheele;
> Where vsurers are choakt with melting golde,
> And wantons are embraste with ougly Snakes,
> And murderers grone with neuer killing wounds,
> And periurde wightes scalded in boyling lead,
> And all foule sinnes with torments ouerwhelmd.
> Twixt these two waies I trod the middle path,
> Which brought me to the fair Elisian greene,
> In midst whereof there standes a stately Towre,
> The walles of brasse, the gates of adamant.
> Heere finding *Pluto* with his *Proserpine*,
> I shewed my passport. . . . (I.i.65–77)

Though Andrea twice calls this place "hell" (I.i.27, 64), from a Christian perspective it is a very curious spot. The classical names and punishments for "sins" are almost *de rigueur* in Elizabethan Christian accounts of hell, but this passage makes no reference to an opposing heaven. Furthermore, at the play's end, Revenge proposes to Andrea: "haste we doune to meet thy freends and foes:/ To place thy freends in ease, the rest in woes;/ For heere, though death hath end their miserie,/ Ile there begin their endles Tragedie" (V.v.45–48). Although there is some sense of punishment for wrongdoing, the judge will be Andrea. Those he wishes to punish are wicked by any standard, but an unbiased observer might not deem Bel-Imperia worthy of "those ioyes/ That vestall Virgins and faire Queenes possesse" (IV.v.21–22). The afterlife shown in *The Spanish Tragedy* is as Virgilian as that in Dante's *Inferno*, but it is a Virgil little influenced by Christianity.

   The Spanish Tragedy, clearly classical in its description of hell, does not resemble either medieval or Renaissance conventions —unlike *Doctor Faustus*, which resembles both.[6] As this touchstone of the English drama depicts Good and Bad Angels exhort-

ing a medieval Everyman[7] and a soliloquizing Renaissance individ-
ualist—including both a medieval show of Seven Deadly Sins in
allegorical presentation[8] and the protagonist's enactment of these
same sins in scenes with dukes and duchesses, emperors and
popes, both a non-causal structure unified by thematic character
development[9] and a possible five-act classical structure complete
with chorus[10]—so also the Bad Angel paints a vivid medieval hell
while Mephostophilis delineates a Renaissance concept. When the
Good Angel exits, warning Faustus that "the jaws of hell" await
him (xix.115), and the hell mouth is shown to the audience, the
Bad Angel describes a hell where "the furies" are torturing the
damned by "tossing" them "On burning forks" and boiling them
"in lead:/ . . . live quarters broiling on the coals"; there is an
"ever-burning chair" for "o'er tortur'd souls to rest them in," and
gluttons "are fed with sops of flaming fire," who had "laugh'd to
see the poor starve at their gates" (xv.118–25). The hell mouth, the
submerged Dives-Lazarus allusion, the specific punishments for
the archetypal sin of gluttony—all are aspects of medieval hell
which have been traced at length in other papers in the present
volume.[11] For comparison, Hieronymus Bosch's well-known *Garden of Delights* pictures the damned as ending up "tortured,
crushed, impaled on an overturned table, or devoured by the bird-
headed specimen enthroned on his royal toilet,"[12] and his Last
Judgment shows them fried, spitted, and prepared for roasting.[13]
The play's conclusion also emphasizes a physical hell with squibs
going off as the devils come to get Faustus and with the scholars
finding "Faustus' limbs/ All torn asunder by the hand of death"
(xx.6–7).

The excruciating medieval detail is exacerbated by the Calvinist pessimism of Faustus' life—especially the last hour. Several
writers have found in Calvin (particularly his concept of the Reprobate) the key to Faustus' inability to accept (or even to see) the
promise of Grace in the Scripture he reads at the play's opening,
his tormented questioning of why he cannot be saved after signing
the pact, and his agonized vision of Christ's blood streaming in the
firmament, but none for him, at the end.[14] Thus Calvinist deter-

minism leads Doctor Faustus to a medieval hell.

However, Marlowe also presents quite another concept of damnation. After signing the Devil's deed, Faustus immediately asks Mephostophilis, "Tell me, where is the place that men call hell?" (v.117). The first lines of the answer are conventional enough: "Within the bowels of these elements,/ Where we are tortur'd and remain for ever" (ll. 120–21); but Mephostophilis continues:

> Hell hath no limits, nor is circumscrib'd
> In one self place, but where we are is hell,
> And where hell is, there must we ever be;
> And, to be short, when all the world dissolves
> And every creature shall be purify'd,
> All places shall be hell that is not heaven. (v.122–27)

In the face of this, Faustus maintains that "hell's a fable," for he is not "fond" enough "to imagine/ That after this life there is any pain" (ll. 134–35). And when Mephostophilis argues that he is "instance to prove the contrary,/ For . . . I am damned and now in hell," Faustus replies, "and this be hell, I'll willingly be damn'd" (ll. 137–38). Faustus is unusual in liking this world-as-hell—perhaps because he is not yet (or does not fully realize that he is) a lost soul. In contrast, Mephostophilis *does* know his true state.

Even before the signing, Faustus had asked Mephostophilis why it is, if he is damned, "that thou art out of hell." Mephostophilis answers:

> Why, this is hell, nor am I out of it.
> Think'st thou that I, who saw the face of God
> And tasted the eternal joys of heaven,
> Am not tormented with ten thousand hells
> In being depriv'd of everlasting bliss? (iii.78–82)

In these two passages, Marlowe reflects Renaissance speculation about non-literal notions of hell. Mephostophilis' definition presages Milton's unforgettable Satan: "Which way I fly is Hell; myself am

Hell" (*Paradise Lost* IV.75).[15] Earlier in Book IV, Milton's sense of the evil will providing its own hell is articulated as Satan wends his way to earth to wreak havoc on humanity:

> horror and doubt distract
> His troubl'd thoughts, and from the bottom stir
> The Hell within him, for within him Hell
> He brings, and round about him, nor from Hell
> One step no more than from himself can fly
> By change of place. . . . (ll. 18–23)

In *Doctrine and Discipline of Divorce* Milton explicitly compares the traditional with a less literal conception: "To banish for ever into a locall hell, whether in the aire or in the center, or in that uttermost and bottomlesse gulph of *Chaos*, deeper from holy blisse then the worlds diameter multiply'd, [the pagan authors] thought not a punishing so proper and proportionat for God to inflict, as to punish sinne with sinne."[16]

Other seventeenth-century writers make the same point, Sir Thomas Browne maintaining its superiority to literal notions:

> Surely though wee place Hell under earth, the Devils walke and pur-
> lue is about it: men speake too popularly who place it in those flam-
> ing mountains, which to grosser apprehensions represent Hell. The
> heart of man is the place the devill dwels in; I feele somtimes a hell
> within my selfe. . . . There are as many hels as *Anaxagoras* conceited
> worlds; there was more than one hell in *Magdalen*, when there were
> seven devils, for every devill is an hel unto himselfe: he holds
> enough of torture in his owne *ubi*, and needs not the misery of cir-
> cumference to afflict him. . . .[17]

Don Cameron Allen traces this non-literal view of hell as ubiqui-tous with the damned soul to John Brenz, a Lutheran heretic, and concludes: "For the orthodox, Heaven and Hell were on the map of the universe, and to think otherwise was a doctrine fathered by those who had the best reason to know better."[18] Despite Mephos-tophilis' memorable lines, *Doctor Faustus* ends with an orthodox hell; later Elizabethan dramatists find Mephostophilis' ubiquism to be useful, and Milton and Browne seem to approve it.

Yet a third concept of hell is mentioned by Milton—and perhaps by Marlowe as well. In the opening scene of *Paradise Lost*, Satan states that hell and heaven are states of mind: "The mind is its own place, and in itself/ Can make a Heav'n of Hell, a Hell of Heav'n" (I.254–55). This relativist notion can be found in Amaury de Bene, a thirteenth-century heretic often cited in seventeenth-century lists of atheists.[19] Satan's speech to his followers distantly echoes Hamlet's to Rosencrantz and Guildenstern upon their disagreeing with him about the world being a prison: "Why then, 'tis none to you; for there is nothing either good or bad, but thinking makes it so. To me it is a prison" (II.ii.249–51).[20] However, Hamlet's relativism, indebted as it is to Montaigne, is secularized and may well be considered distinct from the play's Christian referents—in this context a ghost walking in the "hell" of the staging and a prince dying with the iconographically traditional wish (in V.ii.360) that "flights of angels sing thee to thy rest." (Depictions of small naked souls angelically guided to their rest, an icon based on the Dives-Lazarus story, are common from the twelfth century through the Renaissance[21]). However medieval some of the play's allusions, Hamlet has a thoroughly Renaissance mind, torn between the primitive duty of revenge, Christian moral absolutes, and the "new Philosophy" which, according to John Donne's *Anatomie of the World*, "calls all in doubt"[22] (compare Horatio's "philosophy" [I.v.167], which did not allow for ghosts).

The idolatrous sense that the mind controls its environment as observed briefly in Hamlet and more fully in the Miltonic Satan's early statement finds dramatic presentation in Faustus' mental confusion as he views Helen of Troy: "Here will I dwell, for heaven be in these lips,/ And all is dross that is not Helena" (xviii.104–05). (Compare the somewhat similar confusion of the speaker of Shakespeare's Sonnet 129: "none knows well/ To shun the heaven that leads men to this hell.") But Faustus' words themselves reveal that Helena is hell just as Milton's Satan is in hell, for he will contradict himself later with his view of hell as ubiquitous with the evil soul. The soul divorced from God cannot make a heaven: like Milton's Satan and Marlowe's Mephostophilis, that individual *is* hell. The heretical relativist hell is useful mainly for irony: both Satan and Faustus are deceiving themselves—as are others who think they are in heaven while being led to hell. Of the three concepts of hell put forth in Marlowe and Milton—the traditional, the ubiquitous, and the relativist—the Elizabethan stage usually portrayed the second: the hell of the living person divorced from God.

Of course there are vestigial remnants of older traditions. The two most striking have already been discussed: the classical hell of *The Spanish Tragedy* and the grotesque Christian hell at the conclusion of *Doctor Faustus*. In addition, one must keep in mind that the stage itself was

> thoroughly symbolic. . . . The 'heavens' are represented by a canopy over the acting area. Beneath the stage is the locale of hell, which may be reached through trap doors over which may be placed a hell-mouth such as the one appearing in Henslowe's inventory of 1598/99. Between the heavens and hell . . . is middle earth, upon which all the significant action takes place. . . . This is the Globe, and the name . . . indicates that it is to be thought of as a kind of microcosmic reflection of the great globe itself.[23]

Given a stage of such possibilities—and the Rose and the Fortune are as microcosmic in structure if not quite as felicitously named as the Globe—the closing scene (V.v) of Marlowe's *Jew of Malta* would inescapably suggest the protagonist's descent to hell.[24] Barabas stands "*above*," a "*charge*" is sounded, a "*cable cut, a cauldron discovered*" (V.v.62*sd*), and Barabas dies as "the extremity of heat [begins]/ To pinch me with intolerable pangs" (ll. 86–87)—a device he had devised for others kills him. Not only are cauldrons frequent objects in the medieval scenery of hell, but damned sinners are frequently shown falling into them. The Hours of Cordier de Bignan in the Bodleian Library, for example, depicts unfortunates falling upside down into a hell cauldron.[25] Even more noteworthy, the surviving (though restored) early wall painting in the small church at Chaldon in Surrey shows in the scene of the torments of hell in the lower left another sinner falling upside down into a cauldron (fig. 20) and perhaps indicates by the very fact of its existence in an obscure English church the ubiquity of the icon. Although Marlowe shows Barabas' death, not his punishment afterwards, the scene visually recapitulates medieval pictures of sinners falling into hell.

Other physical details seem related to comic characters as in *Friar Bacon and Friar Bungay* when Miles rides to hell on a devil's back with the promise that he will be tapster there (Scene xv). The piggyback motif is common in the pictorial tradition; for example, a wonderfully elaborate scene from the London Hours shows a devil carrying off on his back five souls in a basket,[26] while painted glass in the west window at Fairford (fig. 15) also illustrates a demonic figure with a damned person carried piggyback toward hell. Yet another devil in the Fairford glass has a nude figure slung over his shoulders as he moves in the same direction.[27] Two mid-sixteenth-century moralities had devils carrying off Worldy Man (*Enough is as Good as a Feast*) and Nicholas Newfangle (*Like Will to Like*).[28] The comic possibilities (Miles threatens to use spurs) inherent in dramatizing the icon perhaps led to its ultimately comic use. A secularized version of this motif appears in *1 Henry IV*. Falstaff's carrying off of Hotspur has been interpreted with reference to Saturnalian rites as "getting rid of bad luck by comedy,"[29] but in the light of the iconographic and dramatic heritage, "that reverent Vice, that grey Iniquity . . . that old, white-bearded Sathan" (II.iv.453–54, 463) Falstaff may also be seen as hauling another lost soul to hell. As William Empson remarked, "Hotspur is the most attractive of Shakespeare's soldiers. . . . The double-plot method is carrying a fearful strain here."[30] The audience must switch perspective quickly, for Hotspur's death speech is barely mediated by Hal's two eulogies when Falstaff jumps up to bear the tragic figure comically away.

Although a piggyback duo might have been thought more appropriately comic than tragic, it may also be that putting traditional hellish motifs in comic scenes served the same function in iconoclastic dramaturgy as the inset scenes of the Last Judgment in Reformation painting. Such insets give perspective without falling into the perceived sin of representing mysteries of faith.[31] (If this insight is correct, Holbein's *Ambassadors* with its death's head inset may not be the best illustration for Stephen Greenblatt's discussion of the Catholic Thomas More.[32])

The piggyback motif is not alone among comic details suggesting universal perspective. Other such referents appear in the *Henriad*. The biblical Dives-Lazarus story (*Luke* 16.19–25) was theologically and iconographically important from the Middle Ages to the Renaissance and inescapably linked to Judgment by its description of Lazarus being carried away by the angels to Abraham's bosom, while Dives *sepultus est in inferno* ("was buried in hell").[33] The scene appeared on wall hangings decorating poorer houses in Shakespeare's England as indicated in Falstaff's description of his recruits: "slaves as ragged as Lazarus in the painted cloth, where the glutton's dogs lick'd his sores" (*1 Henry IV* IV.ii.25–26). If the poor "scarecrows" (l. 38) of recruits are like Lazarus, "blown Jack" (l. 49) must be Dives. In fact, as Christ rejects those who presumed they knew him ("I know you not whence ye are; departe from me, all ye workers of iniquitie" [*Luke* 13.27, *Geneva version*]), so the newly-crowned Hal rejects "surfeit-swell'd" Falstaff in *2 Henry IV*: "I know thee not, old man" (V.v.47, 50). The Lazarus story appears again when the Hostess states in *Henry V* that the dead Falstaff is "not in hell; he's in Arthur's bosom, if ever man went to Arthur's bosom" (II.iii.9–10). At the very least, such comic referents keep the perspective of an ultimate Judgment—however ambiguous—present to the audience.

In addition to comic intimations of Judgment, characters frequently turn their worlds into symbolic hells—sometimes comic ones like Shylock's in *The Merchant of Venice*. Jessica laments Gobbo's leaving Shylock's service: "I am sorry thou wilt leave my father so./ Our house is hell, and thou, a merry devil" (II.iii.1–2). Lancelot himself likened Shylock to "a kind of devil," indeed "the very devil incarnation" (II.ii.24, 27–28). The opposition of place in this play is suggestive: Portia's Belmont with its hospitality, music, moral tests, beauty, love, and wealth versus Shylock's sober, quiet, thrifty house.[34] However reminiscent of a morality this opposition of place and person may be, it is suggestion only. The real world of Venice may waver between Portia and Shylock, but ultimately even Portia's mercy is ambiguous, the ambiguity of this world.

Macbeth also presents a symbolic hell, in yet another comic scene. After Macbeth's murder of Duncan, the drunken porter pretends to be at hell gate. The staging of such a hell gate might recall the medieval hell mouth—also open to receive all who go the wrong way; indeed, the two concepts were frequently joined as in the twelfth-century English illumination in the Winchester Psalter which shows an angel locking the gate to hell mouth and bears the inscription, "Ici est enfers e li angels ki enferme les portes."[35] Macbeth's porter states, "But this place is too cold for hell. I'll devil-porter it no further" (II.iii.16–17). The line is worthy of Samuel Beckett's *Waiting for Godot* in which two clowns compare their torturous waiting to Christ's Passion with the balance in favor of the past where "they crucified quick."[36] Macbeth's actions turn his castle and his kingdom—once earthly paradises of procreation and harvest—to earthly hells where kings and children are murdered and trees cut for camouflage. But heaven and hell are in this case both on earth. This is not to say that the concept of reward or punishment in the afterlife is not operative. Macbeth's "eternal jewel" is given to the "common enemy of man" (III.i.67–68).

Another aspect of Shakespearean drama reminiscent of Last Judgment iconography is the not-infrequent inclusion of a list naming "some of all professions that go the primrose way to th' everlasting bonfire" (*Macbeth* II.iii.18–19). Medieval Dooms and hell-gates often give a visual sampling; the hell scene from the fifteenth-century London Hours (fol. 89ʳ) shows "Kings, nobles, cardinals, and monks . . . dispatched without mercy"—a friar and a naked, yet richly caped lady are prominently placed in the lower level.[37] Macbeth's porter lists a farmer, an equivocator, and an English tailor (the equivocator satirizing the Jesuit role in the Gunpowder Plot[38]).

Hamlet, in another comic scene, lists the first murderer, a politician, a courtier, a lawyer, and a great buyer of land

(V.i.75–112). Of course, Prince Hamlet with the skull of Yorick, King Hamlet's jester, is much concerned simply with death itself, but the *memento mori* has a religious purpose from the Middle Ages through the seventeenth century. (Consider the miniature of the ruler as *le-roi-mort* in the London Hours of René of Anjou—or John Donne sculpted in his shroud.[39] And death itself was considered a punishment for sin; it is no accident that the gravediggers "hold up Adam's profession" (V.i.31). Moreover, Hamlet's list is framed with Judgment references from the graves, which last "till doomsday" (V.i.59), to poor Ophelia, who should "in ground unsanctified been lodg'd/ Till the last trumpet" (V.i.229–30). Sounds in this scene, from the priest's mention of the final trumpet call to Laertes' prophecy that "a minist'ring angel shall my sister be/ When thou [the priest] liest howling" (ll. 241–42), also give an eternal perspective to Hamlet's list,[40] suspect in itself with its allusion to Cain (l. 77) and to a politician who "would circumvent God" (l. 79).

Yet a third list comes from a low comic scene in *Measure for Measure*. Pompey Bum likens the prison to his former bawdy house in their mutual occupants: Masters Rash, Caper, Three-pile, Dizzy, Deep-vow, Copper-spur, Starve-lackey, Drop-heir, Forthlight, Shoe-tie, Half-can, and some forty more, all "now 'for the Lord's sake'" (IV.iii.1–19). Prisons themselves imply earthly judgment and may foreshadow the Last Judgment and hell itself. An angel locking the door of hell is a typical medieval icon, as in the Winchester Psalter cited above;[41] an unusual variation in the Hours of Catherine of Cleves shows the Devil with a hell mouth and a prison grill abdomen.[42] The play's prison is very peculiar itself: a "reprobate" cannot there be executed until he be "fit," for to "transport him in the mind he is/ Were damnable" (IV.iii.68–69, 74). Perhaps here as in *Hamlet* "this harsh world" is itself the prison-hell from which to absent oneself—at least if one has drawn enough painful breaths in it (*Hamlet* V.ii.347–48). Of these three lists, the Porter's sinners are going to hell, Hamlet's are certainly dead and the context suggests damnation as well, and Pompey's have been judged fit for prison on this earth and had better "Look forward for the journey [they] shall go" (*Measure for Measure* IV.iii.58) to "prepare" themselves for the Last Judgment.

Lists of sinners sometimes appear in plays which are explicitly speculative about the afterlife. Although *Macbeth* seems orthodox in depicting Macbeth's and others' choices as leading to a hell on earth preceding eternal damnation, Claudio in *Measure for Measure* runs through various possibilities:

> Ay, but to die, and go we know not where;
> To lie in cold obstruction, and to rot;
> This sensible warm motion to become
> A kneaded clod; and the delighted spirit
> To bathe in fiery floods, or to reside
> In thrilling region of thick-ribbed ice;
> To be imprison'd in the viewless winds
> And blown with restless violence round about
> The pendant world; or to be worse than worst
> Of those that lawless and incertain thought
> Imagine howling—'tis too horrible! (III.i.117–27)

Medieval ideas of hell are present with the "howling," the "fiery floods," the ice, and the winds. But adding to Claudius' fear of physical death and spiritual torment is the fear of going "we know not where," the "dread of something after death,/ The undiscover'd country from whose bourn/ No traveller returns" which likewise puzzles Hamlet (III.i.77–79). The medieval remnants and the Renaissance doubts form characteristic Elizabethan mixtures.

In addition to the appearance of hell mouths, hell gates, and various symbolic hells, specific punishments frequently suggest a medieval hell. Consider Othello. As if he were in a morality, he is symbolically flanked by the "divine Desdemona" (II.i.73) and "that demi-devil" Iago (V.ii.301). After Desdemona's death he muses:

> . . . O ill-starr'd wench,
> Pale as thy smock! when we shall meet at compt,
> This look of thine will hurl my soul from heaven,
> And fiends will snatch at it.
>
>   . . .

Whip me, ye devils,
From the possession of this heavenly sight!
Blow me about in winds! roast me in sulfur!
Wash me in steep-down gulfs of liquid fire!
O Desdemon! Dead, Desdemon! dead!
(V.ii.272–75, 277–81)

The snatching fiends and whipping devils, the winds, the sulphur, and the liquid fire are all familiar concomitants of hell.[43] And alone of Shakespeare's plays, *Othello* ends with torture:

To you, Lord Governor,
Remains the censure of this hellish villain,
The time, the place, the torture, O, enforce it!
(V.ii.367–69)

But these accounts of hell and torture are offset by Othello's awareness that his imagination is superstitious—already implied earlier in this final scene by his relegation of Desdemona to hell for her denial that he was her murderer: "She's like a liar gone to burning hell: 'Twas I that kill'd her" (l. 129). His literalness is corrected by Emilia's "O, the more angel she,/ And you the blacker devil!" (ll. 130–31). Previously, Othello had been credulous in believing Iago and superstitious in his account of his mother's handkerchief with its supposed aphrodisiac charms—merely losing it would mean "perdition" (III.iv.55–68). Othello locates superstition in himself when he looks at Iago after "that viper" appears: "I look down towards his feet; but that's a fable./ If that thou be'st a devil, I cannot kill thee" (V.ii.286–87). Othello does indeed fail to kill Iago, but he does not draw the conclusion that Iago is therefore a devil; on the contrary: "I am not sorry neither, I'ld have thee live;/ For in my sense, 'tis happiness to die" (ll. 289–90). The most one can say is that *Othello* refers to heaven and hell, divinity and devil, but that these serve as reminders of eternity, not as present actualities, for Iago and Desdemona are human beings, however devilish and divine their respective actions.

The punishments of hell are also evident in *King Lear*. Claudio's fear of the howling associated with hell in *Measure for Measure* is echoed when Lear enters with the hanged Cordelia: "Howl, howl, howl!" (V.iii.258). The observers question, "Is this the promis'd end?" A more accurate response follows: "Or image of that horror" (ll. 264–65). The hellish punishment is here, for "he hates him/ That would upon the rack of this tough world/ Stretch him out longer" (ll. 314–15). This sentiment is reminiscent of Lear's earlier comment on being wakened by Cordelia:

> You do me wrong to take me out o' th' grave:
> Thou art a soul in bliss, but I am bound
> Upon a wheel of fire, that mine own tears
> Do scald like molten lead. (IV.vii.44–47)

The rack and the wheel of fire (reserved for the proud, as Clifford Davidson has shown elsewhere in the present volume) are traditionally assigned to hell's torments, but are here related to life on middle earth, for Lear—again like Claudio—is doubtful about the afterlife. Lear knows "when one is dead, and when one lives" (V.iii.261)—Cordelia may be alive, but Goneril and Regan are dead—he thinks (l. 293). What afterlife there is, if any there be, must be in accordance with that reality, but our attention is drawn forcefully to this moment in time, and we are asked to "Look there" and to "see" (ll. 311–12).

The focus on this world seems to be a constant. Huston Diehl has traced Judgment scenes from early to late Renaissance drama, focusing on *The Malcontent, Measure for Measure, The Atheist's Tragedy,* and *The Devil's Law Case* to conclude that "Protestant drama does not attempt to enact the final day of judgment, but rather to remind the audience of that anticipated day through visible signs from the natural world."[44] Her list could be considerably expanded. One thinks of the trial scene in *The Merchant of Venice* with its thematic opposition between Shylock and Portia, Old Law and New Law, Justice and Mercy—and then of the rather disappointing "mercy" meted out in the real world of slave-holding Venice where Christians teach Jews about revenge.

Curiously, mercantilism and realism in a play do not mitigate against the symbolism of its trial scenes. Thus Jonson's *Volpone* seems neo-classical and realistic in its professed aims and world, but its final scene inevitably suggests the Last Judgment with our "Renaissance Everyman"[45] brought to judgment by Celia (whose name means "heavenly") and Mosca (clearly related to the Lord of the Flies). This play also ends with emphasis on punishment: Mosca whipped and sentenced to slavery, Volpone imprisoned and shackled, Voltore exiled, Corbaccio confined to a monastery, and Corvino publicly humiliated—all in Volpone's words to experience "mortifying" (V.xii.125), presumably that mortification of the flesh considered a religious duty but here unwillingly undertaken. Though Jonson's Venice seems more realistic than Shakespeare's, *Volpone* has as much (if not more) of a morality play structure than *The Merchant of Venice*.

An eternal perspective, if not a morality structure, also seems to color Jacobean tragedy of fantastic intrigue in a decadent world. Consider Vindice's entrance with a skull in *The Revenger's Tragedy* and the use to which he puts the skull as revenger of his sister's honor. Or take the somewhat less obvious plays of John Webster—works such as *The White Devil* in which one prays at the burial of the dead:[46] *"But keep the wolf far thence, that's foe to men,/ For with his nails he'll dig them up agen"* (V.iv.103–04). A wolf is a traditional icon for death, as in the Hours of Catherine of Cleves miniature in which a tree grows from Adam's grave with a mouse entering the grave and a wolf gnawing a bone.[47] In fact, medieval works might show the damned turning into the beasts they had been in life; if my interpretation is correct, all those cast into the lake of fire in the Trinity Apocalypse (Cambridge, Trinity College MS. R.16.2, fol. 23ᵛ) are now beasts.[48] Similarly, Webster's Duke in *The Duchess of Malfi* (1614) had been a wolf before he turns into one—the development, ugly enough in a medieval miniature, becoming grotesque in the "real" world of psychology.[49] Nor is the eternal perspective forgotten. "When I go to hell, I mean to carry a bribe," states the mad Duke (V.ii.41–42). "Mercy upon me," muses Bosola when it is clear the "princely wits" have fled, "what a fatal judgement/ Hath fall'n upon this Ferdinand!" (V.ii.85–86). His brother the Cardinal meditates on a book shortly before his death: "I am puzzled in a question about hell;/ He says, in hell there's one material fire,/ And yet it shall not burn all men alike" (V.v.1–3). This book is very like the insets in Renaissance paintings. Set upon by revengers, the Cardinal asks Ferdinand: "Help me, I am your brother." "The devil!" cries crazed Ferdinand, "My brother fight upon the adverse party?" (V.v.51–52), and he gives the Cardinal and Bosola their death wounds, Bosola stabs him, and he dies, appropriately accounting the "world but a dog-kennel" (V.v.67). If the gloomy world itself has become such a "deep pit of darkness" in *The Duchess of Malfi* that "worthy minds" need not fear to leave it, there is "another voyage" still for the guilty (ll. 97–105).

The characters make a similar hell-on-earth in Middleton's *The Changeling*.[50] While in *The Duchess of Malfi* there is a chorus of madmen, here there is a comic sub-plot set in a madhouse. If the former chorus foreshadowed Ferdinand's lycanthropy, the pretended madmen contrast with the lustful compulsions of the "sane" De Flores and Beatrice-Joanna. If Ferdinand's incestuous desire for his sister leads to her murder and his madness, De Flores' obsession with Beatrice-Joanna and her enslavement to his murderous deeds done for her—and ultimately to his sexual power over her—lead to their exposure and deaths. Again, the suggestion of eternal patterns is kept alive even as psychological realism is stressed. When Beatrice-Joanna kneels to De Flores, it is clear she has mistaken her deity—she must "engender with a viper." In this play's last scene, De Flores admits that he had never been under any illusions: "I lov'd this woman in spite of her heart"; and he thanks "life for nothing/ But that pleasure" of having "coupled . . ./ At barley-brake; now we are left in hell" (V.iii.162–63, 165, 168–69). Alsemero, the innocent for whom the murders were done, newly cognizant of the truth, had told them to "rehearse again/ Your scene of lust, that you may be perfect/ When you shall come to act it to the black audience/ Where howls and gnashings shall be music to you" (ll. 114–17). When De Flores admits that he and

Beatrice-Joanna are in hell, her shocked father states, "We are all there, it circumscribes us here" (1. 164). Again, not only is the present the "image of that horror," but the audience is reminded of the eternal perspective on the action.

In Elizabethan and Jacobean drama there are some very close parallels to medieval drama and art: souls carried off piggyback to hell, Good and Bad Angels (not to mention the secularized version of Good and Bad Counselors of *Gorbuduc* and *Cambises*), hell mouths and cauldrons. But the general movement—for intellectual and theological as well as dramatic reasons—is toward the dramatization of this world while keeping the next world present in comic insets (Miles being carried off by a devil), real world resonances (trial scenes), suggestive arrangements of characters (Othello flanked by Desdemona and Iago), and linguistic analogy (Celia is heavenly, De Flores is a viper, the world is a pit of darkness). The purpose of the Elizabethan stage was to "hold as 'twere a mirror up to nature: to show virtue her feature, scorn her own image, and the very age and body of the time his form and pressure" (*Hamlet* III.ii.22–24). Its hell and heaven are on earth and are made such by men's actions. De Flores' and Beatrice's actions make them live in hell; Cordelia's are "like a better way." Nonetheless, the suggestion of "something after death" remains an eternal backdrop to the dramatization of earthly time.

NOTES

1. See Harold C. Gardiner, *Mysteries' End: An Investigation of the Last Days of the Medieval Religious Stage* (New Haven: Yale Univ. Press, 1946), *passim*, and *Iconoclasm vs. Drama and Art*, ed. Clifford Davidson and Ann Eljenhom Nichols, Early Drama, Art, and Music, Monograph Ser., 11 (Kalamazoo: Medieval Institute Publications, 1988), *passim*.

2. David Bevington, *From* Mankind *to* Marlowe (Cambridge: Harvard Univ. Press, 1962), p. 161.

3. Huston Diehl, "'To put us in remembrance': The Protestant Transformation of

Images of Judgment," in *Homo, Memento Finis: The Iconography of Just Judgment in Medieval Art and Drama,* Early Drama, Art, and Music, Monograph Ser., 6 (Kalamazoo: Medieval Institute Publications, 1985), pp. 186–91.

4. See Clifford Davidson, "The Fate of the Damned in English Art and Drama," in this volume.

5. Quotations from *The Spanish Tragedy* in my text are from Thomas Kyd, *The Works,* ed. Frederick S. Boas, 2nd ed. (1955; rpt. Oxford: Clarendon Press, 1967).

6. Quotations from *Doctor Faustus* in my text are from Christopher Marlowe, *Doctor Faustus,* ed. John Jump, Revels Plays (London: Methuen, 1962).

7. See Leo Kirschbaum, ed., *The Plays of Christopher Marlowe* (Cleveland: World, 1962), p. 103.

8. Sherman Hawkins, "The Education of Faustus," *Studies in English Literature,* 6 (1966), 193–209.

9. Bevington, *From* Mankind *to* Marlowe, p. 259, provides a diagram relating *Doctor Faustus* to *psychomachia* drama.

10. G. K. Hunter, "Five-Act Structure in *Doctor Faustus,*" *Tulane Drama Review,* 8, No. 4 (Summer 1964), 77–91. On the question of causation in *Doctor Faustus,* cf. Clifford Davidson, "Doctor Faustus of Wittenberg," *Studies in Philology,* 59 (1962), 514–23.

11. See in particular Pamela Sheingorn's "'Who can open the doors of his face?': The Iconography of Hell Mouth," in the present volume.

12. Carl Linfert, *Hieronymus Bosch,* trans. Robert Erick Wolf (New York: Harry N. Abrams, n.d.), p. 114.

13. Ibid., p. 93. For further commentary on these paintings, see Walter Gibson, *Hieronymus Bosch* (New York: Praeger, 1973), pp. 49–99.

14. See Thomas Paul Cartelli, "Marlowe's Theater: The Limits of Possibility," unpublished Ph.D. diss. (Univ. of California at Santa Cruz, 1979), and Richard Waswo, "Damnation, Protestant Style: Macbeth, Faustus, and Christian Tragedy,"

Journal of Medieval and Renaissance Studies, 4 (1974), 63–99. For a different view, see Davidson, "Doctor Faustus of Wittenberg," pp. 514–23.

15. Quotations from *Paradise Lost* are from John Milton, *The Poems*, ed. Merritt Y. Hughes (New York: Odyssey Press, 1957).

16. John Milton, *Doctrine and Discipline of Divorce*, in *The Complete Prose Works*, II (New Haven: Yale Univ. Press, 1959), 294.

17. *Religio Medici* I.51, in Sir Thomas Browne, *The Prose*, ed. Norman J. Endicott (New York: W. W. Norton, 1967), pp. 59–60.

18. D. C. Allen, "*Paradise Lost*, I.254–55," *Modern Language Notes*, 71 (1956), 326.

19. Ibid., p. 325.

20. All citations to Shakespeare are to *The Riverside Shakespeare*, ed. G. Blakemore Evans *et al.* (Boston: Houghton Mifflin, 1974).

21. T. S. R. Boase, "King Death: Mortality, Judgment and Remembrance," in *The Flowering of the Middle Ages*, ed. Joan Evans (New York: Bonanza, 1985), pp. 187–91.

22. "The First Anniverary," l. 205, in John Donne, *The Poems*, ed. Herbert Grierson (London: Oxford Univ. Press, 1933).

23. Clifford Davidson, *The Primrose Way: A Study of Shakespeare's* Macbeth (Conesville, Iowa: John Westburg and Associates, 1970), p. 22.

24. Citations in my text to Christopher Marlowe, *The Jew of Malta*, are to the edition prepared by N. W. Bawcutt, Revels Plays (Baltimore: Johns Hopkins Univ. Press, 1978).

25. Bodleian Library, MS. Douce 62, fol. 95^r; for a reproduction of this illumination, see Robert G. Calkins, *Illuminated Books of the Middle Ages* (Ithaca: Cornell Univ. Press, 1983), Pl. 158.

26. British Library, Add. MS. 29,433, fol. 89^r; for a reproduction, see Calkins, *Illuminated Books*, Pl. 147, and for another example, see ibid., Pl. 128, an illumi-

nation in the margin of a page of the Breviary of Charles V (Bibliothèque Nationale, MS. lat. 1052, fol. 261ʳ).

27. See also Clifford Davidson, *Visualizing the Moral Life* (New York: AMS Press, 1989), fig. 18.

28. For these two examples, see Diehl, "To put us in remembrance," p. 188.

29. C. L. Barber, *Shakespeare's Festive Comedy* (Princeton: Princeton Univ. Press, 1959), pp. 205–12.

30. William Empson, *Some Versions of Pastoral* (Norfolk: James Laughlin, n.d.), p. 46.

31. Diehl, "To put us in remembrance," pp. 180–85.

32. Stephen Greenblatt, *Renaissance Self-Fashioning* (Chicago: Univ. of Chicago Press, 1980), pp. 18–27.

33. Boase, "King Death," pp. 187–88; also, for the Lazarus example from *1 Henry IV*, see ibid., p. 190.

34. Barber, *Shakespeare's Festive Comedy*, pp. 163–91, contrasts the world of Portia and Shylock but in a rather different context.

35. British Library MS. Cotton Nero C.IV, fol. 39ʳ; Francis Wormald, *The Winchester Psalter* (London: Harvey Miller and Medcalf, 1973), frontispiece and fig. 42. On combining the mouth and gates or doors of hell, see the paper by Sheingorn in the present volume.

36. Samuel Beckett, *Waiting for Godot* (London: Faber and Faber, 1956), p. 52.

37. Calkins, *Illuminated Books*, p. 261, fig. 147.

38. Frank L. Huntley, "*Macbeth* and the Background of Jesuitical Equivocation," *PMLA*, 79 (1964), 390–400, and Davidson, *The Primrose Way*, pp. 59–61.

39. British Library MS. Egerton 1070, fol. 53ʳ; see John Harthan, *The Book of Hours* (New York: Thomas Y. Crowell, 1977), Pl. 90. Hartham describes the likeness as "a three-quarter-length crowned skeleton" (p. 92). The sculpture of

John Donne in his shroud, which survived the Great Fire of 1666 that destroyed Old St. Paul's, can still be seen in St. Paul's Cathedral in London.

40. See Richard Rastall on "The Sounds of Hell" in this volume.

41. Wormald, *Winchester Psalter*, fig. 42; see also Calkins, *Illuminated Books*, p. 186.

42. John Plummer, *The Hours of Catherine of Cleves* (New York: George Braziller, 1966), Pl. 58.

43. Thomas Seiler's paper "Filth and Stench as Aspects of the Iconography of Hell," a useful tour guide to one aspect of the medieval hell, is included in this book, but see also Philip Butterworth's "Hellfire: Flame as Special Effect," above.

44. Diehl, "To put us in remembrance," p. 206.

45. Robert E. Knoll, *Ben Jonson's Plays* (Lincoln: Univ. of Nebraska Press, 1964), p. 96; specifically, Knoll calls Volpone "The Renaissance man awake to his pleasurable world of sensation, asleep to all others" and "a Cynical Everyman yielding to worldly temptation." For *Volpone*, see Vol. V of the standard edition of Ben Jonson's works, ed. C. H. Herford and Percy Simpson (Oxford: Clarendon Press, 1937).

46. Citations in my text are to John Webster, *The White Devil*, ed. John Russell Brown, Revels Plays (Cambridge: Harvard Univ. Press, 1960).

47. Plummer, *The Hours of Catherine of Cleves*, Pl. 82.

48. See Richard Marks and Nigel Morgan, *The Golden Age of English Manuscript Painting, 1100–1500* (New York: George Braziller, 1981), Pl. 13.

49. Citations in my text are to John Webster, *The Duchess of Malfi*, ed. John Russell Brown, Revels Plays (Cambridge: Harvard Univ. Press, 1964).

50. Citations in my text are to *The Changeling*, ed. N. W. Bawcutt, Revels Plays (1958; rpt. London: Methuen, 1961).

Index

Acts of the Apostles, play of 30

Adam, Anglo-Norman play 4, 62, 128, 131

Adel, Ccurch at 28

Albertus Magnus 100

Alkerton, Richard 57

Allen, Don Cameron 191

Anaxagoras 191

Anderson, M. D. 8–9, 53

Angers, tapestries at 1–2, 13

Anthony, St. 22, 25–26, 28, 31

Antichrist, plays of 10, 80, 107

Apocalypse, illuminated manuscripts of 11–12, 201

Apocalypse of St. Paul 44, 59–61, 64, 132, 134

Apocalypse of St. Peter 134

Apocalypse of Zephaniah 133

Apollonia, St. 4, 10

A porta inferi 148

Aquinas, St. Thomas 62

Ashburton, play at 32

Athanasius 22

Atheist's Tragedy, The 200

Augustine, St. 44, 116, 127–28

B., R. 187

Babington, John 98

Baker, Donald C. 15

Bakhtin, Mikhail 6

Baldock, Bishop 142

Barcelona, Corpus Christi procession at 30

Barking Abbey 141–46, 150, 152, 154–56

Barking, plays and ceremonies at 141–55

Bate, John 92, 95, 98

Bayeux tapestry 36

Beck, Christopher 82

Beckett, Samuel 196

Bene, Amaury de 192

Bevington, David 180, 182

Bibliothèque Nationale MS. fr. 616 25

Blankenburg, Psalter from 12

Boccaccio, Giovanni 135

Bodleian Library MS. Gough Liturg. 3 (English Hours) 43

Boethius 115, 129

Book of Kells 23

Bosch, Hieronymus 25–28, 31, 36

Bourges Cathedral 78

Bourges Parade 30

Brainard, Ingrid 121

Braunstein, Philippe 132

Brenz, John 191

Breughel, Pieter 180

Breviary of Love 8

Bromyard, John 133

Browne, Sir Thomas 191–92

Bruges, city of 138

Bucher, François 13

Caesarius of Heisterbach 2
Calendar of Shepherds; *see*
   Shepherds' Calendar
Calendrier des bergiers 56;
   see also Shepherds'
   Calendar
Calleau, Hubert 9
Calvin, John 189
Cambises 203
Cambridge, play at 32
Cambridge University Library
   MS. Add. 4103 (Dutch
   Book of Hours) 9
Camden, William 64
Carcassone Castle Museum,
   alabaster at 8
Carthusian Miscellany 10
Castle of Perseverance 31, 41,
   45, 57, 67, 83–85, 109,
   114, 118–19
Catherine of Cleves, Hours of
   197, 201
Cawley, A. C. 3
Chaldon, church at 55, 193
Chambers, E. K. 70
Changeling, The 202–03
Charles V, Breviary of 206
Charles VI, King of France
   85–86
Charles the Bold 15
Chester, Whitsun plays at 20,
   31–32, 34, 42–43, 45–49,
   53, 58, 60, 63, 72–73, 78,
   102, 105, 107, 110,
   112–14, 120–21, 123,
   125–26, 137, 159, 161,
   163–66, 169–71, 172–74,
   180–81, 183–84
Chicago Medieval Players 141,
   153–55

Cloisters Apocalypse 7, 11
Colette, St., of Corbie 15
Compton Wynyates 29
Conques, Church of St. Foy at
   15, 50–51, 63
Consurgit Christus 151–52
Conversion of St. Paul, Digby
   play 82–84, 86, 89, 111
Cordier de Bignan, Hours of
   193
Cosman, Madeline Pelner 135
Coventry, Church (later
   Cathedral) of St. Michael
   48, 61
Coventry, plays of 8, 17, 33,
   49, 68–72, 106, 112, 118,
   122, 165–69, 174–77, 181,
   184–85
Cranach, Lucas 55
Creacion of the World, Cornish
   play 59, 71, 84, 104, 114,
   116, 122–23
Crescenzi, Pietro di 25
Crispin and Crispinian, SS.,
   play of 80
Crow, Robert 68
Croxton *Play of the Sacrament*
   78–79, 110
Cum rex glorie 149–51, 156

Dante Aligheri 132, 134–35,
   140, 188
Dauntsey, Wiltshire, church at
   1
Davidson, Clifford 200
Dead Mans Song, The 52
Delight, Reynes fragment 115
Denys, St. 4
Desert Fathers 22
Devil's Law Case, The 200

Dewsbury, Church of All Saints
28
Diehl, Huston 200
Doctor Faustus 56–58, 188–
93, 204
Domine abstaxisti ab inferis
148–49
Donne, John 192, 197, 207
Dorrell, Margaret; *see*
Rogerson, Margaret
Dortmund, Antichrist play at
10
Drawswerd, Thomas 169
Dublin, plays at 137
Duchess of Malfi, The 201–02
Dudley, Robert, Earl of
Leicester 74, 95
Dunbar, William 55
Dutka, JoAnna 116–17, 120,
127, 130–31

Einsedeln, Book of Pericopes
possibly from 23
Empson, William 194
Enders, Jody 154
Enough is as Good as a Feast
41, 194
Étienne Chevalier, Hours of 5,
10
Everyman 47, 119
Evesham, Monk of 132–34

Fairford, Church of St. Mary
28–29, 37, 54–55, 194
Felton, Sibille 142
Fitzwarin Psalter 8
Fitz-Simon, Christopher 137
Fouquet, Jean 10
Friar Bacon and Friar Bungay
194

Fulwell, Ulpian 187
Fux, J. J. 130

Galpern, Joyce 7
Gardiner, Eileen 136
George, St. 33
Gesta Romanorum 53
Gibson, Gail McMurray 128
Gillam, Hugh, morris dancer
120–21
Gorboduc 7, 203
Grabar, André 24
Grantley, Darryll 96
Great Malvern Priory 112, 128
Greenblatt, Stephen 195
Gregory the Great 2, 7, 13,
134
Grimm, Jacob 24
Grünewald, Matthias 120–21,
130
Guisay, Hugonin de 85
Gurevich, Aron 2, 13

Haarlem, Rhetoricians' festival
at 12
Hall, play properties at 9–10
Hamlet 192, 196–98, 203
Harewood, Church of All
Saints at 27, 29
Harthan, John 206
Healey, Antoinette di Paolo 60
Henry II, King 127
Henry IV, Pt. 1 194–95; Pt. 2
195
Henry V 195
Herod 28, 45, 106, 118–19,
121–22, 131
Herrad of Landsberg 65
Heywood, John 100

Hildburgh Collection, of
    alabasters 120–21, 130
Hildegard of Bingen 3, 14
Hildesheim, Easter ceremony at
    152
Hilton, Walter 103–04, 125
Himmelfarb, Martha 52, 134
Holbein, Hans 195
Holding, Peter 6
Holinshed, Raphael 95
Holkham Bible Picture Book 4,
    53–54
Hugh, St. 28

Iceland 2; manuscript from 5
Ingram, R. W. 184
Innocent III, Pope 175

Jeu d'Adam; see Adam, Anglo-
    Norman play
Jew of Malta, The 193
John the Baptist 26–27
Johnson, B. P. 135
Johnston, Alexandra F. 6
Jonson, Ben 201
Justice, Alan 137

Katherine of Sutton 141–44,
    154
Kendall Castle, play at 58
Killing of the Children, The,
    Digby play 120
King Lear 199–200
Künzelsauer Fronleichnamspiel
    4, 15
Kyd, Thomas 188

Lazarus and Dives, play of 4
Leeds, Church of St. John 28
Leviathan 1, 21–22, 24, 54

Liber divinorum operum 3
Like Will to Like 194
Lincoln, plays at 71, 95–96
Lincoln Cathedral 1, 28, 45,
    51–52, 64
London, city of 138
London Hours of René of
    Anjou 194, 196–97
London, St. Paul's Cathedral at
    207
London, Midsummer Show at
    69, 82
Lucerne, Passion play at 3, 10,
    30
Ludlow, church at 29, 32
Lumiansky, R. M. 107
Luttrell Psalter 36
Lyche, Robert 32

Macbeth 196, 198
Machyn, Henry 82
Majorca, plays at 49, 80
Malcontent, The 200
Mâle, Émile 41
Mankind 102, 106, 108–10,
    115, 119, 123–24, 128
Mannyng, Robert, of Brunne
    114
Marchant, Guyot 56
Margaret of York 15
Marlowe, Christopher 56–57,
    173, 187, 190, 192–94
Marienburg Castle 4
Marshall, John 10, 183
Marston, John 116
Martin of Tours, St., play of
    31, 81, 84–85
Mary Magdalene, Digby play
    106–11, 119, 122–23

Measure for Measure 197–98, 200
Merchant of Venice, The 195–96, 200–01
Meredith, Peter 30, 120, 130
Methley, Church of St. Oswald 26, 28
Middleton, Thomas 187, 202
Minorita, Alexander 12
Metz, play at 9, 71
Michael, St., archangel 26, 29, 43, 46, 50–51, 55
Michel, Jean 45
Mills, David 107, 127
Milton, John 190–93
Modane, play at 80, 100
Modena, Corpus Christi play at 96
Mons, plays at 68, 71, 89, 99–100, 186
Montaigne, Michel de 192
Monteferrand, Passion play at 9
More, St. Thomas 195
Muir, Lynette 45
Munich Psalter 42
Murphy, John L. 15
Mysteries, The, at National Theatre 73, 95

Nero 4
Newcastle, dragon at 34; play at 70, 82
New Romney, play at 70
Nicodemus, Gospel of 73, 78, 143, 159, 163, 172
Norwich, snap dragon at 33–34; plays at 33, 72
N-town plays 6, 32, 45–49, 58, 110–11, 115, 118–22, 166,

N-town plays (cont.) 182

Office of the Dead 58
Of the Seuen Ages 44–45
Ordinalia, Cornish 67, 104, 114, 116, 122–23, 136–37
Othello 198–99, 203
Otto, Rita 3
Oxford 42

Paradise Lost 190–92
Paris, city of 138; plays at 137, 160
Paul, St. 82
Peckham, John 3
Peke, Richard 47
Peter and Paul, SS., play of 8
Petteur, Roland le 127
Phoebus, Gaston 25
Pickering, Church of SS. Peter and Paul 33, 182
Piers Plowman 127
Platt, Hugh 75–76, 78, 95
Playfair Hours 8, 17
Play of the Sacrament; *see* Croxton *Play of the Sacrament*
Poculi Ludique Societas (PLS) 164
Provençal Stage Director's Book 84, 86–88
Psellus 21

Quentin, St., play of 29

Rankin, Susan 155
Reading, play at 70
Reichenau, Book of Pericopes possibly from 23

Reims Cathedral 51
Revello, play at 73–74, 78, 185
Revenger's Tragedy, The 201
Ripoll, church at 1
Ripon, dragon at 34
Robbins, Rossell Hope 20, 22
Robert de Lisle Psalter 14
Rogerson, Margaret (Dorrell) 6, 177
Rolle, Richard, of Hampole 125
Romans, play at 71
Rotherham, church at 29
Rouen, Passion play at 9
Rouerge, play at 49

St. Gall, Book of Pericopes possibly from 23
St. Lambrecht, convent of 33
St. Martial of Limoges 4
St. Patrick's Purgatory 133
Salisbury, Church of St. Thomas of Canterbury 1, 12, 42, 58–59
Salvator mundi 112
S. Maria Antiqua, Rome, fresco at 23
Sawles Warde 42, 57
Schocken Pentateuch 14
Schiller, Gertrud 23
Seiler, Thomas 207
Selby Abbey 29
Serlio, Sebastiano 76, 95
Seure, St. Martin play at 31
Shakespeare, William 56, 192, 194–96
Sheingorn, Pamela 50, 180, 182
Shepherds' Calendar 56–57

Shibden Hall, Halifax 28
Smith, F. Joseph 129
Spanish Tragedy, The 188, 193
Speculum humanae salvationis 3
Sponsus 4, 15, 64
Sprotbrough, Church of St. Mary 28
Staatliche Museum, Berlin 2
Sterzing, play at 4
Stetchworth, grafitto at 10
Stevens, John 128–29
Stevens, Martin 127
Stock, Elliot 143
Stratford-upon-Avon, Guild Chapel 9–10, 17, 29, 37, 52–53, 56
Stuttgart Psalter 23

Tailby, John 30
Tacuinum Sanitatis 26
Te Deum 54, 174
Temperley, Nicholas 124
Temptations of St. Anthony 25–26
Tertullian 21
Thomas of Chabham 116, 129
Thornhill, Church of St. Michael 26
Tobias, play of 9, 71
Tollite portas 147
Tondal, The Visions of 2, 13
Toronto, medieval drama at 6
Towneley plays 4, 8–9, 42, 53–54, 62, 106–09, 112–13, 123, 125, 127–28, 159–61, 163–65, 169–71, 174, 180
Traité de bien vivre et de bien mourir, Le 56

Très riches heures, of the Duke of Berry 25
Trinity Apocalypse 201
Twycross, Meg 59, 62, 179, 186

Utrecht Psalter 6–7, 17

Vaux, Pierre de 15
Valenciennes, Passion play at 3, 9
Vérard, Antoine 56
Victoria and Albert Museum, Anglo-Saxon ivory at 50
Vigne, Andrieu de la 30–31
Visio Lazari 56
Visio Pauli; *see Apocalypse of St. Paul*
Visitatio Sepulchri 155–56
Volpone 201

Wager, W. 41, 187
Waiting for Godot 196
Wapull, George 187
Watts, Hughe 82
Webster, John 201
Wenhaston, church at 48, 50

Wentersdorf, Karl P. 27, 110–11
White Devil, The 201
Whitehorne, Peter 98
Wickham, Glynne 7, 166
Wierus, Johannes 21
Winchester Psalter 50–52, 63, 196–97, 206
Wisdom 115, 119
Woolf, Rosemary 63
Worcester Antiphonal 142, 152–53
Wormald, Francis 10
Wymondham, play at 32–33

York, city of 135, 137–38
York, Church of St. Michael-le-Belfrey 50; Church of St. Michael Spurriergate 27
York Minster 27–29, 51–52
York plays 6–7, 31–32, 43, 46, 48, 54, 63, 68, 106, 112, 119, 136–38, 140, 159–61, 163–65, 169–71, 173–75, 177–82, 185
Yorkshire Museum, tympanum at 45

1. Detail of Last Judgment. Wall painting (restored) over chancel arch, Church of
St. Thomas of Canterbury, Salisbury. By permission of the Royal Commission
on the Historical Monuments of England.

2. Damned being tormented by Devils and Snakes. Sculpture, Frieze, West Front, Lincoln Cathedral. By permission of the Royal Commission on the Historical Monuments of England.

3. The Damned assailed by dragons. Sculpture, Frieze, West Front, Lincoln Cathedral. By permission of the Royal Commission on the Historical Monuments of England.

4. The Devil tortures two of the Damned. Sculpture, Frieze, West Front, Lincoln Cathedral. By permission of the Royal Commission on the Historical Monuments of England.

5. Fall of Rebel Angels, Creation, Fall of Man. Stjórn's translation of the Old Testament into Icelandic. Rekykjavík, Árni Magnússon Institute, MS. AM 227, fol. 1ᵛ.

6. Doomsday, as staged by the Graduate Centre for the Study of Drama. N-town Pageants, produced by Poculi Ludique Societas (Andrew Taylor, Artistic Director) at the University of Toronto, May 1988. Courtesy of Alexandra F. Johnston.

7. Detail from Doom. Wall painting over chancel arch, Guild Chapel, Stratford-upon-Avon. Engraving from Thomas Sharp, *A Dissertation on the Mysteries* (1825).

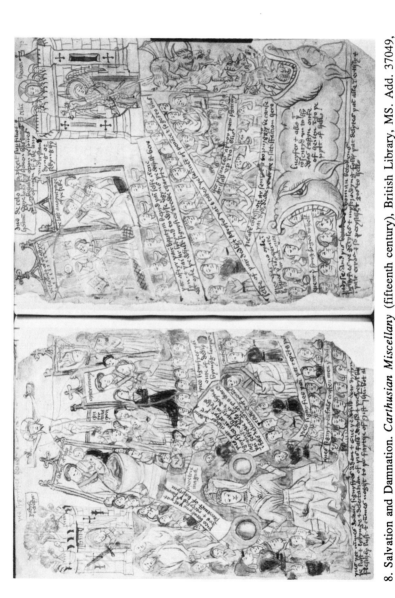

8. Salvation and Damnation. *Carthusian Miscellany* (fifteenth century), British Library, MS. Add. 37049, fols. 72v–73r. By permission of the British Library.

9. *Revelations* 6.7–8. Opening of the Fourth Seal: Pale Horse. Cloisters Apocalypse (early fourteenth century); Metropolitan Museum of Art, Cloisters Collection, 1968 (MS. 68.174, fol. 9r).

10. Opening of the Fourth Seal: Pale Horse. Apocalypse. British Library, MS. Harley 4972, fol. 11ᵛ. By permission of the British Library.

11. Opening of the Fourth Seal: Pale Horse. Alexander Minorita Apocalypse. Cambridge University Library, MS. 5.31, fol. 27v. By permission of the Syndics of Cambridge University Library.

12a. Hieronymus Bosch, Monsters. Bister and pen drawing. By kind permission of the Ashmolean Museum, Oxford.

12b. Hieronymus Bosch, Monsters. Bister and pen drawing. By kind permission of the Ashmolean Museum, Oxford.

13. Mace (fourteenth or fifteenth century). By permission of the Museum of London.

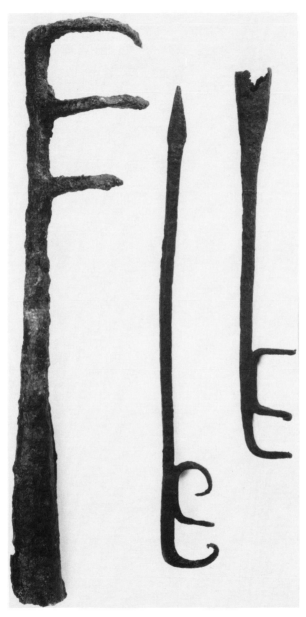

14. Flesh-hooks. By permission of the Museum of London.

15. Detail of Doom. Painted Glass, West Window, Church of St. Mary, Fairford. By permission of the Royal Commission on the Historical Monuments of England.

16. Devil with Flesh-hook; formerly at the right of this figure there was a Fall of Adam and Eve. Misericord, Church of St. Mary, Sprotbrough, West Yorkshire.

17. Hell Mouth, swallowing human figure. Bronze Closing Ring. Church of St. John the Baptist, Adel, West Yorkshire.

18. Harrowing of Hell. *Holkham Bible Picture Book*. British Library, MS. Add. 47682, fol. 34r. By permission of the British Library.

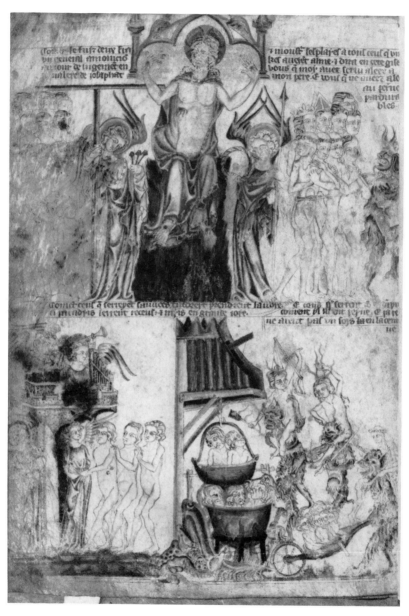

19. The Last Judgment. *Holkham Bible Picture Book*. British Library MS. Add. 47682, fol. 42ᵛ. Permission of the British Library.

20. The Weighing of Souls (above), the Ladder of Salvation, and Hell. Wall painting (restored), Church of SS. Peter and Paul, Chaldon, Surrey. By permission of the Royal Commission on the Historical Monuments of England.

21. Punishment of the Wrathful. *The Kalender of Sheephardes* (c.1570). Bodleian Library, Malone 17, sig. E7ᵛ. By permission of the Bodleian Library.

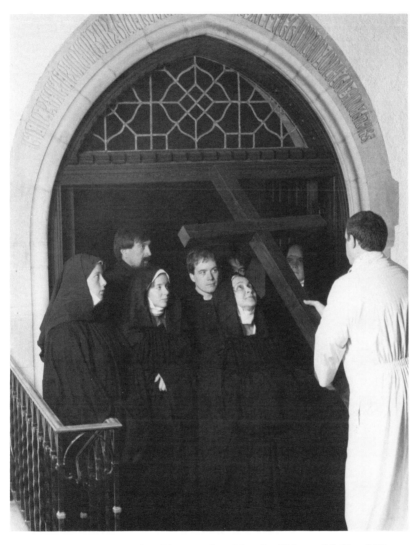

22. The Barking Harrowing Play, produced by the Chicago Medieval Players,
1989.

23. York Doomsday Play, produced by Joculatores Lancastrienses. Directed by Meg Twycross. York Festival, 1988. Photograph: courtesy of Meg Twycross.